SOMETHING WORTH WALKING FOR

GW00708054

John Wilmut

A Lands End to John O'Groats walk for
Christian Aid's work for education
in poor countries

Published 2013 by arima publishing

www.arimapublishing.com

ISBN 978 1 84549 568 8

© John Wilmut 2013

All rights reserved

This book is copyright. Subject to statutory exception and to provisions of relevant collective licensing agreements, no part of this publication may be reproduced, stored in a retrieval system, or transmitted in any form or by any means, without the prior written permission of the author.

Printed and bound in the United Kingdom

Typeset in Trebuchet and Times New Roman

This book is sold subject to the conditions that it shall not, by way of trade or otherwise, be lent, re-sold, hired out, or otherwise circulated without the publisher's prior consent in any form of binding or cover other than that which it is published and without a similar condition including this condition being imposed on the subsequent purchaser.

arima publishing

ASK House, Northgate Avenue

Bury St Edmunds, Suffolk IP32 6BB

t: (+44) 01284 700321

http://www.arimapublishing.com

Except where it says otherwise, all the photographs used in this book were taken by John Wilmut in the course of the walk. Other photographs, taken by friends during the walk and and kindly made available, have been credited in the captions. Photographs supplied by Christian Aid have been identified as such and are used with kind permission.

A few photographs have been taken from Geograph (http://www.geograph.org. uk). In each case the copyright holder has been identified and the photograph is licensed for reuse under the Creative Commons License (http://creativecommons.org/licenses/by-sa/2.0/).

SOMETHING WORTH WALKING FOR

John Wilmut was born and grew up in Bristol. He graduated as a mechanical engineer but switched immediately to science teaching. After doing a masters degree in educational research he worked in that field, specialising in educational assessment, first at the University of Reading, then at the Associated Examining Board and finally as an independent consultant.

He spent a significant part of his professional life working on development aid projects in education and on projects that focused on minority groups and on vocational and occupational qualifications. He became very aware of the terrible waste of opportunity and talent that comes as a result of under-resourced educational provision in many countries of the world where there are not enough schools, classes are huge, books are few in number, teachers are poorly trained and poorly paid and countless children (especially girls) drop out after only a year or two of primary education. The walk described in this book is a direct consequence of this experience.

John now lives in Cornwall, is married to Viv and they have two children and one grandchild.

Christian Aid is a Christian organisation that insists that the world can and must be swiftly changed to one where everyone can live a full life, free from poverty. It works globally for profound change that eradicates the causes of

poverty, striving to achieve equality, dignity and freedom for all, regardless of faith or nationality. It is part of a wider movement for social justice and provides urgent, practical and effective assistance where the need is great, tackling the effects of poverty as well as its root causes.

Contents

To Viv, who encouraged me, tolerated my long absence from home and helped with the walk in so many ways.

And to all the children in countries where opportunities are limited by poverty.

Before we begin

This is a record of a walk from Lands End to John O'Groats that I undertook from May to July 2012 on behalf of Christian Aid. It is a personal account that I'm writing for my own satisfaction and for the entertainment of anyone who might be interested. It is definitely not a guide to walking from one end of the UK to the other; others have already done a good job of describing routes and giving advice on how to go about doing the walk and I gladly acknowledge the help that I've had from their accounts.

This, therefore, is a description of why I did the walk, how I went about planning it and how it turned out. It's also an acknowledgment of the help and support that I had from others and how this influenced the walk. This was a journey in my mind as well as with my feet and I chronicled it on a daily basis on a blog that is one of the frameworks around which this account has been created. It has been suggested that I should simply publish the blog as it stands but I felt that would appear a very incomplete and fragmented account of what was, for me, a coherent and whole experience.

It is important not to take that whole experience too seriously. It wasn't a continuously happy and carefree walk but nor was it sad or terribly difficult; like most experiences, it had high and low points, exciting and boring aspects and some minor irritations. Plenty of people have done this walk before and many more will follow and, as one person told me, "They all think that they've done something unique". I have no doubt that there are people who have made a unique contribution to walks of this kind but I don't think that I'm one of them.

Having said that, I did have some particular purposes in doing the walk and I want to explain these as clearly as I can. These purposes could be applied to a large number of activities like this walk. Of course, people are doing this all the time, usually very successfully and often without much publicity or acknowledgment. My walk belongs in the company of the coffee mornings, sponsored bike rides, bungee jumps and jumble sales that are the fabric of charity fundraising here and in many other countries. People work hard in organising these events, others take part and have fun and many, many people give generously in support of the charities. I see no need to give this a tag such as 'The Big Society' (favoured by our present government); indeed, to do so is to politicise the idea and rob the activities of their spontaneity. I will be offended if my walk is thought to epitomise the Big Society concept.

I've written my account as a fairly continuous narrative that starts with the planning and preparation, continues with a day-by-day description of the walk based on the edited blog, and concludes with some reflections on the whole experience. Statistics of the walk, acknowledgements of help and lists of equipment are added as sections in Chapter 5. In reproducing the blog I have resisted making wholesale changes, only removing irrelevant material, updating information and correcting typing errors and some gross misuses of the language. At the time of producing this account the blog is still live, as is the website that I created to support the walk and you will see that I have lifted some of the website text and used it here.

As they say when they put food before you in a restaurant "Enjoy" (though I am never sure whether this is a command or an invitation).

John Wilmut
Cornwall, January 2013

This book was first produced in electronic format, available for download from the website http://www.wilmut.net/lejog. This version differs only in layout details with some limited additions and corrections to the text. The electronic version will, in due course, be removed from the website.

Proceeds from the sale of this book will be added to donations already made to the walk. But if, when you get to the end of the book, you would like to make a further donation, you can do so by going to my website and following the link leading to donation information which, at the time of writing, covers both electronic and postal gifts. Or you can donate directly to Christian Aid at http://www.christianaid.org.uk/

Children in school in Sierra Leone
Photograph from Christian Aid

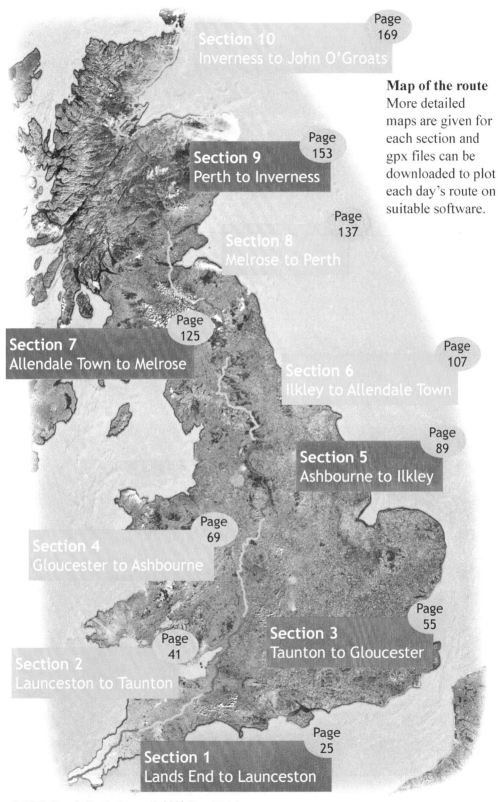

Section 10
Inverness to John O'Groats
Page 169

Map of the route
More detailed
maps are given for
each section and
gpx files can be
downloaded to plot
each day's route on
suitable software.

Section 9
Perth to Inverness
Page 153

Section 8
Melrose to Perth
Page 137

Section 7
Allendale Town to Melrose
Page 125

Section 6
Ilkley to Allendale Town
Page 107

Section 5
Ashbourne to Ilkley
Page 89

Section 4
Gloucester to Ashbourne
Page 69

Section 3
Taunton to Gloucester
Page 55

Section 2
Launceston to Taunton
Page 41

Section 1
Lands End to Launceston
Page 25

© 2013 Google Earth; Image © 2013 TerraMetrics

Children at school in Sierra Leone
Photograph from Christian Aid

Chapter 1

A very long gestation

Beginnings

I daresay that many people of my generation read John Hillaby's book *Journey Through Britain*, first published in 1970, and dreamed of doing the same thing. He had an engaging style of writing that brought out the excitement and novelty of the enterprise without trivialising the difficulties which were rather greater in the 1960s than they are now. However, I don't suppose that I'm very different from the majority of Hillaby's readers in deciding that other commitments took priority and that it was impossible to find enough time to do a walk of this kind. In my case, the idea went onto the back burner for well over 30 years, only to resurface as I approached retirement.

I did work in Nepal for some years and did a good deal of day walking and a long trek and then, in 2004, I walked the West Highland Way. This wasn't a very successful experience; I didn't do enough preparation, my boots were not a good fit and I carried a pack that was far too heavy. Consequently, I got a bad attack of blisters and finished the walk in some pain, having managed an average of less than 12 miles a day. If I was to emulate John Hillaby I knew that I would have to do better than that.

By that time, however, more had been written about end-to-end walks. Several books and internet accounts had been published that were either describing individual efforts or were presented as manuals, describing methods and routes. It was easy to start planning my own effort: I could steal all the best route ideas, throw in a few of my own, set a pace that I could cope with and take others' advice about accommodation and equipment. The internet made research much easier than in Hillaby's day and spreadsheets made the plans look very impressive. The fundamental questions remained, of course: Why was I planning this? What purpose would it serve? I am quite clear that my initial motivation was not altruistic or charitable; it was to demonstrate to myself, and to anyone else who was interested, that I could do the walk. I was particularly enthusiastic about the idea that someone in their late 60s could do this sort of thing; this would certainly give a good impression.

The planning was a very pleasurable process and my enthusiasm for the detail of the walk may have been a little obsessive. I still have spreadsheets that show nine or ten detailed routes and I quite soon realised that the planning was becoming an end in itself and an impediment to making a decision. I made no great secret of my plans and I think that I dropped a number of hints to both friends and family but actually coming out with a clear statement of intent was quite another matter. So four or five years went by during which I polished up the plans but made no commitment to implementing them. To be fair, I was still doing some pieces of work that made it difficult to fit in a 2-3 month absence, but that was only part of the reason for the delay.

I am not sure when I made the link between the walk and Christian Aid, a charity which I had supported in principle and as a donor for some years before I started to think about the walk. I'm not sure that I can fully explain my commitment to Christian Aid and I have been rather evasive when asked why I chose to do the walk in support of its work. Sufficient to say, perhaps, that, although I gained as a child and still retain my fundamental Christian beliefs, I am no longer actively involved with a church but do see my commitment to Christian Aid (and to another charity working in the developing world) as some sort of attempt to come to terms with the ambiguities of this position. I felt quite comfortable with the idea that this walk should be in support of a Christian Aid programme.

Once on the walk, I did expect that someone would ask whether I was on a pilgrimage and I knew that my answer would be 'no', since the motivation for doing the walk was so unclear in my mind. In fact, no-one ever did ask me that question but someone did ask whether it was a penance. I couldn't answer that but, to my relief, the conversation moved on and I was spared the difficulty of trying to frame an answer. I still don't know what I would have said.

By 2011 (but not for the first time) it was clear that the walk would never take place if I didn't make a commitment very soon. I was now 71 and time would soon run out. In mid-autumn 2011, on the spur of the moment, I told a friend that I was planning to do the walk in 2012 and asked whether he'd help out with some of my other commitments during the 2-3 months that I would be away. I was surprised at his readiness to accept the idea and, although he didn't broadcast the news, I regarded that as a commitment that I couldn't abandon. I discussed it with Viv; she didn't object so the walk was on for 2012. The next stop was the Christian Aid office in Exmouth where I explained that I wanted to do a walk that would be in support of an education project or programme somewhere in the developing world.

My reasons for choosing this type of project were simple. I had spent all my professional life working in education and that included work on development aid projects in a number of countries in Asia, Africa, the Middle East, Caribbean and Europe and on projects in the UK that were concerned with educational opportunities for minority groups. I have a clear view of the importance of investing heavily and in the long term in education as a matter both of personal development of the individual and of the advancement of poor countries. I do not limit education to the formal schooling of the young. Enabling families and their communities to support young children's learning is as essential as providing schools. Adult education and training programmes in the community and in industry, commerce and higher education institutions are of equal importance if individuals are to realise their full potential and societies are to be stable and prosperous.

Commitment to all types of educational infrastructure is needed; to schools and colleges; to teacher training and professional development; to books, computers, wall charts, writing materials, desks, school management systems, methods for community governance of schools, distance education systems, laboratories and workshops - the list is endless and the cost is very high. But without the investment over a long period of time poverty cannot be eradicated since people will not have the skills and knowledge to help themselves.

Linking with Christian Aid

My initial meeting with staff at the Christian Aid regional office in Exmouth was very productive and I was cheered by the positive and enthusiastic reception. To some extent that was probably because I went there with a ready-made and developed proposal and I clearly wanted to have charge of the whole undertaking. This was something that I took for granted particularly since I was proposing to do the walk on my own and could organise my own support structures.

This was the point where we made the choice of the education work of Christian Aid and its partners in Sierra Leone as the focus for the fundraising. I've already indicated the reasons for this and I later tried to explain these on my website (http://www.wilmut.net/lejog) and in my blog (included here under Day 31) using material supplied by Christian Aid. I've never been to Sierra Leone but I have worked elsewhere in Africa and in other developing countries and find it very easy to relate to its problems that have been exacerbated by the brutal civil war of the 1990s. We did agree that the wording of the publicity for my walk, whilst being explicitly concerned with education, would not relate solely to Sierra Leone, thus allowing Christian Aid to use the funds for a similar purpose elsewhere, at its discretion. In practice, however, it was always easier to cite Sierra Leone as the principal focus for the walk.

In the panels on the next two pages I reproduce the information on my website (http://www.wilmut.net/lejog) that describes Christian Aid's work in Sierra Leone. The website page identifies Christian Aid's commitment:

"This is just one example of Christian Aid's work. It works in 48 countries with over 500 projects at any one time. It works globally, where the need is greatest, for profound change that eradicates the causes of poverty, striving to achieve equality, dignity and freedom for all, regardless of faith or nationality."

As a result of the initial meeting the Exmouth office began to put round information about the walk to its other offices. Specifically, a request went out for help with overnight accommodation as I walked northwards, basing this on a schedule that I published on my website soon afterwards. This eventually resulted in me staying with Christian Aid supporters for 13 nights and this was augmented by hospitality from friends for another 10 (including the two nights that I spent at home at the end of the first section of the walk). Thus 30% of my accommodation needs were met in this way.

There was other publicity through Christian Aid News, press releases and information sent to Christian Aid offices. However, some of this did not generate as

 # Christian Aid in Sierra Leone

One of the many examples where Christian Aid is tackling the root cause of poverty in a community and is committed to finding long term, sustainable, empowering solutions for the people to lift themselves out of poverty, for good.

A decade after Sierra Leone emerged from a brutal civil war which devastated rural areas, it remains one of the poorest countries in the world with more than half of the population living on less than US$1.25 a day*.

The partner: the Methodist Church of Sierra Leone

The Methodist Church of Sierra Leone (MCSL) is a long-term partner of Christian Aid and has received direct funding since 1997. It is one of the larger members of the Council of Churches of Sierra Leone. Since its establishment, MCSL has been involved in the implementation of development programmes, which include:

- Pastoral care
- Health care services
- Education
- Provision of appropriate skills and tools for self- development
- Supporting youth and women
- Literacy programmes

According to its vision statement "the Methodist Church Sierra Leone is committed to developing, rehabilitating and maintaining human and material resources for self-reliance." In line with this MCSL projects have a particular emphasis on empowering communities to bring about improvements themselves. The project directly helps 4,850 people (2370 men and 2480 women) and indirectly benefits 23,362 people, the population of the three chiefdoms where MCSL works.

Fact box: learning for life

In Sierra Leone, 69 per cent of primary-aged children attend school. UNICEF

Sierra Leone's government spent 2,810,100,000 leones on primary and pre-primary education in 2011. Sierra Leone's total spending on education is equivalent to four per cent of its GDP. UNESCO

Educating girls for six years or more results in improved prenatal and postnatal care dramatically reduces maternal and child mortality. UNICEF

The Sierra Leonean government conducted a census in 2007 to understand the scale of its educational needs. This survey found there were just 141 primary schools across Bonthe District and only 100 were in good condition.

Along with Pujehun and Bombali, Bonthe District has the lowest rate of school attendance in Sierra Leone. VAM, World Bank, 2007

Some 70% of villages in Bonthe do not have a functioning primary school. VAM, World Bank, 2007

* currently (November 2012) 78p a day

The volunteer teacher:
'It's a responsibility I can't deny'

At 33, Saidu Tucker is a man with many fingers in many pies. A key figure in Gbap's development, he is a member of both the Village Development Committee (VDC) and Ward Development Committee (WDC) and a farmer in the production group. But his real passion lies in education. Once a star pupil at Gbap's primary school, he now passes on that learning to a new generation of Gbap students as a volunteer teacher, and to their parents through adult literacy classes. And having helped lobby for the new school building, now that it is nearing completion he devotes part of every afternoon to painting its walls to ensure that it is ready for use as soon as possible.

A new generation of talented workers

With one in three primary-aged children missing school in Sierra Leone, Fatmata Jayah, 13, who is now in class five may consider herself fortunate. But with rafters hanging precariously from the roof – threatening to drop at any moment - and few desks having withstood the ravages of the termites that infest her school, it is hard to really think of her as lucky. Frustrated by the local government's lack of attention to school maintenance, Gbap's VDC lobbied persistently for better facilities. Today Fatmata can look forward to completing her primary education in a new school which will provide more space and a better environment for pupils.

New school will help girls make the grade

Approaching her final year of primary school, 12-year-old Patricia Sawie is busy planning her future. Strikingly smart and confident, she has high hopes of attending secondary school and going on to become Sierra Leone's first female president. While girls are now just as likely to be enrolled in Sierra Leonean primary schools as boys, inequalities at secondary school level remain. Today only 20 per cent of secondary-aged girls enrol compared with some 30 per cent of boys. But this is a challenge for which Patricia seems well prepared and with a better school soon to open in her community as a result of successful lobbying by Gbap's VDC, she is confident she can make the grade.

> "If we have better education, we will have better lives"
>
> Patricia Sawie,
> 12 years old

much response as we'd hoped; perhaps there were two main reasons for this. One was that my initial contact with Christian Aid was too late - our meeting was only 4 months before I was due to start the walk. This was too short a time, particularly because the lead time for getting items published in the quarterly Christian Aid News is quite long and information therefore missed the Spring 2012 issue. Moreover, subsequent information only appeared in the south-west England version of the News which meant that people in areas that I was walking through didn't know about the walk.

The other problem was that arrangements for the walk were being finalised just before Christian Aid Week started; this is a time when the staff are very fully committed. One unfortunate result of this was that general information about my walk wasn't always sent in advance to the people who had offered accommodation. Unless I had told them about it, some of them hadn't seen my website and several said that they could have spread the work locally and arranged a wider spread of accommodation had they known the details of what I was doing.

On the other hand, it was most gratifying to be seen off at Lands End by a representative of Christian Aid, to be met at John O'Groats by a small group of supporters and again at Plymouth station by another group. Without that, the start of the walk would have been much less notable and the end really would have been an anti-climax.

My own publicity

Once all the decisions had been made with Christian Aid I created the website http://www.wilmut.net/lejog, started the donation site http://www.justgiving.com/johnslejog and the blog site http://johnslejog.wordpress.com. I generated some posters and some cards (which could be handed out to anyone who was interested both before and during the walk) and Viv and I sent emails to anyone we thought might be interested in the walk. Almost immediately donations began to come in and friends offered support of one type or another, sometimes bringing me back into contact with people that I hadn't seen for many years. The local branch of Tesco offered me some sponsorship (in the form of items useful for the walk) and an opportunity for some publicity in the store one Sunday morning, as a result of which a couple of local papers carried small news items.

In a very welcome arrangement with my local parish church, publicity was given over the period of the walk which was mentioned in services and shown in the form of a map that charted my progress. Additional news items went into the community newsletter so that local awareness of and involvement in the walk was very high. In many senses this was one of the most satisfying and enjoyable aspects of the whole undertaking which culminated in a very well-attended 'welcome home' party a couple of days after I returned home to Cornwall.

Managing the money

From the outset, the principal mechanism for making donations was through the Just Giving website http://www.justgiving.com/johnslejog. Two-thirds of all donations came through this route and the costs of operating it were charged as a small deduction made at the point of transfer of the money to Christian Aid. It is a well-tried process and, for someone like me whose main concern was doing the walk, wholly painless. It has the added advantage of ensuring that Gift Aid is added to the donations whenever this is appropriate and the donor agrees. It is also possible for a donor to support the walk anonymously if they prefer.

It was clear, however, that there would be a lot of people who would, for convenience or otherwise, want to donate in cash or by cheque. We therefore set up and advertised an alternative to the website that channelled the donations through Viv and then on to Christian Aid in regular payments that included cheques and paperwork to support Gift Aid donations where these were made. We felt that it was important to be scrupulously careful over this aspect since we had agreed that all the money donated would be forwarded with no deductions for the costs of the walk.

These costs were for consumables bought before the walk, transport and materials in connection with organising the walk, training, accommodation during the walk, meals and transport back at the end. I did not keep a very accurate account of these items but have included some estimates in Chapter 5 where it is obvious that a walk of this type is not a cheap undertaking.

Finalising a route

There is no single accepted route for a walk from Lands End to John O'Groats or from John O'Groats to Lands End. More people walk from south to north than from north to south but the arguments in favour of a northward walk have always seemed to me to be less convincing than has sometimes been suggested. A number of considerations might be taken into account in planning a route.

- The walk will benefit from better weather and longer daylight hours making early April to late September the best period.
- The tourist season in Devon and Cornwall from late July to early September makes bed & breakfast or hostel accommodation less easily available.
- The summer midge season in Scotland is better avoided but it is difficult to predict its location and timing.
- Some people have said that walking 'downhill' (north to south) feels better. I don't believe this but, since I live in Cornwall, I did feel that walking towards home might be better than walking away from it.
- The harder part of the walk is to the north (though this depends somewhat on the route chosen); I'm not clear whether it's better to get this over and done with early or to wait until fitness has improved.

- Whether one is walking into the prevailing wind or into the sun or with these at one's back do not seem to me to be relevant issues since both are unpredictable in a British summer.

For a long time I planned a north-south route but switched direction at a fairly late stage because of the difficulties of the route that I chose across the northern highlands of Scotland. As you will see later, I changed my mind about this part of the route but, by the time I did that, I had already completed most of the walk. With hindsight I might have been better to have stuck with my north-south first preference.

Andrew McCloy has described most of the route options available to the walker and I won't repeat these here. One of his possible routes, starting at Land End, involves crossing southern England to the eastern counties and then walking northwards from there. Because of the increased distance involved I rejected this possibility which does, in any case, miss out some of the most attractive hill scenery that England and southern Scotland have to offer. That leaves routes that go through central England or the Welsh borders, up the Pennines or through the Lake District and up through Scotland either to the west or to the east, merging in the far north-east.

I made the following choices.

Through the centre of Cornwall and Devon to Taunton. The obvious alternatives were the north or south coast paths but these, whilst splendid walks, do involve a great deal of climbing and weaving around headlands and coves; not something that I wanted to do early in the walk. The disadvantage of the central route is that there is no long-distance path to follow; all available routes consist of a mixture of short or medium length footpath sections and sections of road walking. It does, however, use part of the Camel Trail, bits of several trails in Devon and the canal towpath and river walk from Tiverton to Taunton.

Across the Somerset levels to the M5 bridge over the River Avon at Avonmouth; then the Severn Way and Gloucester and Sharpness Canal towpath into the West Midlands. Apart from sections each side of the Avon this is a flat and fast walking route. Many walkers head for Bath and then use the Cotswold Way; they then have the choice of dropping down to the Severn Way in the Gloucester area or joining the Heart of England Way to pass east of Birmingham. None of this appealed to me. I also chose not to cross the Severn Estuary in order to use Offa's Dyke Path since I felt that this ended up with an awkward route across southern Shropshire in order to get into south Derbyshire. Some walkers who want to walk into Scotland from the Lake District have chosen to cross Cheshire into Lancashire and then walk north from there but the Cheshire/Lancashire section is not very interesting. However, there is a lot of pleasure to be had from walking some of Offa's Dyke Path and I understand why many walkers would prefer this route.

The Staffordshire Way linking to the Alternative Pennine Way at Ashbourne. The Staffordshire Way is well marked and plots a good route across a county that has a lot of enclosed land (farmland and urban sites). The Way has a minimum of road walking and it would be difficult to find a better way of getting into South Derbyshire.

The Alternative Pennine Way (APW). Most end-to-end walkers choose to walk the Pennine Way from Edale in mid-Derbyshire to the Scottish border. It has the enormous advantage of being relatively well waymarked and well documented with a list of accommodation available and with baggage-carrying services if wanted. I chose to use the Alternative Pennine Way (developed by Denis Brook & Phil Hinchliffe) which starts in Ashbourne and ends at Jedburgh. I accept that my reasons are not altogether convincing; mainly it was that I wanted a route that avoided some of the obvious places that I'd walked before (such as Crowden, Malham Cave and Upper Teesdale) and one that set out to highlight less visited parts of the Pennines. Maybe I was just being different for the sake of being different and the choice of the APW turned out to be a mixed blessing for reasons described for some sections on the walk.

The Borders to Inverness. I did not particularly want to go to Edinburgh and I did not particularly want to do the West Highland Way again nor to walk the Great Glen Way from Fort William to Inverness. I put together a route across the Southern Uplands of Scotland that was adapted from one described by Robinson and which brought me down to the Forth Road Bridge. From there I followed a route described in outline by McCloy that went through Perth, Pitlochry, the Cairngorms and Aviemore to Inverness, largely using cycleways. The only part of this that is a recognised trail is the splendid 2-day route up Glen Tilt and then through Lairig Ghru. This involved one night camping at Chest of Dee. The advantage of this whole route is its directness; its disadvantage is that it involves rather more minor road walking than I wanted.

The coastal route from Inverness. I had intended a walk from Inverness that fitted together routes described by Butler and Robinson and that went through mid-Sutherland to Lairg, crossed the Flow Country to Watten and then followed minor roads and paths to John O'Groats. I abandoned this idea at Inverness for reasons that I describe in the report of that section of the route. Instead I took the much more conventional route up the coast through Dingwall, Dornoch, Helmsdale and Wick to Duncansby Head and John O'Groats. There's a lot of main road walking on this coastal route but I did manage to do that at a weekend when there was very little traffic. I regret abandoning the cross-country route but did get to the end of the walk 2 days earlier than I originally intended.

I'm not generally unhappy with this choice of route. There were some difficult bits and I did not enjoy some of the road walking. On the other hand, I walked many parts of the country that I've never seen before, followed many splendid footpaths and completed the walk reasonably efficiently. Overall I

- tried to do as little road walking as possible
- aimed for an average daily distance of between 24 and 26 km (15 - 16 miles)
- inserted rest days at intervals of about a week
- chose stopping places that would be likely to yield a choice of accommodation and set an accommodation cost limit of £45 per night.

I have put a full description of the route (as I finally walked it) in a table in Chapter 5. The table was compiled using the routes as recorded on my GPS as I walked but with some manual corrections where the GPS failed (usually because I'd let the batteries go flat or had forgotten to turn it on at the start of the day); these have been plotted onto Ordnance Survey maps available on the OS Getamap website from which I can read off the distance walked. I am not publishing these maps but the GPS waypoints (in the form of the final gpx files) are available for download from my website. Instructions for this are alongside the tables at the start of each section described in Chapter 3. Once downloaded the files can be saved and the waypoints plotted directly onto suitable mapping software (such as OS Getamap or Google maps) and then viewed in detail or saved.

My intended route was originally published on my website at http://www.wilmut. net/lejog and will remain there for the foreseeable future. Whereas I used a mixture of imperial and metric units in the original walk descriptions I've now rationalised my records so that everything is shown in metric units with imperial equivalents in brackets where appropriate. Some of the places listed in the table are different from those on the website because I walked further or less far than I intended (usually because of the availability of accommodation) but the basic route sections are very much the same as those on the website with the notable exception of north-east Scotland.

Walking alone

Some people were surprised that I chose to walk alone. For me, there was no question that I would do this and I told enquirers that I do not make a good walking companion, preferring to make my own decisions and set my own pace. I do not get lonely and value having my personal time and space. For almost all of the walk I was happy with this decision; just occasionally I would have valued another opinion or the opportunity to share difficult decision-making.

Accommodation and meals

There are end-to-end walkers who carry tents or bivvy sheets all the way, are only dependent on finding a bit of ground to sleep on and who say that this gives freedom to each day's walk. I'm not convinced, particularly if one is carrying everything in a rucksack and walking for a period of 2 months or more. The most basic camping will add at least 3 kg to the weight carried and this will involve using the smallest of tents. Camp sites are thinly spread outside the main tourist areas so that washing, toilet and laundry facilities will not be available most days. It may be wimpish, but I'm not drawn to the idea of erecting a wet tent every evening, cooking primitive meals, sleeping on the ground and taking a wetter tent down every morning, day after day.

It is possible to get camping gear carried in a support vehicle and it is possible to forgo the pleasures of camping at intervals in order to enjoy the comforts of a hostel or guest house. For me, that wasn't the solution. I did not have (nor want to have) a support system; I don't think that it's reasonable to expect a relative or friend to spend two or more months driving round the country while I walk a daily distance that a car or van can do in half an hour. I am too mean to pay for such a service and would want to be as self-contained as possible (though I have envied people overtaking me with day bags on their backs and their heavy gear being carried in a van). Nor do I want to carry camping equipment unless I have no alternative.

I also know that I am a planner by nature and would find it very difficult to live with the uncertainty of not having a destination each day. I am not one of those end-to-end walkers who is willing to take a chance that someone will offer a bed for the night, perhaps as a reward for a poetry reading or a comic turn in a pub. So, before I left, I trawled the internet to find places to stay. This was an extremely time-consuming task which I cannot recommend. However, without such a list one is dependent on either walking into places and spotting B&Bs, pubs, hostels or hotels and hoping that they have space or on calling tourist information centres and getting them to find accommodation.

However, as I've already described, I wasn't entirely dependent on my list. As a result of the contact with Christian Aid I had a number of offers of accommodation from their supporters and more offers came from personal friends (some of whom I hadn't seen for 50 years!); in all cases I was glad to accept these very kind offers of help for which I am very grateful and which I acknowledge in more detail in Chapter 5. Everything else was B&Bs or pubs within my cost limit of £45 per night; I only used one hostel in the end though I went armed with a YHA card as a standby. I guess that this reflects my wish to have some private space in the evenings; to be able to go to bed early, not to have to talk to people and not to have to share room space. Meals, generally speaking, were in pubs and the cheaper restaurants, keeping costs as low as I could.

I did not book accommodation far in advance because of the unpredictability of the walk. I generally spent some time working through my list, telephoning potential places to stay, not more than 3 or 4 nights in advance. I had very few problems with this and only contacted a tourist information centre once, but found that the information that I had was better than theirs. I only failed to locate accommodation twice though I occasionally had to change my route because I needed to widen the area of search for suitable accommodation. For the most part, the guest houses, pubs and hostels that I stayed in were good though I never knew in advance what each would be like and cost was not a reliable guide to quality. Many of the proprietors took an interest in the walk and a number made contributions, which was unexpected but very welcome. Where I have a comment about the quality of somewhere that I stayed, it can be found in the text on the page or in the blog extract. It would be unwise to treat what I've said as either a general recommendation or a generalcriticism.

There were several places where the accommodation was off route. This most often happened when I was staying with a Christian Aid supporter or with a friend but I did commute by train from Hathersage into Sheffield and back out next morning because I couldn't locate a B&B in Hathersage that had space. I also spent a rest day in Bradford because the B&Bs that I had located in Ilkley were expensive; the travel was cheap and it enabled me to see the city, which I'd never visited.

The cost for a single person staying in a B&B is generally higher than when sharing a room and some proprietors imposed such a large surcharge that it took the room cost outside my budget. A few of the single rooms that I used were very small; acceptable for one night but likely to be intolerable for more.

My main food intake was in the evenings. Whilst staying at B&Bs I normally went to a pub or a restaurant and I've mentioned many of these in the day-by-day descriptions in Chapter 3. Whilst clearly an optional extra, I frequently enjoyed a pint of beer or a glass of wine which gave a mellow feeling to the end of what had often been a hard day. However, in the daytime I studiously (though occasionally regretfully) walked past pubs, not wanting to turn the walk into an almighty pub crawl.

Breakfast and lunch, by contrast, were minimalist affairs. I find the 'full' English or Scottish breakfast entirely unsuitable as a basis for a day's walking and invariably had cereal and coffee, occasionally supplemented with a bit of toast or an egg. I found I could often trade my minimalist breakfast for a slightly earlier start in the morning, though I very rarely managed to get on the road before 7.30 am.

Lunch was the same every day. I make up a mixture of raisins and nuts (peanuts or cashews) and eat it by the handful. It's quick, nutritious, needs little preparation, weighs little and can be carried in a rucksack for several days without damage or deterioration. A chocolate bar and an apple followed and I drank water. This lunch may sound primitive but I looked forward to it every day!

I have estimated the overall costs of accommodation and meals in Chapter 5.

Chapter 2

Gearing up

While all the planning and organising was going on I was also trying to get fit for the walk and making sure that I had the equipment that I would need. This chapter discusses these things and takes me to the point where I set off for Lands End with my wife and a rucksack in a state of some anxiety that was, I hope, well hidden.

Getting fitter

If you go back to my blog (http://johnslejog.wordpress.com/) you will find that the first entry describes training walks that I had been doing since January.

I never was very athletic and I'm useless at sport so I really can't see myself going to a gym or swimming 50 lengths a day. My theory is that all I need to do to get fit for walking is to walk. So I'm doing long walks every few days, making sure that they're over the sort of territory that I can expect once I start in May. So I devise walks that are between 24 and 32 km (15 and 20 miles) long, which involve varying amounts of up and down, which minimise road walking and which I can access using public transport. This isn't something new ... but the end-to-end walk is something rather more ambitious, so I'm not taking it lightly. Everybody says that training is important and I believe them!

As a target for my training walks I use a rule that was devised by Scottish mountaineer William Naismith in 1892. The rule says that the time taken for a walk by a reasonably fit person over typical terrain will be 1 hour for every 5 km (5 miles) plus half an hour for every 300 m (or 1000 ft) of ascent. I map out a route on the computer using a piece of OS software and this gives me a Naismith time which is then my target.

I'm getting better! A month ago I walked from Looe to Par (24 km or 17 miles, also on the coast path) and missed the target by 30 minutes. Not good. A glorious 29 km (21 mile) walk in bright sunshine at the end of February was a circular route from Padstow via Trevose Head and Portcothan which missed the target by only 15 minutes, but I did get lost in a small jungle and had to bail out by crossing a stream balancing on a fallen treetrunk. Last Monday, I walked from Looe to the Cremyll Ferry (22 km or 16 miles, most on the coast path) and hit the target with 20 minutes to spare.

Other similar walks would follow until, by the time I left in May, I had completed 11 long walks, totalling just under 200 miles and 74 hours although only the last couple of walks were done with a moderately full rucksack.

I wrote blog entries for most of the later walks, seeing this as a way of involving people who had already shown interest or donated. Some entries make interesting reading in the light of what happened during the walk - this is from mid-March.

Yesterday Dartmoor looked splendid; once the mist had lifted the light was sharp and clear and it was the perfect spring day. My aim was a training walk of about 20 miles in a large loop that started and finished in Princetown. Perhaps it was a bad sign that I missed the track out of the town and was then harassed by two large and noisy dogs. But things then improved and I made good time on the first leg of the loop, working my way across the moor on good tracks and down through the very picturesque village of Hexworthy, then back up across the high moor where I had a solitary lunch in the sunshine.

Navigation should have been easy – it was bright sunlight and all the landmarks were very clear. But, after lunch, gradually the tracks petered out and I was crossing the great tufts of winter grass that conceal bogs and holes and the rough ground of old mine workings or medieval settlements. Navigating rough and boggy ground saps the energy very quickly and every step carries the risk of a twisted ankle or a boot full of water.

I did find odd bits of tracks but most of the second half of the day was this frustrating battle with rough ground and bogs. I met only one group of walkers – three cheerful lads with rucksacks and a radio tuned to a commentary on the England-France rugby match. The sun still shone and the birds still sang but the walk got slower and slower and my temper shorter and shorter. I may even have sworn at the occasional bog. Mercifully, the last 3 miles back into Princetown did at least follow a clear and well-graded track but, by then, the day had lost its sparkle, I was an hour late and I was tired and rather dispirited. And my opinion of Dartmoor as walking territory had reverted to hearty dislike.

However, training is both a matter of getting fitter and a matter of learning. My route for the walk won't involve much open moorland like Dartmoor – where it does I need to make sure that I allow enough time to navigate the bogs. I just hope it's not raining!

Another post was concerned with my boots and I made a decision that did not turn out as well as I'd expected when, later in the walk, the new boots failed to keep the water out and had to be replaced. I also used this and some other posts to complain about things that I complained about again during the end-to-end walk; these included the annoyances that arose when landowners blocked paths or made access difficult, the ever-pervasive smell of chips that hangs over most Cornish coastal villages and the prevalence of litter.

I have been wondering for some time whether my very comfortable Brasher boots had enough life left in them to cope with 1100 miles without falling apart. A few days ago I measured the wear on the soles, inspected the stitching and decided that they were too much of a risk. So I had an expensive day in the Cotswold shop in Plymouth, taking up a lot of the assistants' time before buying (amongst other items) a brand new pair of Berghaus boots. The assistants who helped with the boots and with the other items were very helpful and very patient and, fortunately, it was a slow day at Cotswold.

No-one is ever happy with this process. The wrong choice of boot and you're in for a crippling time on a walk. But in a shop, all you can do is to lace up a pair of boots and walk round the shop for a few minutes, up and down some stairs if you're lucky, feeling a bit of a prat. You then part with well over £100 and offer a prayer that you've made the right choice because, once those boots hit a hard surface and the first scuff appears, there's no going back.

Well, I got it right this time. I got back yesterday afternoon from 16 miles of countryside and coast path near Tintagel (another fantastic spring day, but if you were working you won't want to know that) and the feet were glowing gently but undamaged. So I now have a pair of boots that will probably survive until John O'Groats. If not, I can always get the old Brashers mailed to me.

Then there was the problem that other things intervened and training and writing the blog both took a back seat for some time.

I know that I'm falling behind with this blog. Hundreds of eager readers out there, waiting for the next revelations and almost 2 weeks have passed since I last wrote. It won't do!

My excuse is that I've been very busy – mixing training walks with getting accommodation, equipment and maps ready for the walk and with getting other essential jobs done. I'd never realised how much preparatory work would be needed for this walk – it's taken over my life! I have, of course, had some less stressful moments – a superb performance of La Traviata by the Welsh National Opera last week, some very enjoyable dinners with family and friends and one of my regular stints as washer-up at the Saturday breakfast at our local community centre. (Did I say that I am the best-qualified washer-up in Cornwall or, perhaps, nationally? No? Interested? I'll tell you about it sometime.)

Everybody's asking me how the training is going. Well, I'm still walking and I feel reasonably fit but I can't honestly say that I'm much slimmer. If I'm truthful, I don't look much like a potential end-to-end walker most of the time but that will improve, I think. I've had a couple of long days since I last wrote and I've a few more to go before I leave in 3 weeks' time.

Then, on my last training walk from Sourton to Eggesford in mid-Devon (a 32 km or 23-mile trek designed to test endurance!) I encountered rain, sheep that followed me across a field and a Citroën on stilts that set me up very nicely for my eventual experiences on the walk, especially the rain.

You could make a good sermon from the behaviour of these sheep. This wasn't the first time that I've been followed by a flock of sheep and it's a bit unnerving. What do they want? What are they going to do? Do I look like another sheep?

The Citroën was just a bit surreal. I'd heard that odd things go on in North Devon, away from the public gaze. But this poor old 2CV was just sitting in a field on top of a steel frame, gently rusting (as I was – it had started to rain). I might have expected this on a garage forecourt but not in a field.

What I took with me

As with blisters, there's no shortage of advice about what to take on a walk like this. Lists differ but everyone agrees that the greatest risk is that of taking too much stuff. Somebody who lifted my rucksack during the walk solemnly told me that you assemble the gear, then throw half the stuff out then throw out a half of what's left and go with the residue. Of course, that's silly - the problem is to ensure that everything packed justifies its inclusion and then tolerating whatever comes out of that process. I guess that everyone discovers some mistakes - both omissions and the inclusion of unnecessary items.

My final list is shown in Chapter 5. I think that I need to explain the inclusion of some items on that list. The total weight on my back, rucksack and all, was a little over 11 kg which was 3-4 kg more than I intended. I later made some reductions but the basic weight that I carried all the way was always in the 10 - 11 kg region. In addition, from Pitlochry to Inverness I carried a total of 13 kg that included the camping gear but with the loss of a few basic items that I sent back home.

A good deal of the weight was created because I wanted a satisfactory record of the walk. At the heart of this was the netbook and its associated bits and pieces, coming in at a little under 1.5 kg. I wavered between this and something like a

Blackberry, deciding in the end that I'd put up with the additional weight for the sake of a much more versatile device, capable of providing backup for the camera, audio recorder and GPS and allowing me to type easily and quickly, all at a reasonable price. I still don't know whether this was the right decision but it did have the added advantage of replacing my elderly laptop and so has a life beyond that of the walk.

Accompanying the netbook were the digital camera, GPS and digital audio recorder. I cannot imagine doing a walk without a camera and took a small elderly digital Pentax that has always been reliable and continued to be so for the walk. The audio recorder was for making notes - more instant than paper and pencil (and marginally better in the rain) and, as it turned out, an excellent investment to support my memory as I wrote the blog and compiled this book.

I had previously had no experience of using a GPS. I spoke to several people about this and was overwhelmed by their enthusiasm for the bells and whistles on their instruments. However, I also decided that I would not want to trust 70 days of navigation to maps on a GPS screen, particularly since these are only available across the whole country at 1:50,000 scale at a hideous cost. The batteries could fail or I could lose the machine and then where would I be? So I went back to traditional map and compass navigation for the whole walk; the maps (a mixture of 1:50,000 and 1:25,000 scales) cost me about £250 and one could easily be replaced if lost. I then bought a Garmin etrex10 GPS - it's cheap and basic but does two things that I needed: it records where I walked (I set it to store waypoints at 2 minute intervals) and, if I got lost, I could get it to tell me my grid reference which I could look up on my paper map. It would also give me a man overboard fix if there was a flood and I could get directions to a specified waypoint if needed; I didn't use these facilities.

With a Kindle (lighter than books), batteries, a dongle (to get me an internet link if I couldn't get WiFi), my phone, batteries, chargers and cables, this electronic gear weighed in at a little under 3 kg.

The list details most of the other items which were normal for this type of walk. I had one change of clothes, some lightweight trainers and the lightest waterproofs I could find without spending a fortune; these and my first aid kit accounted for almost 4 kg. The waterproofs were not ideal - they had only thin inner linings so were slow to wick away sweat so I sometimes got almost as wet inside them (especially the jacket) as I would if I'd not worn them at all. In fact, in light rain, I often didn't. The rucksack was excellent and as light as I could manage at a reasonable price and for the size that I needed. I paid for one with a ventilated back but felt, in the end, that this didn't work quite as well as I might have hoped.

I only carried maps for a limited number of days. I posted used maps back home and Viv mailed or brought packets of maps to me at the starts of some sections. I took the covers off all the maps and cut away areas of each map that I would be unlikely to need. Where I compiled a route for myself (as, for example, in Cornwall, Devon and Somerset) I used 1:25,000 maps. Where walking was likely to be very straightforward (as along the Severn Way) or the 1:25,000 map showed no more information than the 1:50,000 map (as in north-east Scotland) I used the latter since the total cost was lower. As a subscriber to OS Getamap I did use the facility to print my own copies of small sections of maps where it would have been a waste of money to buy a whole map. In addition to the maps I took copies of pages from the book of the Alternative Pennine Way and from Robinson's guide to the end-to-end walk and used these in conjunction with 1:50,000 maps.

I took my walking poles and hardly used them. They are a pair of Brasher poles bought in the late 1990s and weighing only half a kilogram; I thought that they would be important but they only came out on a couple of occasions when I hurt my foot and leg and when I was very tired coming down from Lairig Ghru. I would not, however, go without them since they are, in my view, a great safety aid as was the Blizzard emergency bag that sat in the bottom of my rucksack and did nothing for the whole of the trip.

The camping equipment was in no way unusual and most of it was gear that I already had. The failure of the tent groundsheet (reported on Day 68) was wholly unexpected but I have to admit that I am not in any way in love with this minute tent in which I cannot even sit up. It is, I think, an enthusiast's tent. but it's hard to get lighter than 1.7 kg without spending a large amount of money (lightweight gear is notoriously expensive).

Patricia Sawie in school in
Sierra Leone
Photograph from Christian Aid

Chapter 3

Putting feet and head in gear

Enough of the planning and preparations! I now come to the story of the walk as it actually happened. This chapter is based firmly on the blog written whilst I was walking from Lands End to John O'Groats. I've divided the chapter into sections each of which ends with a rest day or with the end of the walk. I've put a summary map with each section and the gpx files for each of the days can be downloaded from my website: instructions appear alongside the table in the preamble to each section. Each day is dealt with separately and includes photographs, some of which have already appeared in the blog, others not.

I have done some judicious editing on the daily blog posts, removing irrelevant material and correcting errors. I have added some further notes for some of the days where I felt that there were matters that I'd omitted from the blog. The whole may or may not represent a coherent account.

Serious thought (and some fear) before starting; a sunny send-off at Lands End
Photograph by Viv Wilmut

West Cornwall bluebell wood

Lands End to Launceston

Date	Day	No	From	To
2-May-2012	Wed	1	Lands End	Penzance
3-May-2012	Thu	2	Penzance	Four Lanes
4-May-2012	Fri	3	Four Lanes	Truro
5-May-2012	Sat	4	Truro	Fraddon
6-May-2012	Sun	5	Fraddon	Nanstallon
7-May-2012	Mon	6	Nanstallon	Camelford
8-May-2012	Tue	7	Camelford	Launceston

GPX files for each day's walk can be downloaded from the internet and plotted using mapping software such as OS Getamap or Google maps. The download addresses are in the form http://www.wilmut.net/lejogbook/day1.gpx

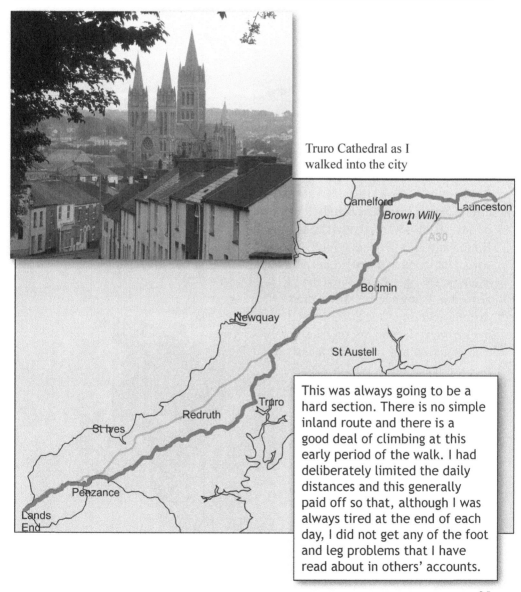

Truro Cathedral as I walked into the city

This was always going to be a hard section. There is no simple inland route and there is a good deal of climbing at this early period of the walk. I had deliberately limited the daily distances and this generally paid off so that, although I was always tired at the end of each day, I did not get any of the foot and leg problems that I have read about in others' accounts.

DAY 1 **Lands End to Penzance**

17 km (11 miles)
332 m of climb
1% completed

It's a mess of paths as you leave Lands End and walk through Sennen, looking back to the unsightly muddle of buildings at Lands End. The small hill that is Carn Brea acts like a magnet and provides the last long view backs to Lands End; I would be looking forward from now on.

I was almost euphoric at the end of the day - I had really started the walk! But it was also a learning day. I found that I needed to develop systems for doing things - a typical example would be ensuring that I put particular items such as the camera or GPS in the same pockets each day and that I switched the GPS on when I started and off when I finished walking. Packing the rucksack would also be a ritual so that I could be sure that I never left anything behind and knew where to find particular items in a hurry. One silly example emerged on this first day; I arrived in Penzance and discovered that the address of my B&B was on my netbook, deep in my rucksack. Thereafter I made sure that I had a piece of paper in my pocket with address and directions. No paperless office for me.

I should add that I decided fairly early on that I wouldn't bother with the Lands End to John O'Groats passport - I would not need to prove to anyone that I'd done this walk and I have better uses for £15.

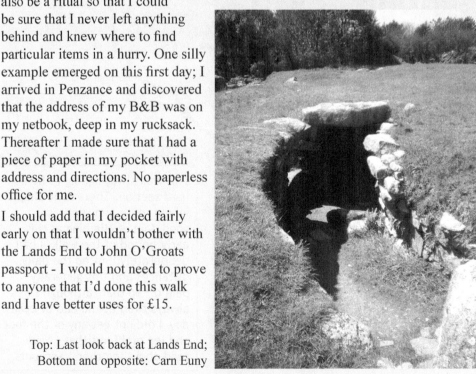

Top: Last look back at Lands End;
Bottom and opposite: Carn Euny

1% done, 99% to go!

Don't worry! I'm not going to keep a statistical record of progress – number of miles walked, number of metres climbed, number of steps taken. But at least a barrier has been broken today. I no longer have the walk to do – only 99% of it. I was photographed at the signpost at Lands End (sandwiched between photographs of a happy couple and of a happy married couple, though I suppose that the first couple may have been married but were shy about it). Then a farewell to Viv, with a wave as I disappeared over the horizon to Sennen. No one cheered, there was no fly-past and Lands End looked much the same after I'd gone as when I arrived.

I should add that, before I left, I called at the hotel and got my Lands End to John O'Groats passport stamped and dated. I now have to get it stamped and dated half a dozen or more times before it is finally presented at John O'Groats for a ceremonial final entry. On payment of £15 I can then get a certificate. If I feel mean I can always frame the passport which will have had the privilege of having travelled all the way with me.

The weather today was fantastic. I may never have another one like it on this walk – it will be hard to beat. I went over the fields and along the lanes to Penzance – only a short distance today but a great start after the awful weather of the last couple of weeks. I went via Carn Brea and then came across the ancient monument called Carn Euny which was, it said, a British-Romano settlement built on the site of an earlier Iron Age village. It looked remarkably like some of the sites that we saw on Orkney a few years ago, and marvelled at. Here, there was a small underground chamber and some bits of walling and what may have been the foundations of dwellings – the information board was a bit short on detail which was a pity. It was a lovely place to have lunch – absolutely solitary.

Later I met a man who approached me up a footpath but stopped to take some photographs of a ruined farmhouse and barn. We exchanged hellos and, in an accent that was either from the USA or Canada, he asked me where I'd come from and where I was going; when I told him he shook me by the hand and asked me how old I was. When I told him he said 'gee', and then asked why I was doing it. I told him that and he looked suitably impressed so I gave him one of my

(quite pretty) little cards. I hope that he remembers it and gives a suitably impressive donation, but I'm not holding my breath. On the other hand, he may be intending to buy the ruin and would feel that a donation would be one way of ingratiating himself with the locals. We'll see.

DAY 2   **Penzance to Four Lanes**   31 km (19 miles)
481 m of climb
3% completed

Four Lanes is a village 4 km south-west of Redruth.

FROM THE BLOG

Bullocks, litter, bluebells and a peacock

This should have been a fairly straightforward day, ending at Praze an Beeble (I'd always wanted to go there – what an address to have!). But the hoped-for B&B didn't work out and the best I could do was 4 miles further on. I modified my route to include more road walking (which is quicker but not as interesting as footpaths) and walked solidly from 7.30 until I settled for an early lunch at about 12.15.

In fact, it was a very interesting day. As I left Penzance, passengers were trekking across to the *Scillonian* (the ferry to the Isles of Scilly) and, further along, the helicopter was taking off. A Cross-Country train left the station as I walked past and I reflected that,

had I caught that, I could have been at John O'Groats by lunchtime tomorrow. I could take the boat to Orkney, find a nice place to stay and write the blog from there. Silly ideas … I trudged on making a small note to myself (I'm carrying a voice recorder) that, even though this is only Day 2, I'm feeling a great deal more relaxed about the walk than I have been at any time in the last 2-3 weeks. I hope that's not tempting providence.

St Michael's Mount looked suitably mysterious in the rather hazy weather and then I turned my back on the sea for the last time and headed inland. People could no longer mistake me for a coastal path walker – I was now definitely headed much further afield. This was where the road walking began, interspersed with stretches of footpath that varied from very narrow and muddy paths to green lanes that were in regular use by farmers and others. At one point I had to follow a rather erratic route across what had clearly been a mining area but most of which was now an enormous pasture, home to a herd of bored bullocks. I was obviously the most interesting thing that they'd seen for a long time and they started to follow me, really quite closely. I didn't want to get jostled by bullocks

Above: Helicopter leaving Penzance for the Isles of Scilly
Opposite top: Bullocks safely behind a gate
Opposite bottom: Peacock perched on a chimney

but I was having real trouble finding the exit to this field – I walked a few yards then turned to flap my map at them, then walked a few more yards and flapped again. Had a gate not appeared this could have gone on for a long time.

This was the start of a very annoying bit of cross-country walking. The footpath went down through woodland which suddenly opened out into a large caravan site. No indication of how to get out! I drifted around, trying to relate my map to what was there, then suddenly came to a bridge across a large stream. This

must be the way out! I began to walk down the other side of the stream looking for the path that went up through woodland; a woman called out to me from the caravan site side of the stream: 'There's no way out down there'. But my map said there was so I carried on … to find that there was no way out. I walked back to find the same woman waiting for me. To be fair, she didn't gloat (though I think that she was secretly pleased to have been proved right) but did point to an unmarked track that she said went up the hill through the woodland but ended in a ploughed field. The footpath sign, she said, had disappeared some time ago.

Again, she was right, but I wasn't going back down for a third encounter. I inched my way round the field, carefully avoiding the crop until I found a gate that led onto a green lane which released me from this wretched valley. I wasn't where I'd intended to be but I was past caring – with bullocks, campsite, missing signs and ploughed field, the whole had probably lost me 30-45 minutes.

I skirted a village called Leedstown, using a bridle way that turned out to be the pits of the place. It was littered with junk, abandoned vehicles and

failed enterprises. There was a very elegant armchair on a tip that was a tempting lunch place, but I just couldn't cope with the surroundings. So I walked on, remembering that the whole of the Cornish countryside is littered with unwanted stuff and no-one seems to care.

The day ended with a walk past a beautiful bluebell wood and a peacock sitting on someone's chimney pot. I'd heard this bird shouting across the valley for some time but hadn't expected it to be on show in this way. We have resident jackdaws at home – a peacock is an altogether more worrying guest.

DAY 3 **Four Lanes to Truro**

20 km (13 miles)
285 m of climb
4% completed

This day was a walk through a large part of Cornwall's mining heritage, now part of the Cornwall and West Devon Mining Landscape World Heritage Site, designated in 2006. So I shouldn't have been surprised at encountering the Hayle Railway which provided me with good views across towards Redruth where I remember enjoying a very interesting town trail a few years ago.

I'm not very good at spotting wildlife - I tend to walk along looking at my boots. But, in addition to yesterday's peacock I encountered a female fox walking nonchalantly towards me along the tramway path but disappearing into the undergrowth as I approached.

Gwennap, passed through later, was once famous for the extent of its copper mines and the area was described in the late 18th and early 19th centuries as the richest square mile in the world. A mile or two from the village is Gwennap Pit which is an open air amphitheatre made famous by John Wesley, the founder of Methodism. Possibly a hollow created by mining activities, it has remarkable acoustic properties

and became one of Wesley's favourite open air preaching places; he came there on 18 occasions between 1762 and 1789. The Pit, now owned by the Methodist Church, is still in use today.

Above: View over Pennance;
Left: Viaduct on the Falmouth branch line
Top Right: Granite plaque;
Bottom Right: Cornish miner (photographed on an information board; note the candles, one stuck on his hat)

Short day, short blog

It should have been a short day but ended up feeling like a long one and, by the time I reached Costa in Truro, I really was ready for a large cappuccino. I guess that it was because I chose to use as many footpaths as possible and most were very muddy or complicated or inhabited by bullocks (but no more bullock stories, I promise). So it got slow, my right foot was sore from the efforts of yesterday and I began to feel a bit sorry for myself. But I'm typing this in Costa, revived by the coffee.

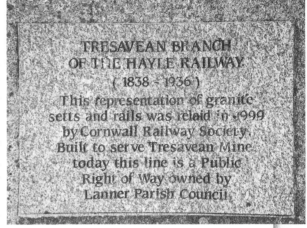

Though short, the walk wasn't without interest. One of the best bits was joining a footpath to discover that it was part of the Tresavean branch of the Hayle Railway, opened in 1838 to serve the Tresavean mine and closed in 1936. A good notice board explained the details (though why did they have to put it so high that no child could read it?) and the view over Pennance was superb.

Some nice villages too – places that really would make good postcards without any great effort. I saw a church in Gwennap with what looked like a detached bell tower and wished afterwards that I'd gone in to look at it. There was also a pub in Frogpool that would have tempted me had it been open. And there was a surprising number of very smart large houses tucked away in picturesque corners, many of them converted farm buildings. There's plenty of money somewhere though I wouldn't be surprised if a lot of them weren't second homes. How much of this wealth rubs off on Cornwall, I wonder?

I'm having some senior moments with my GPS which I carry for two reasons

only. First, it's my fallback if I get lost – I can read the grid reference and locate myself on a map. Then, I use it to record my route – it logs a waypoint every two minutes. At least, that's what I set it to do but I wasn't at all sure today that it was working properly. I will study the manual this evening and see what I may be doing wrong – if this machine can do 'man overboard' records than it surely can meet my modest needs.

That will do for today. I'm on my second cappuccino and it will soon be time to go off to find my B&B. I might walk round to the cathedral first.

22 km (13 miles)
416 m of climb
5% completed

I felt the need, from time to time, to prove to those reading my blog that I was actually walking through Britain and not holed up somewhere, living a luxurious existence and inventing stories about the walk. I therefore took pictures of myself, using my Gorrilapod which makes it possible to mount my very petite camera almost anywhere and use the timer. One such is below and it was included in my blog for

Day 4 though, unless you knew the location of this bridge, I could have been anywhere! But at least I do look as though I'm doing some serious walking and, if you look at pictures like this taken through the walk you can see that I'm losing weight and looking progressively more dishevelled.

I also include another picture of Truro cathedral that does dominate the centre of the city; I spent some time there at the end of Day 3. I did hear someone in Yorkshire describe it and one or two others as not 'proper' cathedrals since they are not of medieval origin. I was not impressed by this argument.

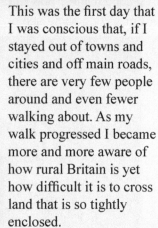

This was the first day that I was conscious that, if I stayed out of towns and cities and off main roads, there are very few people around and even fewer walking about. As my walk progressed I became more and more aware of how rural Britain is yet how difficult it is to cross land that is so tightly enclosed.

FROM THE BLOG
Valleys and smells

I did stop off at the cathedral last night and then found myself with something rather different for accommodation. It was right in the centre of Truro and was very laid back, friendly and inexpensive. I had a good evening meal in a crowded and noisy pub and then returned to some undemanding TV and an early night. After a self-help breakfast (I did wash up my dishes!) I sneaked off very quietly though hadn't expected it to be raining. But this didn't last for very long and, since then, the day has been fitfully sunny.

The exit from Truro was up a hill under the railway viaduct and very abruptly into a delightful valley. The transition from urban to rural was very sudden, surprising in these days when we're used to ribbons of business parks, retail parks and industrial parks, generally ugly and not really parks at all. In fact, coming into the city the day before had been like that – one moment countryside, the next cityscape. It gives a good feel to a place.

Today was, sadly, heavy with road walking. I had a good footpath up the valley and a long climb on a forestry track, seeing only a jogger and girl on a bicycle, both of whom looked very cheerful – no doubt the effect of a Saturday. After that it was country lanes with attractive views and very, very few vehicles. I have learned something in my few days of walking: bashing on for hour after hour, especially on roads, is bad for me. My feet get tired and I get bored; better to stop and have a break. I did that this morning, high up on the side of another valley where it would have been easy to go to sleep in the sunshine. I remember reading a Lonely Planet guide that said that Cornwall had a beautiful coastline but an ugly interior. Well, on the evidence of 4 days' walking, that's really not true. I have come across a lot of very attractive places in my walk so far and this valley was typical. It was just trees and fields but the whole was very tranquil. It reminded me of my days in the sixth form in the 50s when we went out onto Mendip to go caving. Afterwards there was a lot of sitting around in the sunshine chatting. I think that we were rather pleased with ourselves for going caving and I guess that it wasn't sunny all of the time, but this valley reminded me of that time when the worst thing that could happen was A levels.

I must have been dozing because I remember thinking about smells (though this valley was odour free). Where do they all go? Is the planet getting steadily more malodorous? I suppose that smells are molecules that we detect with our noses but that must drift off somewhere – perhaps there's a special layer in the atmosphere (the pongosphere) that will grow to trouble our descendants. Or perhaps sunlight or the act of smelling alters the molecules and makes them harmless. In that case we can easily deal with global ponging.

I've gone down the cappuccino route again – this time in a shopping mall by the A30. It's a good way to spend the afternoon before I go off to find my quarters for the night. Then only 3 more days to go and I will have my first rest day and my first county will be behind me. A probable cause for celebration. First, I must find a WiFi connection.

DAY 5 **Fraddon to Nanstallon**

19 km (12 miles)
316 m of climb
6% completed

In case you have a problem locating these places on a map, Fraddon is a village close to Indian Queens and to the A30 while Nanstallon is a village to the south west of Bodmin.

This was a day when, as I skirted Goss Moor (a heathland area noted for its wild-life), I first struggled with overgrown footpaths - something that would become more and more common as I walked north and as the summer progressed. Battling through long grass has three disadvantages: it's hard work, you can't see where you're putting your feet and (especially in the morning) trousers and legs get soaked. Other than by finding another route there's not a lot that can be done about the first two while the third can only be solved by either putting waterproof trousers on or stripping down to shorts, though this option is not available when stinging net-tles are amongst the grass. I will return to this problem later in the walk.

Left: Luminous fields; Right: Unacceptable behaviour; Below Left: Nostalgia near Nanstallon; the cycleway on the right now follows the route of the old railway to Padstow; Below: More unacceptable behaviour

FROM THE BLOG
Nice day, nasty day

Actually, mostly a nice day – just a bit of nastiness. However, I'm wary of the word 'nice'. It all stems from the criticism of one of my English teachers at school, who disliked the word, suggesting that it had become debased by association with soft prettiness rather than what she said was its original association with suitability and precision. Anyway, sorry Miss Broad, but I'm going for the sentimental meaning.

It was very nice to be accommodated last night by Tony and Doreen White who were most welcoming, They gave me a splendid dinner and breakfast and the most comfortable night's sleep that I've had so far. To cap the feelings of good-will, the morning was fine – a bit chilly but with splashes of sunshine. I'll settle for chilly sunshine any day – the alternatives are much worse. I was cheered by glowing oil seed rape fields and the walking was good – alternating bits of country lanes and footpaths which took me steadily away from the noise of the A30 road and into a very rural part of Cornwall.

I won't harp on about missing footpath signs or awkward stiles, though I will probably come back to this later. I wouldn't want Cornish landowners to feel that they were being singled out! I passed through several very tiny places which had very

large churches – how can these huge buildings be supported? But they are such a prominent and integral part of the countryside. Close to one of them was a building site for what appeared to be some sort of community hall which (as far as one could tell at this stage) was very successfully integrating a modern style and structure with traditional building materials and shapes. Just the sort of building that one would want to see in a 21st century village.

The nastiness came towards the end of the day. I was walking up a steep green lane when, over the hedge I saw the first mess; then a bit further on, another one. This wasn't some flytipping stranger, dumping his rubbish and then speeding back to his urban paradise. These two spots were so difficult of access and so far off the beaten track that they had to be the work of local people. What right does anyone have to misuse the environment in this way? What is the point of planning and environmental management regulations when this can happen? Where are the parish council and the county council?

My rendevous with friends who had offered a bed for the night was close to the terminus of the Bodmin and Wenford Railway and I was early so I walked down to the station. It was deserted. I stared long and hard at the timetable to see if a train might come and entertain me, but I couldn't understand it. Nor could a woman who came along a little later. So I and my rucksack took advantage of a station seat for half an hour. Having rested and warmed in the sun I was just leaving when a train came round the corner and sidled to a stop. At least I got a photo.

It's good to be staying with friends; very easy to relax. Tomorrow is said to be a wet day – ah well, so far it's been drier than expected.

Nanstallon to Camelford

25 km (16 miles)
504 m of climb
8% completed

I had had some small amounts of rain earlier in the walk but this was my first really wet day, though only in the afternoon. It was particularly unfortunate that it came just as I was making a king-sized mess of navigating across a corner of Bodmin Moor and I learned another few lessons that were important to the success of the walk. One was to get waterproofs on as soon as possible, another was to get the GPS out as soon as a navigational error was suspected and the third was not to expect too much when I sloshed my way into a small town.

I have checked and now know that the River Camel has nothing whatsoever to do with camels of the 4-legged irritable variety but derives from Cornish for 'the crooked one', a reference to its winding course. That in no way deters me from putting in a picture of Sonya and Michael Jackson who deserve just a little fame, having been

ridden in such a leaden way. The other pictures are proof that I walked onto the Camel Trail and through St Breward. I did not photograph Camelford. Sorry, Camelford.

Left: Leaving Nanstallon
Photograph by Dee Edwards;
Lower left: Old road sign at St Breward;
Below: Sonya and Michael Jackson - a photo taken in Rajasthan

FROM THE BLOG
Sloppy navigation day

Dee and David, who had provided me with a very enjoyable evening, a good night's sleep and an early breakfast, took me back to my pickup point of yesterday evening and took pictures of me standing in various 'raring to go' poses. I then strode off down a hill and they, I think, went back to gardening. For most of the morning I was headed up the Camel Trail in bright sunshine – the rain had conveniently fallen overnight. I was full of goodwill and wellbeing, which was the start of the trouble.

How I missed the sign I can't say. I only realised the something was wrong when I saw a board that said 'Welcome to Bodmin'. Very civil of Bodmin but I was supposed to be going the other way. That was the first 2 km diversion, entirely down to my careless assumption that I knew where I was going.

The Camel Trail is a cycleway created from a disused railway. The bit I walked today was delightful. The River Camel was down on my left and roaring down its valley, powered by the overnight rain. There was no-one around – I suppose people had given up on the bank holiday and either gone home or sought out wet weather attractions. But the clouds were high above and the sun shone for most of the time, and I was enjoying my walk; though how much better it would be if the railways in North Cornwall had survived and were now at the hub of a discovery network for visitors.

Incidentally, I have a little experience of camels. Viv and I rode two of the creatures in the desert in Rajasthan some years ago. Hers was called Sonya and mine was called Michael Jackson (or it may have been the other way round). I don't have a natural affinity with animals; the bigger they are the less interested in them I am and they almost certainly realise it. Riding Michael Jackson was difficult and uncomfortable – I didn't fall off but it was a close run thing. I was quite pleased when the whole trip ended but I suppose it contributed to the pleasure of all involved and to the wellbeing of one or two Indian families. I wonder whether my camel now has a new name: Vladimir Putin would be appropriate, I think – it had a bleak look in its eye.

Thinking about camels probably contributed to navigation error number 2. By then I had climbed up through St Breward (a very vertical village 235 miles from London) onto the edge of Bodmin Moor and was crossing fields with quite a lot of enthusiasm and not much attention to the map. Suddenly I was in a thicket and there was a wooded valley in front of me where no valley should have been. That's when the rain started – it quickly got to a point where I needed the full wet-weather gear and I got my GPS and compass out as well. The GPS told me that I was several hundred metres from where I should have been and the compass told me that I was heading west and not north. The sun, which is an unerring guide to direction, was, of course, behind dark clouds.

I had to do a lot of backtracking before I rediscovered the route only to lose it again by over-compensating for my first mistake. My track was pretty erratic – think of a sailing boat tacking into a gale and you'll get the idea. Camelford, when I arrived, was shut though there were dim lights in the Liberal Democrat and in the Conservative party buildings. Serve them right.

DAY 7   Camelford to Launceston

28 km (17 miles)
417 m of climb
9% completed

This was, in a rather modest way, a very satisfying day though rather too dependent on roads. The weather improved, the route was peaceful in the extreme and I was heading for a rest day. Later on, I wondered whether I should have spent that at home. I'm still not sure; it was good to be there and to see Viv and I got some tasks done that would have been more difficult elsewhere. But it felt wrong - an intrusion into the walk.

In their own ways these three pictures taken on this walk from Camelford to Launceston are typical of Cornwall. I particularly liked the trees which seemed rather like commuters waiting in the wet and wind at a bus stop though surely the larger ones should have taken pity on the baby at the right-hand end and protected it. The sheep by

the old airfield runway at Davidstow seem to be permanent settlers in a damaged world - they have no use for the concrete and simply ignore it and get on with their own thing. And, although it's hardly visible on the horizon (picture on the right) the creamery is an ugly blot on the landscape that is nevertheless very important to the local economy.

Last post in Cornwall – I saw Devon in the distance

It is good to have completed my first county. It's taken a long time to get through Cornwall and it will be a good morale booster to get into another county, especially one that is a sensible shape that can be traversed in 4 days.

I stayed in a small hotel in Camelford which was very comfortable and didn't cost too much. And the Mason's Arms delivered an excellent dinner to complement a pint of Proper Job. (I need to make it clear that this end-to-end walk isn't going to be one of those that's lubricated by a substantial daily beer intake; this Camelford pint was only the third since I started the walk). What will make the small hotel memorable was something that happened after I left at about 7.30 this morning. I was walking up a track towards Davidstow when a car pulled up – it was the hotel owner who'd found my small bottle of contact lens cleaning fluid left on my bedside table, had guessed my onward route and had taken the

trouble to get his car out and find me. What service! If you're in Camelford, the Countryman Hotel is the one to go for.

Davidstow still has its concrete airfield runways that date from Word War 2 though sheep and trees now occupy some of the land. It's a slightly weird place where I guess the local petrolheads can go for a spin. It's not a pretty place and is the site of a large cheese and cream factory that dominates the horizon. It is the sort of place where you'd like to see a huge wind farm that would justify the space, but there isn't one.

Most of my walk today was through tiny villages and hamlets where the population density must be one of the lowest in England. I saw almost no other humans and very few vehicles but I did spot some very typical north Cornwall trees. One feels a little sorry for the one on the right which probably gets no thanks at all for the protection that it gives to the others.

I now have a rest day which I'm spending at home; Viv collected me from the cafe in Launceston Tesco and will deliver me back there on the day after tomorrow. I have been looking forward to this rest day ever since I left Lands End but now that it's come I feel strangely out of place here at home. Anyway, unless I get completely hooked on home comforts, this blog will resume in 2 days' time. Thanks to everyone who's taken the trouble to keep in touch with my walk and thanks to everyone who's posted comments. Do tell your friends about the walk – I have still some way to go before I reach my target!

PS I've just added up my mileage in Cornwall – it was 100 miles which is 3 miles less than I'd planned. As promised, I won't tell you that this is 9% of my total planned distance. Bring on Devon, I say (but not just yet).

The River Exe at Bickleigh

Launceston to Taunton

Date	Day	No	From	To	GPX files for each day's walk can be downloaded from the internet and plotted using mapping software such as OS Getamap or Google maps. The download addresses are in the form http://www.wilmut.net/lejogbook/day9.gpx
10-May-2012	Thu	9	Launceston	Bridestowe	
11-May-2012	Fri	10	Bridestowe	West Gooseford	
12-May-2012	Sat	11	West Gooseford	Crediton	
13-May-2012	Sun	12	Crediton	Tiverton	
14-May-2012	Mon	13	Tiverton	Thorne St Margaret	
15-May-2012	Tue	14	Thorne St Margaret	Taunton	

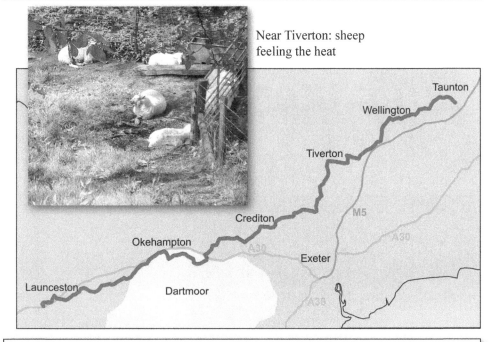

Near Tiverton: sheep feeling the heat

Crossing the border into Devon did little to reduce the hilliness of the walk, at least until I got to Tiverton when I took to my first canal towpath and river bank and had a fairly flat walk to Taunton. The weather, however, after a poor start, improved far too much and I started more than two weeks of high temperatures which, if not a problem, were certainly not comfortable.

This section coincided with the first half of Christian Aid week. I would have welcomed a little more interaction with the Week although I was always wary of commitments that slowed up the walk. Perhaps I had over-planned it, but I was very anxious not to fall behind the schedule that I'd set myself. Practical reasons for this were first, that I couldn't afford to end the walk much after the planned finish date and second, that I had made commitments to take up offers of accommodation and didn't want to change these. However, if I'm truthful, I also needed the schedule as a reassurance that the walk was under control.

Launceston to Bridestowe

23 km (14 miles)
422 m of climb
11% completed

Bridestowe is a pretty village about 9 km to the southwest of Okehampton now thankfully freed from the A30 by two by-passes (not many villages get that sort of treatment). I was firmly corrected in my pronunciation of the name - I had called it Bride*** as in a bride at a wedding, but was told to call it Brid*** as in Bridport. It may even, in the mouths of locals, be Brid-e-stow. I took no pictures of Brid-e-stow or of any other part of the day's walk because the weather was higher in my consciousness than anything else; this was a mistake since you are undoubtedly just as interested in what, for example, the Lifton bus shelter (where I took refuge from the rain for a while) looks like in the rain as you are in what it looks like on a gloriously sunny day. My apologies - I did realise at the time that I had been at fault and I think that I have at least one photograph (and normally many more than one) for every other day of the walk.

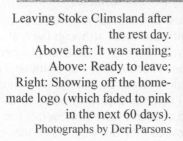

Leaving Stoke Climsland after the rest day.
Above left: It was raining;
Above: Ready to leave;
Right: Showing off the home-made logo (which faded to pink in the next 60 days).
Photographs by Deri Parsons

Obsessions in Devon (and elsewhere!)

Today I have been thinking about what I'm thinking about during this walk.

I know that there are some obsessions that take over a large slice of my consciousness when I'm walking. Probably the most important is my physical well-being, particularly the well-being of my feet and legs. Every twinge is noted and analysed to see whether it's a passing moment or a threat of worse to come. So far, nothing much has lasted for more than a few minutes.

Somewhere beyond physical well-being are weather and navigation. I can easily obsess about the weather, especially when it is poor, as it has been today (which is why there are no photographs with this post). Some people are indifferent to rain (or allege that they are) but I don't like walking in it. I have yet to possess a perfectly waterproof set of garments that aren't outrageously heavy or that don't bathe me in sweat, so I get cross with rain.

Navigation is a very variable obsession. A few days ago I was able to put the map away and walk for several miles up the Camel Trail without any need to check that I was on the right path though, as I said on the blog, I was a bit too casual about it at one stage. But you'll remember a bit later the same day when I was significantly off track, stumbling about (in the rain) map in one hand and compass in the other. Today, navigation was not an important issue; I had walked most of the route a few weeks ago, whilst training, and remembered enough to be able to walk for most of the way with my map in my pocket.

I had a good rest day yesterday though 'rest' is perhaps not the right word. Although I feared that having my first day off at home would be a distraction from the walk, it was actually a very useful opportunity to make a few changes and adjustments in the light of the first 7 days' walking. I set off this morning with a slightly lighter pack and a few improved items of clothing. Very agreeably, several local friends turned out at the parish hall at 7.30 to see me off. That was very kind and I do appreciate their good wishes. Some photographs of me were taken though I wished later that I'd thought to get a group picture with everyone in it. I must try to fix that when I get back. After the farewells Viv drove me to the Tesco car park in Launceston to resume where I left off two days ago.

I'm staying tonight with Jenny and Neon Reynolds, new friends acquired through the link with Christian Aid. My first such were in Cornwall and I'm now enjoying more hospitality in West Devon, for which I'm very grateful; more is due to follow as I move northwards. My next rest day is in Taunton in five days' time when Viv will come up for a couple of days and we can find out whether the Somerset Levels floods have gone down enough to let me walk through on the route that I've planned. If not, any alternative is likely to take a good deal longer.

Just to come back to the obsessions: I wouldn't want you to think that there's nothing else in my mind but feet, rain and maps. I do look round and appreciate the countryside which is at its greenest at present and I do hold one-sided conversations with sheep and (sometimes) with cows as I pass. They seldom reply but m
people who I encounter do give me a cheery 'hello'. And I do reflect on why
doing this walk and the anticipated and unanticipated impacts that it may hav

Ouch ... was that a right knee twinge?

DAY 10

Bridestowe to West Gooseford

26 km (16 miles)
535 m of climb
12% completed

Gooseford is a very small village about 12 km ESE of Okehampton and close to Whiddon Down on the A30. This area is on the northern edge of the Dartmoor National Park and close to the area where access is controlled by the military which uses it for training. The army manages the Ten Tors Challenge but in my view this does not compensate for its shameful intrusion into a national park.

PLEASE KEEP TO THE DEFINED PATH
TO DEVIATE IS TO TRESPASS

The sign on the left intrigued me when I walked here before; it still does! It has a very high moral tone suggesting that only conformity is acceptable; 'straight and narrow' comes to mind. Above: Climbing onto Belstone Common; Top Right: the dereliction at Meldon Quarry; Bottom Right: East Okement River

FROM THE BLOG

My hate affair with the A30 is almost over

A splendid day! A grey start that ever so slowly turned in to a sunny afternoon with all the colours of a Devon spring on view. And a good mix of walking - a bit of road then across fields, then a long trek along a cycleway, some moorland and, finally, minor roads and green lanes to this B&B on a farm near Whiddon Down. And tomorrow I shall part company with the A30 which I have been hearing and seeing all the way from Lands End.

think that there was a time when the A30 was a romantic road - it linked London to the resorts of Devon and Cornwall, projecting images of exciting rural journeys in open-topped cars. But in my lifetime it became first a bottleneck t started in Exeter and went all the way to west Cornwall and then a motay-style highway that now spreads noise across the landscape like treacle.

To 's walk repeated parts of two of my training walks. I went from Bridestowe to Sou n and then along the cycle trail that crosses Meldon Viaduct and passes so h of Okehampton, meeting various dogs and their owners and two very cheery lady cyclists. Bridestowe is a very pretty and seemingly lively village that has benefited from having the A30 moved away as have Okehampton (almost as notorious a bottleneck as the old Exeter bypass) and Sticklepath, which I went through later today.

Meldon Viaduct is probably the best known viaduct in south west England and it's splendidly high to cross and gives good views. Just after it is Meldon Quarry which was the source for much of the track ballast laid on railways over a wide area. I gather that some quarrying still goes on but the place looks derelict and a shadow of what it once was. It was, however, the reason for the line from Exeter to Okehamp-

ton escaping the Beeching axe and now becoming the Dartmoor Railway which has its terminus at the Quarry but which seems to offer a rather limited summer service. The roar from A30 traffic overlays everything.

My route then took me up the East Okement River valley and across onto Belstone Common – a much more pleasant moorland experience than my foray onto Bodmin Moor earlier on the week. In the distance I could see the encampment for the Ten Tors challenge which is this weekend – they will have fine weather, it seems. Then down into Belstone which is typically pretty, sitting at the moor's edge.

I have a sad memory of Belstone though I've never visited it before. In the 1990s I briefly met the wife of a close colleague – she worked in the same organisation as her husband and I guess that she was in her late 20s and a very lively and very able person. They went to Belstone on holiday quite often, I think, but suddenly the news came that she'd developed an aggressive breast cancer. She died soon after what both of them knew would be her last visit to Belstone. I went to her funeral

in the chapel in a large London cemetery and we were all shocked at the loss of someone of that young age.

I have to say that I felt fitter on the walk today than I've felt for some years. The walking isn't easy but I can readily cope with it. I think that I'm losing weight and, whilst I wouldn't claim to be agile, I am moving relatively easily. So, having made good time during the morning I sauntered to Gooseford in mid-afternoon – not wanting to arrive too early. But here I am, in a very friendly farm B&B, with a near-cloudless sky outside and having just eaten a very good (and large) farmhouse dinner.

Who needs to walk 2 miles to a pub?

West Gooseford to Crediton

24 km (15 miles)
343 m of climb
13% completed

This was obviously a blue sky day - the weather had not yet become unpleasantly hot and the rain was behind me and would not seriously return for over 2 weeks. Walking here was a great pleasure and I felt that I was making good progress. However, crossing mid-Devon from west to east does have its difficulties; most of the waymarked paths go from north to south and I was obliged to use short lengths of local footpath linked together by bursts of road walking. These local paths are very variable in quality. The one in the woodland photograph was excellent - easy to follow, in good condition and very pleasurable. You will see from the blog posts for other days that some local paths are in very poor condition and inadequately marked; this discourages people from using them so that they deteriorate further. Sadly, we cannot expect things to improve in the foreseeable future since local authorities have very little money to spend on path maintenance. But I am glad to acknowledge many places where new stiles and new signage are in place, sometimes as a result of action by local or national volunteer groups. I do hope that landowners will recognise the value of well-maintained and well-marked paths.

Above: The conductor - an hallucinatory fancy;
Right: Woodland in the valley of the River
Troney near Spreyton in mid-Devon

The sun shone on Devon

Now, what can I say about today? Well, it was pleasantly uneventful! Weather? Very good indeed – wall-to-wall sunshine with a good cooling wind. Scenery? Magnificent, especially some marvellous woodland that I walked through this morning and some splendid views across central Devon later in the day. My feet? In excellent order for their age. General interest? I didn't see anything outrageous (like a camel or naked nymphs dancing in dappled sunlight) but I did speak to one or two people who seemed very pleasant.

And I did see a tree that seemed to me rather like a hairless squirrel conducting an orchestra. That may have been because I watched the TV programme last night where some celebrities were conducting operas. Or perhaps because I saw several squirrels in the woodland I walked through today. Or I may just have been bored.

I'm staying tonight with a friend from my student days (which are some time ago). I walked into Crediton rail station (our agreed meeting place) to find him there already, ordering a cup of tea. As I've said before, I have been very cheered by the support that I've had from people that I haven't seen for a very long time. But probably the ultimate offer has just come from someone that I was at school with – now that is some time ago! I'm going to check how I can get to him but it will be great to see him and his wife (who was also at the same school). So gradually the peripheral personal benefits from this walk are extending.

Finally, a reflection on the fund-raising for the children of Sierra Leone and elsewhere. I feel quite detached from this process, having been heavily involved in it before the walk started. I do hope that we can make the £10,000 target,

though this will probably not happen until after the walk has finished. What I tell myself is that I must make sure that I tell people about the walk as I go along and give them the cards that I'm carrying with me. I've missed a number of opportunities and kicked myself afterwards – I just have to be more brazen.

But, thanks to my short home stay a couple of days ago, my rucksack does now carry a Christian Aid logo with LANDS END – JOHN O'GROATS written across it in laundry marker. I do feel a bit conspicuous but I think it helps.

I'm really a sad retiring type.

FROM THE BLOG

Sun, tea and a parrot

The day started well. I had enjoyed Richard Law's hospitality, rounded off with an excellent breakfast and a return trip to Crediton station where we'd met on Saturday afternoon. With the church bells ringing I walked out of Crediton where preparations were being made for an archery contest and, I think, a marathon or fun run of some kind. I knew it would be a hilly day and I found myself struggling a bit with the gradients with a recurrence of some tummy trouble that started last week. A sojourn in a field improved that (I

It was picture postcard stuff and Thorverton is a very pretty place where I sat for half an hour and ate an apple (in lieu of the water) and just enjoyed the sunshine. A less abstemious walker might have been tempted by the pub and the very reasonable price for a two-course Sunday lunch with a pint.

The way out of Thorverton was not nice: an interminable steep lane that kept promising to level out, but only did so just before it plunged down and down into the Exe Valley; at least I could be glad that I wasn't walking the other way. Then past Bickleigh Castle (toting for wedding business at what were probably astronomical prices) and to the honeypot site at Bickleigh where pedes-

don't want to conceal any aspect of this walk from you, but we'll say no more than that) after which I plodded a series of paths and roads to the village of Thorverton, discovering along the way that I'd forgotten to fill my water bottle before I left.

By now I was in the immaculate Devon that used to be pictured on 1930s railway travel posters: rolling green hills, red soil and cows, thatched houses and seagulls hovering over a very blue sea.

trians dice with death on the bridge over the river. Surely a place for traffic lights and a decent footpath.

By now I was ready for a proper liquid intake. Bickleigh Mill was excellently positioned and produced a teapot that was capable of delivering four large cups of tea which I drank with an excellent apricot slice. This was traditional Sunday afternoon stuff – a gentle procession of families enjoying the sunshine and food – there was one

Above: luminous fields; Top Right: Bickleigh Castle; Right: the parrot

particularly happy large family group with an age range of, I guess, at least 70 years with children playing, self-conscious teenagers, gossiping parents and grandparents who might easily have enjoyed a sleep in the sun.

A group of bikers also came – parked their bikes, took off the helmets and then had their roll-ups and excursions to the loo before deciding what they would eat. They were a buxom lot (men included), festooned with badges stuck on their leathers, and very jolly. The waitresses (thin teenagers with the shortest of miniskirts) were, I think, a little in awe of them, but they couldn't have been nicer.

The whole scene was supervised by a gaudy parrot with a very high opinion of itself, probably because lots of people took photographs of him (or her – how does one tell?). It would have been easy

to have sat there for the rest of the afternoon but I still had 3 or 4 miles to go to Tiverton, walking along a path through woodland and fields by the Exe. A very pleasant route, away from sight or sound of the main road and with quite a number of Sunday afternoon walkers. True, it went past a sewage works but these things have to be somewhere.

A darker aspect of the walk was the amount of plastic in the river. Most of it was caught on branches at the water's edge and I remembered a news report a few days ago that said that (I think) 20% of the fish caught in some parts of the Pacific Ocean now have small pieces of plastic in their digestive systems. I also remembered the horrifying amounts of rubbish in the rivers in Bosnia and Albania and recalled that hymn that praises the beauty of creation and then says that 'only man is vile'. Well, I don't want to be part of a vile species that wrecks the environment that we have and I'm appalled that my civilisation is responsible for this sort of mess.

I passed some dozing sheep and then a pleasant memory was stirred by the smell of wild garlic as I walked towards Tiverton. I think that I was in the first year of secondary school when we were taken on a day trip that included seeing (and climbing) the Tyndale monument at North Nibley in Gloucestershire. I think that it was a joined-up history and environment trip but it was along the footpath to the monument that I first became aware of the smell of wild garlic.

We never ate garlic then, but do so all the time now.

DAY 13 | **Tiverton to Thorne St Margaret** | 24 km (15 miles)
231 m of climb
16% completed

Thorne St Margaret is a very small village 4 km to the west of Wellington.

I have driven through and around Tiverton many times but not realised that the town centre is on a small hill above the River Exe. It really is very pleasant with a good number of local shops and a well-mannered demeanour.

It was good to be walking along a canal towpath – my first canal of several on this walk. Flat towpaths can get monotonous and this is not the most exciting canal in the country but it is clearly a valuable local recreational asset with horse-drawn barge trips as a tourist attraction (though no horses were in evidence whilst I was walking through).

I did relieve the boredom by counting paces between bridges and referred to this in the blog. Much later in the walk I repeated the exercise and refined my calculation so that I now believe that I walked 2,111,307 steps, 10,000 more than my initial estimate. I should say that this was based on walking reasonably level tracks or roads at my normal pace and that the actual figure is probably rather higher. But I am amazed by the size of this estimate and you should be as well.

Views seen along the Grand Western Canal.
Above: Through a bridge near Tiverton;
Left: Limekilns near Greenham;
Right: Swans and young

Easy day, new county and some statistics

There's been a small change of plan. I've stopped tonight at a (very) small village just west of Wellington and, instead of having a rest day tomorrow, will walk on to Taunton and stay there for 2 nights. After that, the schedule is as on my website.

Today's walk was mostly along the restored part of the Grand Western Canal that terminates in Tiverton at one end and in the middle of nowhere west of Wellington at the other (originally it connected to the canal that still runs from Taunton to Bridgwater). It was easy walking along a well-managed towpath though it rained quite a lot this morning.

The canal doesn't have all the usual apparatus of canaldom. There are no locks, only one movable bridge, a short aqueduct and a very short tunnel. There are very few boats and, once clear of Tiverton, none of the mooring areas, water points, pubs and pump out stations that most canals now have. The northern end of the canal is a filled-in lock and it looks as though very few boats make it that far; in fact, there's no place that a normal narrow boat of 50′ or 60′ could turn. Before that, there is a rather splendid set of limekilns, now partly restored, but these are the only evidence of commercial activity on the canal. That said, the restored canal has a very clear role as a local amenity and as a wildlife area and is very attractive.

Just beyond the end of the canal I went from Devon into Somerset. There was no notice to say that this had happened, no trumpets sounded, no member of Somerset County Council was there to greet me and no passport was demanded; a bit of a let-down really. But this event does give me an excuse for some statistics! As of this evening, I have completed about 16% of the total distance spread over 12 days' walking at an average daily distance of about 15 miles per day. This includes a planned short first day so I am, generally, at or a little above my planned average daily distance. I have traversed two counties which are, by popular consent, hard going and the graveyard of many attempts at an end-to-end walk. The next counties (Somerset, Gloucestershire and Worcestershire) will be much easier though possibly not so interesting.

Today I worked out an estimate that I have promised myself for some time. On the basis of three timings on my towpath walk, I can now reveal that I expect

to have completed 2,101,678 paces by the time I get to John O'Groats. This will probably be an under-estimate since I'd expect to do more paces per mile over fields, up hills or over moors that I will do on a flat towpath.

(Those of you of a statistical bent will want confidence limits for this estimate. Dream on.)

DAY 14

Thorne St Margaret to Taunton

17 km (11 miles)
98 m of climb
17% completed

I need to make two comments on the blogs that I wrote at Thorne St Margaret and Taunton.

First, it is worth recording the Bounty Bars, though not an essential part of my walker's diet, remained a pleasure through the whole of the 77 days though occasionally replaced by a Snickers Bar. There was the continuing problem that the milk chocolate variety was far more readily available than the dark chocolate one but a milky Bar is better than no Bounty at all, and I'm largely in them for the coconut anyway. Any guilt that I may have had about this self-indulgence was swept away a little later in the walk when a friend, who was a plant engineer for Mars, pointed out that my addiction to Bounty Bars was securing the future of his pension.

Almost every day I met dogs and their walkers. The dogs came in all sizes, some excessive, and all temperaments. I was also barked at by many dogs, thankfully captive behind bars or fences; some appeared manic and ready to bark at anything moving within 100 metres. One apparently nice and normal lady with 2 dogs said "Beware, he can be a bit bouncy, that one" as if that was my responsibility to avoid the dog rather than hers to control it. I don't like dogs and sometimes would prefer not to encounter their owners.

The footpath, though signposted, disappeared into the old canal - pretty but unnavigable

Play the interval music

Do you remember the time when, faced with a breakdown or a short gap, the BBC used to play uplifting music? I now have a rest day, so you need some music to bridge the gap that will follow this post.

Before that I must briefly report my day. I stayed in a manor house last night (B&Bs come in all shapes and sizes!). I felt a little shabby in my creased clothing (you try and keep clothes smart in a rucksack) but it was a very friendly and extremely comfortable place. The only problem was that the village of Thorne St Margaret is extremely small and, when I looked at it on the map, very unlikely to have a pub. So, on the way there yesterday I stopped at a shop and bought a Ginsters pasty and a Bounty Bar* to add to my small stock of basic food as insurance. It was good thinking – there was a pub about a mile from Thorne St Margaret but it was closed on Mondays. Two others, 2 and 3 miles away respectively, also shut on Mondays. A cold pre-packaged pasty is not fine dining but in those surroundings it tasted quite good and I made the most of an excellent breakfast this morning. Monday is clearly a day to be missed in Thorne St Margaret.

The walk to Taunton was first along the remains of the Great Western Canal and then down the valley of the River Tone. Nice and flat, only a small amount of road walking and a bracing wind to take the heat out of the sunshine. It was mostly surprisingly dry underfoot – earlier reports of flooding in Somerset had led me to expect that I would be sloshing about in mud but, apart from one impassable bit of old canal, it was as dry as I would expect in high summer. Somerset is clearly porous underfoot.

Unexpectedly, I came across a restoration project on the canal: at Nynehead an aqueduct crossing an entrance drive to Nynehead House is being restored and, next to it, one of the first ever boat lifts is also being rebuilt some 200 years after its inauguration. I see that there's a lot about the Grand Western Canal and the Nynehead restoration on Wikipedia so I won't fill space here describing it, but it looks like a major enterprise spoilt only by the fact that little or none of the canal survives. So, unlike the restored Anderton Boat Lift in Cheshire or the Falkirk Wheel in Scotland, this won't be a part of a rejuvenated waterway. Probably still worth a visit when it's finished, though.

I am now enjoying the fleshpots of Taunton. Then it's 6 days until the next fleshpots – in Gloucester. There I'm told that my departure will be celebrated with the carrying of a burning torch through the city centre, but I'll believe that when I see it.

* There will be one reader of this blog who will be pleased to know that I savoured her gift of Bounty Bars over the first 3-4 days of the walk (yes, I can spin out a Bounty Bar) and am now replenishing the stock as I go along. My best (otherwise frugal) lunches always end with a Bounty Bar and then an apple, which you can, if you wish, regard as good overcoming evil.

Reflections in the Gloucester and Sharpness Canal

Taunton to Gloucester

Date	Day	No	From	To
17-May-2012	Thu	16	Taunton	Cossington
18-May-2012	Fri	17	Cossington	Axbridge
19-May-2012	Sat	18	Axbridge	Nailsea
20-May-2012	Sun	19	Nailsea	Amondsbury
21-May-2012	Mon	20	Amondsbury	Berkeley Road
22-May-2012	Tue	21	Berkeley Road	Gloucester

GPX files for each day's walk can be downloaded from the internet and plotted using mapping software such as OS Getamap or Google maps. The download addresses are in the form http://www.wilmut.net/lejogbook/day16.gpx

In many ways this section was when I settled properly into the walk. I had developed the strategies and tricks that would make the walk manageable and as easy as possible and I was learning how to pace myself. Comments on the blog suggested that that was also getting bedded in and that people were enjoying reading it and keeping track of where I was and what the walk was like. This section also included that first important milestone: leaving the southwest peninsula for Gloucestershire and the Midlands. It would soon be possible to look forward to being half way on my journey to John O'Groats.

I was also on home territory; I was born and grew up in Bristol and, although I wouldn't see much of the city on this walk, I felt that I knew exactly where I was going and how my route related to the countryside around me. That feeling would disappear once I got into the Midlands.

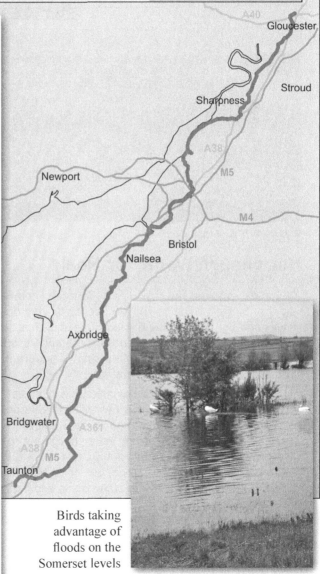

Birds taking advantage of floods on the Somerset levels

DAY 16

Taunton to Cossington

33 km (21 miles)
147 m of climb
19% completed

Below: My path between river and flood; Right: The ruined church at Burrowbridge looks down on the junction of the Rivers Tone and Parrett

Opposite: Tradition on the Somerset Levels: willows lining the rhynes and reeds drying

FROM THE BLOG

Not enough water for Noah

Viv and I enjoyed my rest day in Taunton, comfortable in a small hotel close to the centre of the town. We spent the day drifting around sampling shops, cafés and sights including the very fine churches dedicated to St Mary Magdalene and to St James and the splendid Somerset Museum. And we managed to top it off with a very good dinner in a small restaurant with a relaxed and pleasant atmosphere. Beats walking any day!

I had failed to get my next accommodation in or near Westonzoyland as intended but had located a B&B on a farm a few miles further on. That made today quite a long slog though all on the level. I had worried that the Somerset Levels might still have been flooded and, indeed, they were though not so extensively that any footpaths were impassable and certainly not enough water for an ark though swans and ducks were happy. I strode (yes, strode) out of Taunton along the canal that led to Bridgwater but soon left it to walk along the raised banks of the River Tone to Burrowbridge where it joins the Parrett on its way to the sea at Burnham. Both rivers were flowing fast and fields on both sides were flooded but the ground underfoot was dry.

I was passed by a husband and wife cycle team who were also bound for John O'Groats. They told me that they live in Ilkley which is one of my stopping places later on and they kindly offered me accommodation, though whether we'll manage to get that fixed up I'm not sure. They did say that, on the previous day, they'd met a couple of joggers doing a north-south JOGLE. Not my idea of fun at all. They disappeared into the far distance and I resumed my striding.

Much of the Levels that I crossed today felt very remote – I saw very few people and very few vehicles. Good on a reasonably fine day but horrid, I would think, with the rain lashing down – there would be no shelter. I'm not a flatness fan but this scenery could grow on you. I discovered from an information board that many areas of land were enclosed by 'walls' in medieval times. These were embankments designed to control drainage and keep flood water out and are still one of the principal features of the flood control systems of the area. I also saw willows being dried.

My route went close to the site of the Battle of Sedgemoor in 1685. In Taunton yesterday there were museum exhibits devoted to the battle and its aftermath – said to be the worst thing that had ever happened to Somerset. Certainly, it was not good for those tried by Judge Jefferies who apparently gave increasingly severe judgements as his various bodily ailments worsened. I don't know whether you can visit the battle site or whether, if you do, it makes any sense. Certainly the landscape would not have looked as it does today though Westonzoyland church would have been as much a landmark then as it is now.

A little later I found myself on a footbridge over what turned out to be the Chedzoy New Cut. What place names! Every bit as good as Praze-an-Beeble. I remember a statistician in the mathematics department at Bath University who was a great help when I got bogged down with some research sums. He had a name to conjure with – Olaf Chedzoy.

Enough of this: I resolved today that I would use tonight's blog to take stock of the walk. How it was going, how I felt about it, what things are going well and what could be better, how my feet feel. That sort of thing. Well, in the feel-good atmosphere of the local pub, this seems a much less interesting idea so I'll just say that all is OK. OK?

Cossington to Axbridge

22 km (14 miles)
138 m of climb
20% completed

The main road carrying traffic to Cheddar and Wells now bypasses Axbridge which is now a quite tranquil place. At one time the landlord of the Royal Oak Inn was one Nick Barrington who, in the early 1960s, produced a guide to caves in the Mendip Hills, a book which set the standard for guides of this type for some years. In 1970 we had one of the interminable early meetings of the National Caving Association at his pub in Axbridge – probably the last time I was there. I remember the meeting particularly since, against all the odds, some of us managed to get the nascent Association to adopt a conservation policy.

Above: Looking north to Axbridge from Brinscombe Hill; Top Right: The magic lawn-mower; Bottom right: The risks for the long distance walker.

FROM THE BLOG

Brief encounter in Axbridge

My B&B host at Cossington was great. I had a bit of trouble finding the farm but eventually arrived (with the kind help of a local man who insisted in walking there with me) to find her in the garden. Keeping her company was a lawn mowing robot that looked like a small dark grey sheep with wheels. Now I'm the only lawn mowing robot that I know so I took a particular interest in this one which trundled across the grass, mowing as it went, and then turned when it came to a border and trundled back along a different line. When it was tired it docked itself, recharged, and then started again. It continued all night and was still going when I woke up.

The room was comfortable and the welcome was accompanied by tea and sponge cake after which my host volunteered to take me to the pub for an evening meal and collect me afterwards, refusing my protests that I could walk. So that's how it was and I left this morning with a donation to Christian Aid. What a lovely lady!

However good the accommodation it's very good to get back into the walk each morning. I think that some people were very surprised that I was doing this walk by myself - as if this were dangerous or unnatural. But I do value the solitude of the walk - I can do and think what I want, go as fast or slow as I wish and stop when I feel like it. Successes and mistakes are down to me so, while it's good to get to the end of the day, have a shower and a meal and be comfortable, there's nothing quite like the excitement and quiet of the first few miles each day.

the docking station   the mower

My walk today was made easier and shorter by my efforts yesterday. It did have rather a lot of road walking to begin with but I later took to the footpaths and promptly got lost. I blame the cloud – had the sun been visible I'd have noticed that I was walking southeast instead of north. My tendency in these situations is to blame the map (not up to date) footpath people (signposts and markers missing), farmers (why not?) and the GPS. It was only when I got my trusty Silva compass out and retraced my route that I grudgingly admitted to a personal error (or rather, since this is sackcloth and ashes time) several errors.

In the final stages of today's walk I felt rather weary and was pleased to get to Axbridge where I eventually found a teashop where I had a pot of tea for two and a toasted teacake. These did me no end of good and I spun them out for as long as I could since it was too early to go to my B&B. As I walked out of the teashop my brother was standing there – a matter of some surprise.

Before I began, Richard, who lives in Trowbridge, had tried to work out a convenient way of joining me for a day of the walk but had failed and we'd abandoned the idea. I now know that he had second thoughts and had set out earlier in the day to walk towards me from Axbridge, following the planned route on my website. He wasn't to know that I'd made another (very minor) mistake in my navigation which I'd corrected by walking on a parallel track rather than backtracking. So he'd failed to find me and had returned to Axbridge where we met and went back into the teashop, consumed another pot of tea, and had a long chat before his bus came. Very surreal.

I leave you with a picture that gives some idea of the extreme dangers to which your correspondent is exposed on this walk. Tomorrow I stay in Nailsea – my last night before I cross the Avon on a not entirely different bridge and (symbolically) leave the southwest peninsula.

Progress ... progress.

Axbridge to Nailsea

21 km (13 miles)
235 m of climb
22% completed

Right: The ideal B&B (the white foreground building) opposite the pub (also white, behind it)

Resting on the memorial seat for the Wrington Vale Light Railway 1901-1963

FROM THE BLOG

Strawberries, caves and dog poo

I thought that I should say something about the B&Bs that I've used (I've already said something about the friends who've very kindly put me up). But the B&Bs have been uniformly excellent - all picked from lists because they were in the right place or charged the right sort of price, but all have offered a great welcome, comfortable bed and good breakfast. And, yesterday, another B&B proprietor made a donation to Christian Aid. I'm not going to give ratings to the B&Bs - it will very quickly become dated and I can't expect that others will necessarily follow my route. I'll let you know if I have a bad experience.

I forgot yesterday to mention that I passed something described on the map as Roman Salt Workings. There was nothing visible but I assume that these were seawater salt pans of the type that we saw a couple of years ago on the Dalmatian coast, operating here in the days when the Somerset Levels were regularly flooded by the sea. It's one thing to evaporate seawater in the Adriatic but quite another, I would have thought, to make salt by this method in this climate. Perhaps they were very patient or there weren't very many of them needing salt.

Today's walk was a very gentle affair which I enjoyed very much. It started out along another disused railway - this time the branch that ran from Yatton to Wells. Now

called the Strawberry Line (for that was one of the principal commodities that was carried) it was a branch of the Bristol and Exeter Railway that was laid in Brunel's broad gauge. It has a short tunnel built to accommodate this gauge, unlined at the southern end which is through limestone but lined in the northern end through the marl. Nowadays it has solar powered cats eyes down the middle!

Further up is the place where the Wrington Vale Light Railway joined. I remember this from my youth when we went caving on Mendip. The railway was on its last legs at that stage but it marks for me a period when, having been useless at sport at school, I found something physical that I was reasonably good at. Caving had the added advantage of a bit of mystery and excitement but I think that my mother despaired of the mess that I made of clothes and probably worried quite a lot every time I went. I was, however, a interest that has stayed with me. I no longer do recreational caving but I have continued my involvement with a cave studies trust and with the educational and conservation work that it does.

As it was Saturday there was a large number of people on the Strawberry Line, walking or cycling, many with dogs. One couple had, between them, eight dogs on leads. They ranged from poodle-size to alsatian-size (I don't really know one breed of dog from another). Perhaps they were dog-walkers or ran a kennel but, otherwise, how do two people keep eight dogs!!

Which takes me to dog poo. I am pleased to see people with polythene bags, doing their duty. But I have passed quite a lot of small full plastic bags left by the side of a path – a couple more today. What do these people think they are doing? Who do they expect to deal with these bags if they don't? Like the litter dumping, this

seems to be the height of selfish and disrespectful behaviour. As communities we have to persuade fathers, sons, mothers, daughters, friends, distant relations and others that the environment is something to be respected, not dumped upon.

I am becoming a bore about this.

I came across an elegant stile alongside a farm gate. If the gate hadn't been open I would have used the stile. But it's is a nice way to finish this post.

DAY 19   Nailsea to Almondsbury

30 km (19 miles)
526 m of climb
23% completed

Above: Pill and the River Avon, muddy and mysterious as ever. Pill was a traditional Avon ferry crossing and the base for the Bristol Channel pilots who were a formidable group of men.

Left: The M5 bridge: no beauty here

Bridge to the future

I was royally entertained in Nailsea. Judy and Keith Norwood were very generous with their welcome, were gratifyingly interested in the walk and gave me a splendid dinner, most comfortable bed and a good send-off breakfast. Characteristically, I got lost within 20 minutes of leaving them. However, I fell in with one of the participants in a Nailsea Rotarian charity walk who had a piece of paper that described a route that also happened to be where I wanted to go. So we followed each other for some distance before it was clear that his future lay with the route to Long Ashton and mine lay on the way to the M5 bridge.

But before getting there I walked through some hidden valleys and very attractive woodland that lies just to the side of the M5, largely out of sight, as it drops down to the River Avon. This is an area of some wealth – a sort of millionaires' row that feels a million miles away from the Bristol that I remember. At one stage the footpath lay through the grounds of a prep school where an archery contest was taking place. I walked past and through the playing field, fearing that my boots may be damaging their cricket square. If they did, no-one shouted at me.

And so to the M5 bridge. What can I say about it? Well, it's hard to get onto, a tortuous route even following the cycleway signs. When you do get onto it the first impression is how very noisy it is, after which you are aware of how high it is. Part way along are the travelling cradles used by the maintenance crews. I'm sure that they're safe but I wouldn't want to climb onto one of them with my brain fried by that noise. The bridge takes a long time to cross but I stopped half way to celebrate my departure from the south-west peninsula and my potential transition to the English midlands. And to wallow in the pleasure of knowing that almost a quarter of the whole walk was now finished.

I know that there's still a long way to go but I cannot help feeling that a huge hurdle has now been crossed. I have a routine to my days, I am enjoying most of the walking, nothing hurts unduly and I can anticipate the rest of the walk with some degree of confidence. That said, I will probably fall in a ditch tomorrow.

Tonight I am staying near Bristol with two people who were at school with me in Bristol. That's rather a long tine ago so there's been a lot of remembering of past events and catching up with more recent history. That, of course, is an especial pleasure and I look forward to seeing them again this autumn when we will attend a reunion dinner together.

Now for Gloucestershire where much of my family came from. I will gladly drift away from the clutches of Bristol and start to enjoy the more hidden bits of countryside, some of which I have never seen before.

I must now go and do a bit more reminiscing.

Left: These are South Gloucestershire buttercups.
As my blog records, buttercups were in flower
throughout my walk and their pollen often coated
my trousers with yellow dust

Almondsbury to Berkeley Road

30 km (19 miles)
177 m of climb
25% completed

The Severn is both dangerous and mysterious. It is a navigator's nightmare with the second largest tidal range in the world, sandbanks, mudbanks and underwater cliffs and swift-running water that swirls and eddies round obstacles. Once it had numerous ferries but they have all gone, replaced by huge bridges. It had two rail crossings; the tunnel remains but the bridge was demolished by a boat in the 1960s. Once the industries were salmon fishing and the piloting of boats into small ports

and up to Gloucester; now there are two mothballed nuclear power stations with another further downstream in the Bristol Channel. Gloucestershire surrounds most of this part of the river but Wales broods over it to the southwest. The picture on the left shows old and battered wooden pilings driven in to protect the banks south of Berkeley.

FROM THE BLOG
When we were very young...

I felt a bit of an old codger yesterday, remembering schooldays with my hosts at Filton, though they seemed to remember things that I'd forgotten. I think that we felt that our schooldays had been interesting and constructive and that we'd enjoyed our subsequent careers. Jane, Laurie and I had been part of the group that went caving and took trips to the Lake District before higher education took us into its clutches and away from Bristol. So I set out this morning with a small warm glow, working my way across from north Bristol to the banks of the Severn near Oldbury.

Now this bit of coast has a number of associations for me. In 1962 I was sent on a 3 month placement at Berkeley Nuclear Power Station which was at the stage where reactor 1 was just being brought up to power and reactor 2 was in the final stages of commissioning. It couldn't have been a better time to be there. Some of the temporary site buildings were being demolished so two of us lived for 6 weeks at the Oldbury site down the coast before I moved into a flat in Dursley. At that stage Oldbury was just a very large hole in the ground and only the civil engineering contractors were on site. But digging big holes is thirsty work so the site had what was said to be the longest bar in the country. To be truthful, there was very little to do in the evenings but, as we got more familiar with the work at Berkeley, we found ourselves staying on site there late into the evenings and sometimes through the night.

Berkeley was in a race with Bradwell in Essex to be the first commercial nuclear station delivering power to the

Nuclear power at Oldbury: the station is now mothballed for the next few decades

grid. It lost the race by a few weeks but we all felt part of what Harold Wilson would later call the 'white heat of technology'. Whatever I may now feel about nuclear energy, the 1960s was a very exciting time, with a manufacturing base that could deliver complex installations like Berkeley. Inept and short-sighted governments of the 1970s and 80s threw away or sold that expertise so that we now buy it all from elsewhere.

[A man has just left the bar where I'm drinking tea and typing this, calling "Awright luvver?" over his shoulder - I know I'm back in Gloucestershire.]

I didn't know it at the time but Berkeley was where my mother's family came from. I'm not sure whether she knew it – her grandparents had left in the late 1890s to settle near Chipping Sodbury. She was the product of generations of agricultural labourers, laced with the occasional craftsman, shopkeeper or Severn pilot. When I came back to Berkeley, 40 years after my first visit, I found a very attractive small town where I could easily locate where her ancestors lived and worked. There's a castle, an estate where the tenant farmers employed my ancestors and there's now a museum to commemorate Edward Jenner's success in developing a vaccination against smallpox. Interestingly, he had one consulting room in his house (now filled with the gruesome surgical appliances of his day) and another at the bottom of the garden for the poor people.

Berkeley also boasts an imposing church where many ancestors were baptised, married and buried – a few family gravestones can still be deciphered. I feel oddly at home in this area but I know that it's all in my head!

Finally, I find it slightly incongruous that I'm walking from one end of the country to the other, mostly along insignificant footpaths or country lanes. I feel that it should be a broad path across the top of a moor with signposts pointing one way to Lands End and the other to John O'Groats. And perhaps cheering crowds? Don't they realise what an effort this all is?

DAY 21 **Berkeley Road to Gloucester**

30 km (19 miles)
108 m of climb
27% completed

Above: Superannuated engineers with partners and a young relation; there was no more tempting place than this to give up the walk and lie in the sun.

Left: Slimbridge church early in the morning - a most elegant spire;
Below: There is still commercial traffic on the Gloucester and Sharpness Canal.

Good day, hard day, great day

I'm writing this a day late and have been trying to understand the dynamics of yesterday. Socially I had a very good day indeed; physically, it turned out to be the hardest day's walk so far.

Let me start at the beginning. Once again, I received hospitality at Cam, arranged through Christian Aid with Shirley and Matt Welsh and it was very enjoyable and comfortable. This type of support for my walk has been a joy – I have met new friends and have been gratified by the readiness with which they have taken a complete stranger into their households and worked so hard to meet my every need.

In the morning Matt took me to the point where he'd collected me the night before and I set off through lanes and paths to Slimbridge where I joined the canal towpath which would be my route to Gloucester. This was my second canal of the walk but this one is much more a working canal than the Great Western. There are seagoing boats moored alongside narrow boats and a lot of what appear to be live-aboard boats. There are no locks but the swing bridges are all manned and the whole has a gently busy feel to it.

Slimbridge is, of course, home to the Wildfowl Trust established there by Peter Scott many years ago. Viv and I have been there several times and it's clearly a very special place – I could happily have diverted there yesterday morning. But I had a tryst at a campsite at Frampton on Severn with friends from student days and the morning was getting hotter and sunnier as I neared the site. So it was good to sink back into a camp chair, drink tea (I am drinking far more tea than usual), catch up with everyone's news and eat an early lunch.

It was hard to prise myself from the chair (quite a lot later than intended), put the boots back on and go back to the canal towpath. Perhaps I'd eaten too much or the day had become too hot or the towpath was just too hard on the feet but the 3 hours' walk in the afternoon was very hard going. It was flat but felt like a perpetual uphill, I had a sore muscle in my leg and the temperature went up into the mid 20s. Perhaps it wold have been easier if there had been more of interest to look at but I walked into Gloucester feeling very jaded. I was then joined by Mike (one of the student friends) and I stumbled round Gloucester to a place on the north side where I will be well clear of the Olympic torch celebrations tomorrow morning. I have to say that the route marking for the Severn Way through Gloucester could be improved and we ended up trespassing over some private property before we reached where we wanted to be.

Things were markedly better in the evening when we all met up again for a meal in a local pub. I'm now staying with Rosemary and Mike, gently exercising the sore leg and hoping that tomorrow's walk to Tewkesbury will be cooler and softer on the feet.

And I don't suppose that I'll see another large teddy bear sitting by the water.

NANTWICH
32
MILES.

AUTHERLEY.
JUNCTION.
7, MILES.

NORBURY.
JUNCTION.
8¼ MILES.

Shropshire Union Canal milepost

Gloucester to Ashbourne

Date	Day	No	From	To
24-May-2012	Thu	23	Gloucester	Tewkesbury
25-May-2012	Fri	24	Tewkesbury	Worcester
26-May-2012	Sat	25	Worcester	Blackstone
27-May-2012	Sun	26	Blackstone	Blakeshall
28-May-2012	Mon	27	Blakeshall	Nurton
29-May-2012	Tue	28	Nurton	Penkridge
30-May-2012	Wed	29	Penkridge	Abbots Bromley
31-May-2012	Thu	30	Abbots Bromley	Ashbourne

GPX files for each day's walk can be downloaded from the internet and plotted using mapping software such as OS Getamap or Google maps. The download addresses are in the form http://www.wilmut.net/lejogbook/day23.gpx

Typical Midlands: a narrow boat on the Shropshire Union Canal

I had chosen to walk up the Severn Way because it would be easy and quick and so deliver me into the Midlands with minimum fuss. So it turned out: this section of the walk took me past Birmingham and the Black Country without me really being aware of their presence. I was then into Staffordshire - a county that I've travelled through hundreds of times and know hardly at all. It was on this section of the walk that I realised how easy it was to be cut off from the normal ways of living and to pass through countryside meeting almost no-one along the way. Of course, hidden eyes may have been watching my every move but that's no worse than being spied on by cameras.

69

Gloucester to Tewkesbury

16 km (10 miles)
83 m of climb
28% completed

I felt that there was a need to demonstrate that I really was doing this walk (one comment on my blog asked how people would know that I was not sitting at home). So here I am, striding into the jungle of the Severn Way (photo by Mike Ellis) and, later on, eating my lunch under a noble tree. I know that I look miserable, but that's normal and I have only chosen moderately flattering pictures.

Right: A narrow boat navigating down to Gloucester along a very enclosed part of the river.

FROM THE BLOG

The cathedral, the cuckoo and the stinging nettle

After Tuesday's stresses I wanted an easy day and here it was. On the last leg I'd walked beyond Gloucester before stopping and today I had the reward of a reduced distance and, wonderfully, a cool morning. Only later in the day, after I'd got to my B&B, did the temperature rise to the promised mid 20s. I walked at a sedate pace and the muscle strains from Tuesday eased out as I went along.

The recovery was helped by a good rest day, used well, I think. Rosemary and Mike were splendid hosts who gave me a map and loads of information about Gloucester where I strolled in the sunshine for the best part of the day. In fact, the coolest place was the cathedral where I spent quite a lot of time just sitting and trying to properly connect myself to this walk and to understand what it is that I'm doing and why. I may be getting closer to it but I'm not sure. Anyway, the gentle exercise was exactly what was wanted so I set off today with some bounce back in my walking - a good feeling.

I left Olympic Torch hysteria well behind me as Mike kindly dropped me off at Tuesday's arrival point and photographed me under the Severn Way signpost. However, I have to say that the Severn Way out of Gloucester does need a bit of

TLC. The waymarking is poor and the path almost unnegotiable in places. I had barely turned the first corner before a rather sheepish-looking man emerged from the jungle having, I think, satisfied an urgent need. Then I was just getting into my stride through the nettles when another man and his dog sprang from the undergrowth where, perhaps, the dog had had its own urgent need. The river was very brown and fast flowing between high tree-lined banks and we were the only signs of life. Slightly sinister, I'd say, though later on some boats passed, labouring upstream, and the church tower at Deerhurst Park peered over the trees.

I mention the nettles. I had walked into Gloucester in shorts on Tuesday. I'm not a natural shorts wearer, being pasty of leg, but it was a very hot day. However, the last mile or two were spent dodging stinging nettles so I decided that I'd not take any chances today and would wear trousers. I'm glad that I did; north Gloucestershire stinging nettles are large, very prolific and very sneaky, leaping out from behind other plants. They're also capable of stinging through trousers – surely a measure of their formidable nature. I do think that these nettles should be prepared to negotiate a deal – especially with anyone walking for charity. I would have been perfectly willing to promise to walk quietly and respectfully past and not to trample them if I could have found a representative to negotiate with but there was no evidence that they were organised. A job for the TUC, I think.

I have heard several cuckoos on this walk – the first about 10 days ago and then a couple today with one flying round me cuckooing as it went. Like the nettles they are predatory but do, at least, make a pleasant sound though this does become a bit monotonous. Rather like Ravel's Bolero.

My B&B tonight is a pub by the side of the Severn where I arrived earlier this afternoon, following a lunch that included a Bounty Bar, presented to me earlier (I am glad that I mentioned this to Rosie Nevill when she interviewed me all that time ago). When I announced my arrival at the bar a man noticed the logo on my rucksack (which says that I'm walking from Lands End to John O'Groats) and said that they'd had a lady walk through a month or so ago, doing the same walk. I think that this must have been Mrs Smith whose exploits and accidents featured in several press reports. People I met had spoken of her and Shirley and Matt Welsh in Cam had actually met her, black eyes, broken glasses and all.

I understand that she's now on the last lap having passed Inverness but that her walk has continued to be a chapter of misfortunes. Whether she's brought these on herself I can't say but I'm sure that the publicity has done her cause no harm at all, though she may have suffered. Perhaps I should have danced naked around Gloucester docks or something.

Or not.

Tewkesbury to Worcester

31 km (19 miles)
156 m of climb
29% completed

By now I was beginning to get fed up with hot weather though the breeze had made this day tolerable. I was drinking a lot of water and needing more and was in a perpetual sweat. It seemed a long way to Worcester and when I got there it was already on holiday, getting ready for the weekend. In the city centre I felt rather scruffy and out of place as I searched for a coffee shop.

Top Left: Brutal curves of the M50 crossing the Severn; Left: Incredible vegetation and shades of green; Below: Regimented agriculture on the red soils of the Midlands

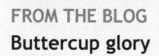

FROM THE BLOG
Buttercup glory

I left the riverside pub where I spent last night in a sun-kissed, breeze-cooled early morning. Ideal walking conditions though it was bound to get hot sooner or later. However, the breeze continued through the day, making this riverside walk a great pleasure, though my feet were tired by the end.

The first milestone was my transition from Gloucestershire to Worcestershire – another county bites the dust! I was heading for Upton on Severn which turned out to be a pretty little town that wasn't quite overwhelmed by the main road going through it. Just before I got there I cam to Upton Ham, a Lammas Field of about 60 hectares. I didn't know about Lammas Fields but it seems that they were pastures that were grazed between Lammas Day in August and the new year; this one had been scheduled as an SSSI because of its grasses and flowers and was a very attractive introduction to Upton.

I was looking for a WiFi connection to upload yesterday's blog and to consult a map that would show me where tonight's accommodation was. I bought a coffee close to where I could connect but it was too bright outside to see the screen and the signal disappeared when I went inside the cafe. I re-established contact in an adjoining churchyard but ended up crouching under a tree in order to see the screen. I managed to upload the text of the blog but gave up after that, packed my rucksack and left Upton. Not a worthwhile stop.

The early part of the day was plagued by long wet grass. I mean waist-high and carrying a lot of water from morning dew. Everything below the waist got very wet and I did think that I might post a Shakespearian soliloquy on wet grass (something like 'night-kissed jewels upon the grass', 'waiting upon the passing trouser' and 'dew-soaked pantaloons') but now I come to try to write it, inspiration has gone. You're probably quite pleased about that. Later, the grass had dried out and seemed shorter – perhaps the north is approaching.

I have to say that the vegetation along the Severn is extremely lush. What a profusion of plants of all shades of green with plumes of flowers! The dandelions have clearly had successful matings and are now shedding seeds on the wind like driven snow. And willow catkins float downstream, presumably to be lost at sea somewhere off Lundy Island. But it's the buttercups that are so exciting: a million small suns gazing into the sky from every meadow.

There was a deviation in the Severn Way, some distance south of Worcester. It suddenly veered away from the river and took to a road past the grounds of the 18th century castellated mansion Severn Bank House that looked across the river to the Malverns.

The diversion went out to the main road (the A38) and turned down the other side of the House, back to the riverside. I suppose that the diversion protected the owners' views and water frontage but it added over a mile to my route which I resented.

But the contact with the A38 did remind me of 1962 when I was home in Bristol for Christmas from my temporary digs in Manchester. In those days we worked between Christmas and the New Year and I was due to drive back north on Boxing Day. There was a big dump of snow overnight and I set off in my pre-war unheated Morris Series E, clad in a lot of sweaters and a duffle cost and equipped by my mother with a thermos of something. I followed the snowploughs very slowly as far as Gloucester, getting steadily colder. By Worcester the snow had become sleet and I got to Manchester, where it was raining, very late in the evening, almost frozen to the steering wheel. Next day was work and there followed one of the coldest Januaries of my lifetime. I do not have warm feelings about Manchester.

But I'm not going there on this trip.

30 km (19 miles)
216 m of climb
31% completed

Blackstone was a convenient country park car park on the A456 about 1 km southeast of Bewdley.

As a family we had taken many holidays on canal narrowboats including one Easter when we hoped to do a circuit down the Staffordshire and Worcestershire canal to Stourport, down the Severn then up the Birmingham and Worcester Canal and back through Birmingham to our starting point. In fact, we only got part-way to Stourport when we heard that the Severn was in flood and navigation was not allowed. At Stourton we attempted to turn up to Birmingham along the Stourbridge Canal but discovered that there was not enough water in the canal and had great difficulty in reversing the boat back out. Then it was back up to Wolverhampton and we improvised a great trip northwards up the Shropshire Union. On this day of the walk I saw the canal junctions at both Stourport and Worcester and, not for the first time, envied those who were gently chuntering along the canals at a speed comparable to mine.

Above: A riding school near the river; Right: A River Severn lock

Don't go down to the woods today

Somehow, Worcester and I didn't click. I've been there many times before and like the city but this time …

I arrived in Worcester with a B&B booked but no idea where it was. So I walked into the city centre and settled myself in Costa with an iced coffee and started up the netbook – no usable WiFi signal! Downed the coffee quickly and went across to WHSmith and surreptitiously consulted a Worcester road map, located the correct road and walked there.

There was no reply when I rang the bell and knocked on the door. Nor was there a back entry where I could do the same thing. I waited for a quarter of an hour, ringing the bell and thumping the door then gave up and walked up the road to another B&B and did the same there. I got a room immediately – it was a bit expensive but I couldn't complain. But it was in the attic where I had a choice between being deafened by the traffic and being fried in the heat. I chose the traffic but it wasn't a great room. I also couldn't get a reliable WiFi signal so I took my netbook down the road to an Italian restaurant where I managed to write the post for the blog but had to put up with a noisy party of people who seemed to be on an office evening out. The food was good but I ate too much and then went back to the B&B to add the photos to the blog and to do some emails.

I couldn't put up with the traffic noise any more so I closed the windows and consequently slept badly, waking at 5am. The proprietor had only been able to offer me an 8am breakfast – my choice was to wait for this or to pack up and go. I went well before 6am, breakfasting on two biscuits and a cup of coffee from the supplies in my room. It was a splendid early morning and I strode out of Worcester feeling pleased with myself and calculating that I'd be in Bewdley by lunchtime – I had visions of sitting in the cool of a cafe, supping tea and writing a very memorable blog. That dream was destroyed in a patch of woodland that had a way in but no visible way out.

I got very angry with this woodland and, in particular, with the people who had either failed to put up markers that told walkers not to go there or who had removed said markers. I am in a position to describe in great detail all the characteristics of this woodland and am available to speak about it at dinners or other functions at any time – just contact my Stoke Climsland agent. In the end I backtracked and took another route that was also poorly signposted so that the whole episode probably cost me between 1 and 2 hours.

I was left rather disillusioned by the Severn Way. Well-marked in places, it often left the walker (me) guessing and confused. I have already mentioned sore and wet feet and the Way had both of these. It was not always the highway into the Midlands that I'd hoped for though, at its best, it was delightful with splendid locks, comfortable sheep and jumping horses. Today, despite the problems, I managed to have an ice cream in Stourport (which was celebrating the sunshine in style) and then arrived early at my rendezvous just south of Bewdley. I elected to walk on into the town where I downed two large mugs of tea and a big glass of water, sitting on the waterfront promenade. Then back to the pick-up point where my arrival coincided with that of Sue Cowen – she and Kevin are my hosts this evening.

I can now relax – no woodland dead-ends here.

DAY 26 — Blackstone to Blakeshall

17 km (11 miles)
339 m of climb
32% completed

Blakeshall is a village 2 km south of Kinver.

As I said in the blog, this was a delightful walk through the edge of the Wyre Forset that stretches a considerable distance to the north and west of Bewdley. It includes a National Nature Reserve, a good deal of access land, adventure playgrounds and holiday parks and is mixed deciduous and conifer woodland across a very hilly area. I was walking through on a sunny Sunday and there were many day walkers about; this weekend was undoubtedly the most crowded part of my whole end-to-end experience. Oddly, no-one commented on the large red logo on my rucksack which announced that I was walking from Lands End to John O'Groats; in fact, throughout the walk it attracted very few comments! I appreciated the anonymity

but I was anxious to get the donations flowing in again - the total had been stuck for some time at just over £4000 and there was very little that I could do about it that I wasn't already doing. However, a little later Viv sent out some reminder letters and emails and things began to take off after that, with a surge when I arrived at John O'Groats.

Above: Sailing on Trimpley Reservoir. This reservoir is at the treatment works for water brought from the Elan Valley in Wales.

Farewell Severn

A mercifully short day today – I have had enough of long slogs in this heat.

Sue and Kevin Cowen had been teachers so we had a lot in common last night. With Kevin's stir-fry backed up by a couple of local beers, we reminisced about TVEI, GNVQ and other forgotten initiatives of the 1980s and 90s. Sue had collected me at a rendezvous just south of Bewdley and I stayed with them in Kidderminster, returning to the pick-up point this morning, rather later than usual. Another delightful stay for which I am, once again, very grateful.

The Severn Valley north of Bewdley is lovely. The river no longer has the sullen look that it develops further south and the valley is fringed by steep and extensive mixed woodlands that look especially attractive at this time of year. I walked at a sedate pace, pausing at a halt on the Severn Valley Railway to see a train go through and then again where the railway crossed the river. People were doing normal Sunday morning things that, in this case, included sailing on a reservoir that was part of the water supply route from the Elan Valley to Birmingham. This crossed the Severn on an aqueduct, though I didn't appreciate the purpose of the strange covered bridge until I was well past it.

Then I left the Severn – having followed it for most of the way from Bristol – and climbed through woodland on the Worcestershire Way which was well marked and very pleasant. These were the first significant hills for 5 or 6 days and my legs seemed to have stiffened into level walking mode. Again, a very attractive area – it was difficult to imagine that, beyond the hills in the middle distance, lay Birmingham. This was clearly commuter country with all the paraphernalia of commuterland including what I thought was a rather unwelcoming sign that said 'REMEMBER – our dog can get to the fence in 25 seconds. CAN YOU?'.

And so to a very small village just south of Kinver where I'm the guest of Ruth and Andrew Stilton in whose splendid garden this is being typed, thankfully in the cool of the evening. I can see Staffordshire from here so Worcestershire will become a memory in the first few minutes of tomorrow's walk. I wouldn't say that the counties are beginning to tumble like ninepins but from tomorrow it's only 4 more days to Derbyshire when life starts to get gritty.

And cooler, I hope.

Severn bridges past and present. Opposite: a dismantled bridge on the railway that ran from Bewdley to Ludlow; Left: Victoria Bridge of 1861, now on the Severn Valley Railway.

Nurton is a small village about 8 km west of Wolverhampton on a minor road to Pattingham.

Enville Hall sits close to the junction between the Staffordshire, Worcestershire and Shropshire borders on an estate of 6500 acres rising to more than 200 m. The original Tudor House, owned by a family whose members seem to have been executed rather frequently, was incorporated into an 18th century re-build and it remains a private home. It is in stark contrast to the cave dwellings of Kinver and the industrial homes of the Black Country!

I was seeing rural Staffordshire but, as I've already noted, industrial Staffordshire was only just over the horizon. It was also a county where the industrial revolution took root in the latter part of the 18th century and was the stamping ground of those men of the enlightenment, Josiah Wedgwood, Joseph Wright, Erasmus Darwin, Matthew Boulton, James Watt, Joseph Priestly and others so beautifully portrayed in Jenny Uglow's *The Lunar Men*. This is the story of a group of men, largely from the Midlands, who met every month in the latter part of the 18th century to discuss matters of common interest, particularly in science and manufacturing. They chose the Monday nearest the full moon so that they could meet in the afternoon, eat a good dinner and then be able to journey home by moonlight. Read the book - it is a revelation!

Above: Enville Hall and grounds;
Right: looking north over Kinver from Kinver Edge

No longer a solo walk

I said, at the outset of this walk, that I would be starting each day's walk at 7am. Well, I've fallen lamentably short of that target on almost every day. Until this morning! My hosts were early breakfasters, arranged so that they could travel into Birmingham for work and school. I was very pleased to be on the road so early – it was cool and the first part of the day was through quite dense woodland across Kinver Edge, with a splendid view over the village, and down past the caves (dug as habitations and now managed by the National Trust) and onto the Staffordshire Way.

I won't grumble about the Staffordshire Way – for the most part it was excellently signposted and very walkable. The miles flew past (in a manner of speaking) as I approached a rendezvous with David Jones somewhere beyond Enville but short of Highgate Common – it was a real Livingstone-Stanley moment.

Anne and David Jones had offered me accommodation for tonight and David had said that he'd like to join the walk for the day so we marched in unison to a very small place (Nurton) near another quite small place (Pattingham) where Anne picked us up and where I will be dropped off tomorrow to resume the northward trek.

I'm not, on the whole, a particularly companionable walker. I may have been once but I've probably become more crotchety as time has gone on and am generally better off by myself. But, for two strangers, David and I went well together today and I enjoyed the experience. It's a matter of walking speed and style (stopping when necessary but not too often), taking joint responsibility for navigation and talking when there's something interesting to say but otherwise simply enjoying the walk for its own sake. I'm now at their home on the edge of Wolverhampton and enjoying their hospitality - one again, they are both ex-teachers!

On the way I had passed Enville Hall which is large and impressive and not obviously a National Trust property or a conference centre. It turns out to be an ancestral home still inhabited by the family – I had rather assumed that it might have been the country seat of a successful 19th century industrialist. It had the benefit of its own cricket ground where it would be very nice to spend a Saturday afternoon and a small village with some picturesque vernacular buildings. It was hard to imagine the old industrial world over the horizon and made me realise that, by routing my walk along rural paths, I am not really getting a very true picture of Britain.

But it is good to look at.

FROM THE BLOG

The bored heron and Walsall memories

If anyone asks me, in some years' time, what I most remember about this walk it's likely that I'll say that it was the people that I met as much as the sights that I saw. The people I shall most remember will be those who offered me overnight accommodation since, in all cases so far, this has been a hugely enjoyable experience. Anne and David in Wolverhampton have already been mentioned and I was very sorry to leave them this morning; I hope that they enjoyed my company as much as I enjoyed theirs.

Wolverhampton is, of course, at the northern end of the Black Country which has not been in sight as I've walked but which was once a dominant part of British manufacturing. Once upon a time I made a tiny contribution to that manufacturing – I will bore you for just a moment by telling you of Marg and the Hilltop Foundry. I was there on one of the 3 month industrial placements that I did as part of my engineering degree. I lived in Walsall at Marg's establishment – her household also included her husband (rarely seen as he worked nights at the postal sorting office), five children – ages roughly 4 to 18, two of us students and a reporter with one of the Birmingham evening papers.

You will understand if I say that we were all pretty innocent in those days. But not after living at Marg's. It was very difficult to eat the evening meal (especially the soup) while her older daughters flaunted their attributes as they prepared to go out on the town. But with little money to spend we found that there wasn't a lot to do in winter in 1960s Walsall so I read a lot and went to bed early. My only memory of Walsall entertainment is that I saw *Psycho* there when it was first released.

It was unfortunate that the place that we worked at was in Wednesbury, some miles away and involved either cycling in the rain or a slow bus journey. In those days buses reeked of tobacco smoke and the windows streamed with condensation. The workplace was called Hilltop Foundry (though it was in a valley, sandwiched between

two railway lines and a stream) and castings in iron and aluminium were made there. The iron foundry was the more spectacular. At least it was dry and warm but otherwise was an inferno of smoke, huge noise and the dazzling glow of molten iron being tapped from the cupolas into large tubs which were trollied round to the moulding stations where the iron was poured into moulds (and quite often on the floor as well – you had to be nimble when that happened). There was real skill there – this was a traditional industry developed over thousands of years and now a rarity in this country. Each day I learned

Above: Cruising the Shropshire Union canal

more about working people and their attitudes, humour and values, and then went back to Marg's and learned a bit more.

Today was cooler and only sunny towards the end of the walk – something to be grateful for. The walking was easy, though the route was a bit ordinary by the standards of previous days. I did make a small navigational error and walked through the middle of a golf course when I should have been on a track hidden from view by trees, but no-one shouted at me.

And I used my third canal towpath – this time the Shropshire Union, one of Telford's great canals, engineered to be fast and economical and now a favourite amongst the leisure boaters. I joined it at Brewood where we hired narrow boats in times past, including a memorable trip to Telford's masterpiece, the Pontcysyllte Aqueduct near Llangollen. Today the canal was quiet – even the heron seemed bored.

Later I was sitting on the ground, leaning against a fencepost on the edge of a field, eating my lunch when a couple approached around the edge of the field and said 'hello'. They asked where I was heading and I said 'John O'Groats'; this answer is always followed by a short pause and people ask questions about when I started and when I'll finish and whether my feet are suffering. I generally try to produce one of my cards in the hope that the recipient will take the trouble to look at my website and blog and, perhaps, make a donation. Which this couple seemed willing to do and I'd be very grateful for that. It then turned out that the woman had had eye surgery a few days before and that this was her first outing after a rather boring time sitting at home, probably being able to do very little. So I hope that her eyesight improves and that she'll soon be able to go walking unaided.

Slightly odder was a car that later passed me on a field track, waving thanks as I stood aside. Odd because this track gave access only to crop fields and a mass of huge polytunnels that glistened in the sunshine – perhaps they were visible from space. A bit later he returned saying that he had thought that the track would give access to a main road. Given the general appearance and state of the track I'd say that his judgement was slightly suspect. His car was rather dustier than it had been earlier.

I am writing this in a pub that calls itself a hotel in the smallest room that I have so far occupied. It is a small miracle of economical space usage and I look out onto rooftops. Tomorrow I walk a similar distance to today but stay with a friend from my student days.

I'm quite glad not to be still living in Walsall (which is, no doubt, a splendid place now).

Top: Bored heron; Bottom: one of dozens of huge polytunnels.

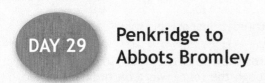

DAY 29 **Penkridge to Abbots Bromley**

31 km (19 miles)
210 m of climb
37% completed

I'm aware that I have included a lot about canals and a lot of canal pictures. I'm sorry if you find canals boring but I don't and I have to work with the pictures that I took which included a lot of canals. If you have a problem with this, I do have a set of paste-on pictures of Mongolian political leaders of the 20th century which you can have on application (accompanied by a small donation to Christian Aid) and can stick over the canal photographs. I do have to admit, however, that canal

towpaths lack variety on an end-to-end walk though they are not as monotonous as old railway tracks and much much better than roads. They are at their best when there are plenty of bridges, locks and boats to look at and the odd special feature to admire. But I do begin to hope for a bit of real up and down and even some stiles and long grass.

Above: Yesterday on the Shropshire Union; Right: Relaxing along the Trent and Mersey Canal; Below: Blithfield Reservoir with Abbots Bromley in the distance.

Feet and canals (again)

I may have said before – everyone asks whether my feet are standing up to the rigours of this walk. Do they ask this of everyone they see walking? Or do my feet look abnormal in some way? Or is it just a conversational gambit? "Hi. How are you? How are your feet?"

Yesterday something went wrong with my right foot. I'm not sure whether I trod heavily or awkwardly but in the later part of the walk into Penkridge it was really quite painful. This morning it was very painful and I was hobbling about my miniscule bedroom (not more that 2 steps in any direction) thinking that this could be a serious matter. Anyway, I strapped the foot with one of my excellent Boots elastic bandages, laced my boot up tightly to give maximum support and set off. It wasn't very nice to begin with; the citizens of Penkridge must have thought it unlikely that such a cripple would make it to Stafford, let alone John O'Groats.

The first part of my route (which was again along the Staffordshire Way) lay along the towpath of the Staffordshire and Worcestershire canal – my fourth of the walk. Towpaths are generally easy walking – they're flat and well used, so making few serious demands of a poorly foot. The route was due to leave the towpath some way from Penkridge and go through fields and woodlands to join the towpath of the Trent and Mersey Canal but I decided to stick with the Staffs and Worcs all the way through Stafford to Heywood Junction where it joins the Trent and Mersey. That gave my foot an easier walk and also enabled me to see a canal that I last travelled along in the 1970s.

There is a fairly unique feature of the canal as it nears the junction; it enters Tixall Wide which is, I think, a natural lake of some size, though rather bounded by reedbeds. I remember that I took the risk of steering the boat that we had in a large circle and got away with it. That's a luxury that is available nowhere else on the canal system, I think. It was here today that I passed a moored boat called *A Perfect Sin*; the owner was seated at the back with a telescope – either trainspotting or twitching, but looking very relaxed, though not obviously sinful.

Towpath walking along these two canals added a couple of miles to my route but the foot eased out a lot. I did take an ibuprofen to ease the discomfort but arrived at Abbots Bromley (where I'm staying with a friend from my student days) in reasonable shape though the foot is still bruised and I'll need to be careful tomorrow. I'm also very aware that I tend to speed up as I walk so that I find myself marching rather than walking and consequently getting hot and fed up rather quickly. This is a tendency that I must curb. But when asked in future I can at least truthfully say that my feet are OK or, perhaps more exactly, that they have recovered.

There's little else to report today but I'll leave you with a nice picture of a boater relaxing at the tiller and enjoying the Trent and Mersey – canals really are enticing places and I have a few more to encounter yet!

Abbots Bromley to Ashbourne

33 km (21 miles)
362 m of climb
39% completed

Colour on a dull day: Rhododendrons to the left and Dove-side wild flowers opposite

I think that I should explain about the patronising gent mentioned in my blog - one of only a very few people who was neither friendly nor welcoming. I was walking down a wide gravel path, clearly defined on the map, which turned out to be the driveway to an imposing house shrouded in trees and with those electric gates barring the way. As I approached the gates opened and a 4x4 came out and stopped by me. The gent said (in words that I remember as best I can) "Do you know where you're going?" and I said "Yes - there's a path marked on the map". He said "That's alright then - so many people of your ilk have no idea. There's a stile on the left down there - you go across that". And he wound his window up and drove off. It was only afterwards that I wondered what 'your ilk' signified; was it that I was a walker, a visitor, a slightly grubby person, an intruder or what? I do wish that I'd asked him. Perhaps I'm being paranoid but I still feel annoyed at the encounter.

Tutbury Mill was one of a series of textile mills built by Richard Arkwright. Less well known than his famous mills on the Derwent at Cromford, it remains a fine and relatively unchanged example of a water-powered mill. It has now been adapted for use as the JCB Academy. This photograph was taken in 2006 before the conversion started.

© Copyright Alan Murray-Rust and licensed for reuse under the Geograph Creative Commons Licence

New county, same old feet

I am writing this in Derbyshire. Welcome to t'north.

I left the genial company of Chris and Rob Ray in Abbots Bromley in mid-Staffordshire early this morning following a very enjoyable evening with an excellent meal and a good and comfortable night. Their house is a 17th century building in the middle of the village – a dwelling with unexpected corners including a splendid vaulted cellar and a fireplace larger than some sitting rooms.

So far everyone in t'north, including a patronising gent in an imposing motor, has smiled at me. I should have responded sharply to the gent but, as always, I thought of the smart and cutting comment after he'd driven away. Perhaps he got it telepathically and is writhing with shame as I write.

My welcome to t'north was wet – not very but enough to warrant wet weather gear. It was also a long slog which rather hurt my sore foot. But I now have a rest day which will undoubtedly do the foot some good. Much of the day was spent walking in the valley of the River Dove which is very attractive and the route included Uttoxeter and Rocester. Now the latter is home to the JCB factory where large earth-moving machines are made. I have seen the factory before – passing it on the road from Uttoxeter to Ashbourne - and

it's very modern and smart. But it seems that JCB has commandeered large swathes of land around Rocester and landscaped this as only they can do, though they do have large yellow notices that say, in effect, PRIVATE. KEEP OUT which is not very friendly.

The most interesting JCB site in Rocester is a mill established by Richard Arkwright in the 1780s. This was the very beginning of the industrial revolution when just a handful of mills were being built and the industrialisation of northern towns had yet to take place. Most industry up to that time had been located in small workshops in rural areas, depicted by Joseph Wright in his very atmospheric paintings of the period. Anyway, Arkwright's mill is now a JCB research and training centre and very smart it is too. And if you're wondering about Rocester it is, I understand, pronounced like rouster.

The Dove is clearly a big tourist attraction though best known north of Ashbourne rather than on its route from Ashbourne to join the Trent. It's a sparkling river though I did wonder whether it would be so highly regarded if it were called the River Bosh or the River Sludge or even the River Mersey. I walk up part of the valley again in 2 days' time but, for now, I'm on a rest day. However, I have been thinking about some educational matters so I may write a second post for the blog today or tomorrow.

But for now I'm resting.

I'm doing this for education

Everyone values education. When Tony Blair declared his priority as 'education, education, education' no-one demurred about the principle of the matter though perhaps they were less impressed with the implementation. We would all want our children to have the same educational opportunities as everyone else's, partly because that is only fair but mainly because we wouldn't want them to miss out on the benefits that may follow a 'good' education.

My walk is for children in developing countries, based on the beliefs that children everywhere should have the same educational opportunities as we enjoy and that relief from poverty is impossible without universal education. But we should be clear what education is for. There are three types of response to this question.

First, government ministers and business people often relate educational provision to the economic benefits that their country wants. All countries need doctors, engineers, carpenters, nurses, bricklayers, lawyers and so on, and we know that we can't have these people unless there is an education system that will deliver the knowledge and skills that these specialists need. A country can buy in the skills from elsewhere, but that's an expensive and sometimes divisive option.

This is a utilitarian view of education that directly relates educational provision to economic well-being. It is widely promoted by bodies such as the OECD and the World Bank; it does not neglect the wishes of individuals but it assumes that these can be subsumed within the general good. However, in totalitarian regimes any personal wishes or aspirations may be over-ridden by decisions of the state.

This type of answer also surfaces when something goes wrong and children do, or fail to do, things that we think they should such as crossing the road carefully, behaving respectfully or being able to do long division. Quite a lot of this is simply the disconnect between generations and we know that there are limits to what education can do to promote a society of which we'd all approve. We also know that, in some of these issues, we're treading a borderline between our responsibilities as adults and the responsibilities of an education system (state or private) to teach and encourage children to be effective and responsible adults.

A second type of answer is concerned with the participation by individuals in their societies. It says that democracy can only operate if there is widespread participation by members of the public with a suffi-

cient level of educational attainment. It is common for western countries to promote democracy in places where regimes are seen to be oppressive, inadequate or inappropriate. But democracy is far more than having the chance to vote periodically. It is a critical and participative process that needs everyone to have at least some degree of education that would minimally provide a capacity to read and write but would more appropriately include some understanding of a national culture and the capacity to find out what is happening, to distinguish between points of view and thus make personal decisions.

The third answer is one that is grounded in notions of liberal education that were commonplace in the west until about 40 years ago but that have been rather squeezed out by the more utilitarian views that I've already described. Here we are concerned with the individual child – how do we, as a society, foster the development of what we would regard as an 'educated adult'? Being educated clearly involves being able to do a whole range of fundamental things like reading, writing, speaking and understanding number. But we are much more likely to describe it in terms of being able to find things out for oneself, having an appreciation of different areas like the arts and sciences, having a capacity for critical analysis, with an ability to evaluate alternative courses of action and being able to participate in discussions on a range of topics. Here, being educated is much more to do with the possession of skills than it is to do with the amount of knowledge that an individual has.

In general, these skills are acquired through a broad base of learning activities spread over a long period of time. In fact, they are a natural extension of the learning processes that start at birth and that we have all wondered at as we watch a baby developing. However, it has always been difficult to see education in this way whilst, at the same time, providing the grounding that will enable an individual to become an engineer, nurse, plumber or lawyer. Utilitarianism naturally tends to take over and, particularly in a developing country where skills are in short supply, this is probably inevitable.

So what am I walking for? Well, in the first instance it's for individuals – so that some children can have the opportunity for personal fulfilment. This means giving them chances to learn and to go on learning for as long and for as much as they are willing and able to do. Creating opportunities like this will, in the end, enable them and their countries to function as they should.

Of course, this also applies to adults - education is not just concerned with children - so that we should regard apprenticeships, adult literacy classes and degree programmes as every bit as important as the provision of schools. This will all take a long time – educational investment is for the long term and people will undoubtedly get impatient with the slowness of the progress. But there is no obvious alternative and it is vitally important that agencies like Christian Aid get into and stay in the education business for the long haul since poverty can never be eliminated until every country has the levels of expertise, acquired in the family and through education, that will enable it to stand on its own feet with its own citizens in charge of its development.

As far as I'm concerned, this is an essential consequence of the Christian message.

Opposite: School in Sierra Leone; Christian Aid photograph

The parish church at Howarth

Ashbourne to Ilkley

Date	Day	No	From	To	
2-June-2012	Sat	32	Ashbourne	Youlgreave	GPX files for each day's walk can be downloaded from the internet and plotted using mapping software such as OS Getamap or Google maps. The download addresses are in the form http://www.wilmut.net/lejogbook/day32.gpx
3-June-2012	Sun	33	Youlgreave	Hathersage	
4-June-2012	Mon	34	Hathersage	Flouch Inn	
5-June-2012	Tue	35	Flouch Inn	Marsden	
6-June-2012	Wed	36	Marsden	Hebden Bridge	
7-June-2012	Thu	37	Hebden Bridge	Haworth	
8 June-2012	Fri	38	Haworth	Ilkley	

Light and shade in the south Pennines

One of the pleasures of variable weather is the contrast in luminosity as clouds cast shadows over the landscape. There were plenty of wide views to be had for much of the rest of this walk although I'm afraid that I haven't done a great job of capturing them on camera. Although in the blog I often complained about the weather, there were some glorious moments as well as days when drizzle blotted out almost everything.

This was undoubtedly harder walking than I had had further south but, at its best, it was more rewarding.

DAY 32 **Ashbourne to Youlgreave**

34 km (21 miles)
691 m of climb
41% completed

I need to do Ashbourne justice: it was a good place for a rest day, though there are no outstanding tourist attractions in the town itself. I did stroll around, enjoyed

some peace and quiet in a local church and in the public library and discovered an excellent Indian restaurant on the first night and an excellent Italian restaurant on the second; neither was outrageously expensive. Perhaps my only irritation was the cobbled streets which were very testing for my poorly foot.

FROM THE BLOG
Derbyshire Dove and drizzle

Above: Setting up the market in Ashbourne;
Right: Dovedale in the rain

Today's 34 km (21 miles) included a bit of mucking around trying to find a perfectly obvious route off the Tissington Trail north of Ashbourne. Which just about summed up the day, really.

It began well. I had had an excellent B&B in Ashbourne and its proprietor made a donation to the fund, which was very kind. If you want a good B&B there at any time just give me a call. I left Ashbourne as market traders were setting up their stalls under the bunting and things went uphill (to get to the Tissington Trail, which is an old railway line) and downhill (organisationally and psychologically). The Trail is a good way of getting out of Ashbourne towards Dovedale. I'm still not sure what I did wrong but I added a mile and lost half an hour and some patience.

And the drizzle started – a grey miasma settled over Derbyshire for the day. Sad really. It robbed me and Dovedale of a little of our sparkle; this is a spectacularly beautiful valley, especially in the very steep-sided part just north of Thorpe. At least the drizzle kept the day trippers away – the people walking the valley were almost all kitted out for serious walking – probably escaping Jubilee celebrations somewhere.

After a good dose of Dovedale beauty, the route continued up Biggindale which doesn't have a pretty river but does evoke memories of several residential programmes held at Biggin Hall (a small country house hotel in the village of Biggin) when I was a member of a research team at Nottingham University; it was our custom to do an afternoon walk down Biggindale to Dovedale and back, designed to energise the grey matter. That was when I could think, so the effort was worthwhile.

During these residential programmes we also developed the habit of going to the village pub which in those days had its own miasma made from chip fat fumes and tobacco smoke. Enough of each and you have a smell that will stick to your clothes for days. I remember demonstrating my total incompetence at darts in that pub, causing hilarity amongst my colleagues. Truth was, I couldn't see the dart board through the haze. The pub today looked rather smarter outside and there was no smell of chips and, of course, I have to assume that there was no smoking inside. Biggin village was *en fete* but the drizzle gave a grey look to the bunting

and to the many effigies of our monarch and various peripheral royals. I don't suppose they noticed.

And so it went on. I encountered several groups of young people whom I later learned were doing Duke of Edinburgh awards – they were cheerful enough and said hello (or maybe it was something else). I went down Grattondale and then over fields to get to Youlgreave which seems a nice sort of place. But at several stages in the day, to keep cheerful, I found myself striding along to hummed versions of marching tunes: things like John Brown's Body, Onward Christian Soldiers, Old Macdonald had a Farm and various classical bits that were never really meant to be marched to. Drizzle does this to a man.

In passing, I also reflected on the greetings between walkers. A cheerful 'good morning' is OK up to midday – most people, pleased to be up and about early, respond to this though with varying degrees of warmth. Anyone under the age of 20 is more likely to respond to 'Hello' or 'Hi' but younger teenagers often look away as though it was all too much trouble. After midday 'Good afternoon' sounds too formal and I tend to revert to 'Hello' or, the slightly more patronising 'Hello there'. Many women, especially those walking alone, look away – perhaps this is a defensive response which is a bit sad. And one has to be careful to stop greeting people in towns – it's just not the done thing. Cyclists are usually very chummy.

Tomorrow it's a similar distance to Hathersage and the forecast is poor. I'm not sure why I'm bothering to dry things off.

DAY 33 **Youlgreave to Hathersage** 26 km (16 miles)
586 m of climb
42% completed

You will see that I mention the Alternative Pennine Way here and in Chapter 1
where I say why I chose to follow it and say that it wasn't altogether successful.
I also mention it at various point between here and Day 52 when I finally left it.
It's difficult to give a balanced view of the route - parts of it were splendid and
very solitary but I expect that most of the Pennine Way would have been equally
splendid and solitary. It avoided some of the worst slogging through the peaty
wasteland of the Kinder Scout area but it had its own share of peaty wastelands. It
was more suitable for an end-to-end walk in that it started at Ashbourne rather than
Edale and finished at Jedburgh rather than Kirk Yetholm.

I probably have two other significant reactions: first, that some parts of the Way
seemed to follow obscure paths almost for the sake of it and second, that the lack of
regular walking made some paths very difficult to follow. But this last is not unique
to the Alternative Pennine Way. Would I recommend anyone else to use the APW?
Possibly, but I would mention a number of specific difficulties and suggest that
these may not be a feature of the Pennine Way. And if you wanted luggage carrying
or other support services these may not be readily available on the APW. And any
path looks better in the sunshine than in the rain.

This is a bad photograph of Chatsworth in the rain. It's the only picture that I took
on this wet day when my camera seemed to have lost the incentive to focus. Baslow
Edge is just about visible above the buildings.

It rained on me today ...

... and rained and rained and rained. And blew somewhat. Not my best day in any way.

I was in no way cheered by the fact (learned afterwards) that the Thames pageant had also been rained upon. In fact, I would have resented wall-to-wall sunshine in London when Derbyshire was being washed so thoroughly. It was raining as I left my B&B at Youlgreave which was, I think, a rather unique place. It was run by a middle-aged gentleman who evidently had a passion for cats (2), books (masses), ceramics (loads of pots) and art (pictures on every wall space). I should have asked him – was he just a collector, perhaps an art historian or a teacher? Anyway, he knew a good deal about the local area and knew also about the Alternative Pennine Way which I am following.

This route was the invention of Denis Brook and Phil Hinchcliffe who published it in the 1990s as an alternative to the official Pennine Way. My B&B host described it as 'the pretty route' and said that, when the book was first published, a lot of people doing the route stayed with him. Though now out of print, I managed to get a used copy and decided that I'd try it as part of my end-to-end walk.

After Youlgreave and some ups and downs I came to Haddon Hall which was the setting for one of the TV or film costume dramas – I can't remember which one. Then through woodland and over another hill and Chatsworth hove into view (just about seen through the mist), Here I met (by arrangement) with Elizabeth and Roger Murphy, sometime colleagues at Nottingham University, who took pity on me and bought me a coffee in the Edensor tea room and then walked with me in the rain to Baslow. We passed some forlorn sheep that had just been shorn and were clearly suffering from the cold and wet – they were huddled under trees in groups. For me, it was good to update on news of colleagues, children and grandchildren and I greatly appreciated their company on such a dreary day.

Then to Baslow edge – one of a series of edges to be traversed on this Alternative Pennine Way. It seemed to take for ever to get up onto the Edge and then to battle along it in the rain and wind and I eventually decided that this was unnecessary suffering (there's more to an end-to-end walk than getting wet in Derbyshire) and dropped down to the Derwent valley to take a long traipse into Hathersage. Here I got the train to Sheffield where I had booked a cheap hotel which turned out to be a sort of student dive in rather poor condition. But I managed to dry most of my stuff and am typing this after a good Italian meal.

Tomorrow it's an early start back to Hathersage and the rigours of Stanage Edge. But the forecast shows sunshine and higher temperatures so perhaps I shall enjoy this one.

DAY 34   **Hathersage to Flouch Inn**   31 km (19 miles)
954 m of climb
44% completed

This was the day of the edges: Stanage, Derwent and Mickleden with a couple of reservoirs and plenty of climbing in between. It ended at Flouch Inn which sits close to the roundabout at the intersection of the A616 and the A628, 5 km west of Penistone. Stanage Edge is the most prominent and longest of the Derbyshire gritstone edges overlooking Hathersage and the Derwent valley. It stretches for 6 km and the Edge itself is up to 30 m in height. It is a very popular place for rock climbing and the gritstone has been used for millstones. I was easily able to climb up onto the Edge from Hathersage and, once up there, could walk northwest before dropping down to the road and then climbing onto Derwent Edge.

Top: Walking along Stanage Edge; Above: Dovestone Tor on Derwent Edge; Top Right: A good, informative, durable footpath sign; Right: Climbing onto Midhope Moors; Opposite: Climbing the path onto Stanage Edge

94

Sun, but not too much of it

The student dive in Sheffield turned out to have a sting in its dingy tail – they had a band night running until 4am. I was near the top of the building at the back so it wasn't as bad as it might have been but sleep eluded me until the early hours and I then woke at 5, decided that I might as well get the very early train back to Hathersage, so went for that with the help of a very cheerful trolley man on the train who sold me stuff that made an acceptable breakfast.

I walked out of Hathersage station well before 7am and climbed to Stanage Edge in a passable amount of sunshine. The wind on top was rather strong and cold but the view was clear and splendid and I made good progress in contrast with my wet stumblings on Baslow Edge the day before. This seemed a day when the walking sticks needed to be used so I got them out for the first time on this walk and they did, indeed, make the going up and coming down (of which there was a lot today) rather easier.

I made another transition today – from Derbyshire into Yorkshire. So I'm really in the north now and will be for quite some time – Yorkshire is a big county. I came down from Stanage Edge to the A57 (which goes across Snake Pass from Manchester to Sheffield and gets snowed up most winters) and then climbed up onto Derwent Moor. I passed enclosures called 'shooting butts' – small hides from which, in the season, people take pot shots at birds.

Nowadays many of the paths across the moors have flagstones which encourage walkers to keep off the peat which has, in the past, become seriously eroded. But some unflagged paths have attracted mountain bikers who climb and descend at some speed and thus are doing as much damage as the feet of many walkers. The flagstones are not, I guess, good to ride on but they are good for quick walking, so they suited me well.

Curlews and skylarks were much in evidence and the rhododendrons when I dropped down to Derwent Reservoir were in full bloom and very splendid. By that time there were whole families out on their Bank Holiday walking and cycling on the paths around the reservoir and I was glad to escape up a side valley for my third and last main climb of the day, the 3-4 miles over to Flouch Inn. This turned out to be closed (so I couldn't get a cup of tea whilst waiting for my hosts to pick me up) but I did manage to book a couple of B&Bs for tomorrow and the day after.

Flouch Inn to Marsden

27 km (17 miles)
559 m of climb
46% completed

At the end of today's blog I issued a challenge which was taken up by several people. I have reproduced most of the entries in the Dongle Interlude on pages 104-5.

Right: View across to Holmfirth (home of Last of the Summer Wine);
Below: Mowing a dam;
Bottom: Waterfall and rhododendrons near Marsden

FROM THE BLOG

A hard day but the band played me in

I had a lovely time yesterday evening with Marie and Julian Raffay – they were great hosts and very interesting to talk with; Marie is an officer with Christian Aid and Julian is a priest working in the NHS with people with mental illness. They picked me up at Flouch Inn (which would be an ideal overnight stopping place if it were still open) and returned me there this morning. A highlight of the evening was an excursion to see the lighting of the Jubilee beacon in their local park – an event attended by their MP and a lot of citizens. The singing of the National Anthem and Rule Britannia would have benefited from some instrumental accompaniment and a conductor since not everyone was singing the same thing at the same time in the same key. But fun was had by all – especially the children.

After the splendid day that I had yesterday I had hoped for a good day today but, for some unaccountable reason, it didn't work that way. Perhaps I was just out if sorts but I felt very weary and anxious that threatened rain would come while I was out on the moors (it didn't). The route wasn't nearly as arduous as yesterday's – the ups were less uppish and the downs not so downish but I just got cheesed off with the whole thing until very late in the day when I began to enjoy the long long downhill stretch into Marsden. It then rained a little as I got to the pub where I'm staying.

This area is dotted with smallish reservoirs and I walked round several of them and across the dams of two, one of which was being mowed by 4 or 5 men with strimmers and a mower. The reservoirs were built to supply the human and industrial thirsts of the area from north Sheffield, through Barnsley to Huddersfield and they now look very integrated into the landscape. This does look very barren in places – sheep have seen to that – with the farmsteads and villages concealed in deep valleys. It's a land of muted greens, browns and greys, which makes the flowers of the rhododendrons all the more startling. It's also the land of moorland birds and I was mobbed a couple of times by anxious curlews, fearful for their eggs or chicks. I finally left the Peak District National Park just before entering Marsden.

My room at the New Inn at Marsden was splendidly different from my last pub lodgings in Penkridge where the room was only 2 paces wide and 3 paces long. Here I have a 4 poster bed (posts but no canopy), a settee, two armchairs, a jacuzzi and heating that works. It's splendid and I'm savouring every moment of it. As the room door closed behind me a brass band struck up (not in the room, you understand – it's large but not that large – but in some nearby building) as if to welcome me to the delights of the town. I did wonder whether I shouldn't just stay here and forget the rest of the walk.

I have been in Marsden before. A few years ago Viv and I, son Ian and his partner, Ruth hired a narrow boat to do the newly opened South Pennine Ring, formed of the restored Rochdale and Huddersfield Narrow canals, with some linking bits. We knew it would be a strenuous 2 weeks and indeed it was. There are over 200 locks on the Ring (I think I remember that number correctly) and some of those on the Rochdale Canal were heavy and malign. It also rained a lot but one major highlight of the trip came at Marsden which is at the east end of the Standedge tunnel. There are 3 tunnels through the hill – the canal tunnel and two railway tunnels, one of which has now been abandoned. Linking tunnels were driven so that spoil could be removed on the canal as the later railway tunnel was bored so that there is now the occasional glimpse of a passing train as you go through on the canal.

But the canal tunnel is very narrow, is poorly ventilated and has a kink where the two ends didn't quite meet so British Waterways is not willing to let boaters loose in such a high-risk place. So it is necessary to book a tow by a BW electric barge. To prevent damage to narrow boats they are sheeted in rubber matting. Their crews sit in a special enclosed barge and the whole entourage bumps through at, I guess, about 2mph and taking more than an hour to do it. It's a damp and chilly experience but quite unique; long may it continue since, without this link, the exciting South Yorkshire Ring would not be possible.

This post is late – I'm sorry for this but access to WiFi and the need to do other things in the evening (sleep, have a meal) mean that I easily get distracted. And I have a backlog of photos to add - it will get done, I promise. To my annoyance, the dongle that I bought specifically for the walk doesn't want to connect to the internet. There's a lesson there – never trust a salesperson who's selling you a dongle.

Here's a personal challenge for you - write exactly 100 words, fantasising on a dongle. It must not be rude.

My comment in the blog on the farm located between the carriageways of the M62 resulted in a short exchange of comments which are reproduced on pages 187-190.

You will see that I got rather lost in the mist and rain above Hebden Bridge and was very concerned that I'd added substantially to the distance that I'd

walked. Having now seen the record of my route on the GPS I find that I took just about the most direct route that I could have chosen; for once, my navigational instincts did not let me down. I wish that I'd known that at the time; though it would have made no difference to my wetness or tiredness it would have made me feel a lot better.

In loving memory of
JANINE MARIE SUTCLIFFE
1951 – 2008

"I go to nature to be soothed and healed and to have my senses put in tune once more"

Clockwise from top left: The Huddersfield Narrow Canal; Looking back at Marsden - a mill town; Farming by the M62; Plaque on my lunch seat .

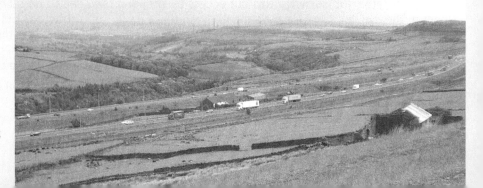

Another motorway, another two canals

It all started very well. I climbed out of Marsden along a route that I'd walked before, though only for a couple of miles. It started by crossing the Huddersfield Narrow Canal which I mentioned in my last post and then climbed onto the moor. The weather was not bad and got better so people I met said 'It's a grand day' and I had to agree. So I was marching across the moors in a good mood when I came to a notice that said 'FOOTPATH CLOSED' and another that said 'PEDESTRIANS THIS WAY' with an imperious arrow.

Now I tend to distrust such notices but these looked official enough so I did as directed. It turned out that some work was being done on a reservoir spillway so human beings were being diverted. I would have minded less if the new route had been engineered in some way. Why should Yorkshire Water and its contractor think it appropriate to send walkers across a mass of boggy ground, deep down into a valley out of which they have to climb and over a distance at least 3 times the length of the designated path? Did they really need to divert the path anyway? It didn't look like it from where I stood, getting crosser by the minute. I noted that they'd taken the trouble to erect new fences but not to lay any sort of surface over the bogs or even strim the grass.

I did consider writing to Yorkshire Water and its contractor, Mott Macdonald, objecting to this diversion and hinting that a donation to the walk would placate me. But, like most irritations, it wore off and I found better things to do with my time.

I crossed under the M62 at the point where the carriageways diverge around a farm and several fields. Who could possibly want to farm in that noise? You couldn't even hear the sheep bleat.

There was a lot of up and down on this stretch – the last up was a lung-bursting climb out of Cragg Vale onto the moor above Hebden Bridge. I had started to hurry in order to escape the rain. In vain – it caught up with me on top of the moor and there I was, floundering in yet another series of bogs. I quite lost the route I was supposed to be on and eventually dropped into Hebden Bridge by the long and not so pretty route that eventually crossed the Rochdale Canal into the town.

I had forgotten to locate my B&B on a map and ended up by going into an estate agent's shop, dripping all over the carpet, and asking for directions, which they readily gave me. I found that the B&B was up a very steep hill which I have to climb again as soon as I've posted this blog, paid my bill and walked out of this warm and congenial pub where I'm typing it.

And I've forgotten to bring the photos with me, so you'll have to wait for those. I have a rest day in a couple of days and I'll try to tidy everything up a bit. Whatever you do, don't stop reading the blog – I have a little counter that tells me how many hits there have been and I will get terribly dispirited if the number falls. And do tell your friends – you could suggest to them that this is the next Booker prize in the making.

PS. I see that I have a photograph (left) of a bench that I sat on to eat my lunch. I was very taken with the dedication plate.

Above: Main Street, Howarth with The Old White Lion in the background where I had an excellent dinner.
© Copyright Nick Macneill and licensed for reuse under the Geograph Creative Commons Licence

I would probably have enjoyed Haworth more in sunshine (or even plain honest cloudy dryness); there were quite a lot of damp tourists about and trains were tooting as they pulled in and out of the station at the bottom of the hill. There's no doubt that a good steam railway (especially one where *The Railway Children* was filmed) pulls in the tourists and Haworth also has the great benefit of a classical literary association that does marvels for a place.

Haworth dates from the 13th century and was a rural settlement before industrialisation brought the mills, now long closed. Remakably it is twinned with Machu Picchu in Peru which it in no way resembles.

Left: Haworth parsonage is difficult to see from either the road or the churchyard and I was too mean (and too wet) to pay to go inside.

Right: The proprietor of my Howarth B&B was clearly a railway enthusiast, perhaps because the B&B is right next to Howarth station on the Worth Valley Railway. He has posted this (undoubtedly fake) notice in the bathroom of my room. I must be going daft to find this funny!

SOUTHERN RAILWAY
QUIET PLEASE
AVOID ANNOYANCE TO RESIDENTS KEEP YOUR ENGINE QUIET AND TAKE CARE TO AVOID SMOKE AND STEAM

Short and wet

Haworth is soggy today. Even the Japanese tourists, normally smiling through anything, look slightly dissolved around the edges. The forecast said 'rain' and rain duly came and accompanied me over the moors to here – a relatively short walk today but well lubricated.

Did I say yesterday that my B&B in Hebden Bridge was half way up the moorside? Well, it was, and very good it was too, though for an evening meal I had to go down the very steep hill and then back up again later. I did notice, part way up, an infants school, no doubt placed there to ensure that small children developed the muscles and bone structure necessary for living in the town. But one of the advantages of the B&B was that I was able to escape Hebden Bridge with part of the climb out already done. No small advantage this morning.

So my walk to Haworth went well, though wetly and I arrived at lunchtime with nothing much to do until I could access my B&B at about 4pm. So I've viewed the Bronte sights, looked at the shops (mostly for tourists), drunk speciality tea and eaten excellent expensive cake in a posh coffee shop, made a brief excursion to the Worth Valley Railway station and am now sitting in a pub, spinning out a pint of coke while I type this. And you thought that this walking was a dawn-to-dusk toil across barren moors, didn't you? As I sit here various people in boots and waterproofs have drifted in, clearly looking for a space where they can dry out. Perhaps pubs like this love wet days.

Looking at a map of this area you get the impression that it's all built over – a hotchpotch of towns spreading up hillsides and merging into a single urban mass. But for the last week I've been walking through remote moorland most of the time, seeing very few people and feeling cut off from civilisation. The settlements are hidden in the valleys and remain out of sight until you've almost stumbled into them. This is a wild open area that owes a lot to industrialisation that is largely out of sight though there are reservoirs and roads and powerlines that give away the secret.

I'm not sure why Haworth is here. There must have been mills, I suppose, though I haven't yet seen any remnants. I daresay that the town now owes a lot of its income to the Brontë family. I went into the church but saw a building that is now largely Victorian – not the church that the Brontë family knew, though, with the exception of Anne (who is buried at Scarborough) they are all buried here. The parsonage is a museum and I suppose that it's the major visitor attraction.

Tomorrow I walk to Ilkley and then have a rest day; it's another short walk – only about 12 miles though I'm not sure what the weather will do. I won't be staying in the town since I couldn't get a bed for the 2 nights at a reasonable price so I'll be getting the train into Bradford which I've never visited. Then back on Sunday for the walk to Pately Bridge that will take me past the halfway point. Magic. At least, that's what I'm telling my feet.

And a tiny item of good news – for me at least. This morning I searched everywhere for the small pack that contains my rucksack cover, couldn't find it and decided that I must have left it on the moor above Hebden Bridge when I frantically put on my waterproofs. More magic: it was in the bottom of my rucksack all the time and came to light as I unpacked this evening. One thing to cross off the shopping list for Bradford.

The Bingley 5-rise locks vewed from below and above;
Opposite Top: Top: Worth Valley railway engines;
Opposite Bottom: Plaque at the top of the locks

FROM THE BLOG

Hatless on Ilkley Moor

Despite the rain yesterday I was very comfortable in Haworth – another B&B that I can recommend. And I was very grateful for a donation – thank you again, Caroline and Adrian. And also to the unknown gent in a Range Rover who stopped on a deeply muddy and potholed track and asked where I was going. When I told him (and passed over one of my cards) he seemed dumbfounded and reached in his pocket, gave me a fiver and wished me luck. That's well over a £ a mile for today's efforts – very cheering.

Yesterday's forecast said rain so I put on all the gear before I left. The trouble with it is that, once I start to climb the hills hereabouts I sweat mightily and get very uncomfortable. Which was silly since it wasn't actually raining at all, though a little came over when I was on Ilkley Moor. But, by that time, I'd shed most of the waterproofs and managed to dry out.

Except for my boots!!! They (especially the left one) are now giving me so much trouble with leakage that I will have to get the spares sent up. After all the complimentary things I said about them when I bought them in March! I take it all back – they have some serious defect that allows water in around the tongues. Which is useless in heavy rain, when walking through long wet grass or when walking over boggy moorland. I've been doing all three in the last few days and my feet are suffering from the continuous wetness. ARGHHHHHHHH!!!!!

To cheer myself up I took some photographs today, after a few days when I didn't manage too many or the ones I took were not good enough to include in the blog. I thought that I should have at least one photograph of the Worth Valley Railway, so here is a picture, taken at the sheds at Haworth, of one of the locomotives being readied for the day's journeys.

There is a superb view over Haworth from the east side of the valley but it needed sunshine to make it look good and I didn't have any. So on to my last English canal

of this walk – the Leeds and Liverpool Canal goes through Bingley where there is one of the wonders of the English canal system – the Bingley 5-rise. It's 5 locks pushed together so that the bottom gates of lock 1 are also the top gates of lock 2, the bottom gates of lock 2 are also the top gates of lock 3 and so on. The opportunities for causing major disasters and widespread flooding are immense, so British Waterways lock keepers direct operations.

I can vouch for the scariness of these locks which are very deep indeed. When you're in a boat coming up the flight you face huge gates that are holding back an immense wall of water. You just have to have faith in the technology. The lock keepers work very hard though they rightly expect the boat crews to do a lot of the paddle winding and gate pushing. These are wide locks so a pair of narrow boats can go down or come up at a time or one boat can come up and another go down, passing somewhere in the middle.

The Five-Rise Locks

Designed By
John Longbotham of Halifax
And Built In 1774
By Local Stonemasons
**Barnabus Morvil, Jonathan Farrar,
William Wild** all of Bingley
and **John Sugden** from Wilsden

The Locks Raise Boats 59 ft. 2 ins.
Over A Distance Of 320 ft.

Distance By Canal
To Leeds   16 miles 2 furlongs
To Liverpool   111 miles

National Heritage Award Winner 1975

I do like the notice at the top which records the building of the flight and names the engineer but also names the masons who did the work. Too often, it's the name of the celebrity who performs the opening that takes pride of place or the credit for the achievement goes to the senior people only. But it's the craftsmanship that has ensured that we still have these engineering monuments working today.

The walk from Bigley to Ilkley looked straightforward on the map and indeed it was though there was a sharp climb up onto Bingley Moor and a sharp descent from Ilkley Moor and a great deal of bog in between. I did have the pleasure of seeing a couple of curlew chicks close to – their parents had flown up from the trackside nest in a panic and the chicks were scuttling for cover as I walked past. And then it was down over the most famous moor on the Pennines into the classy town of Ilkley where, I guess, many of those who made their money from the mill towns built their houses.

And I have a rest day! Marvellous! So probably no post tomorrow and the next should come from Pately Bridge.

THE DONGLE INTERLUDE

In my blog posting for Day 35 I issued a small challenge: to write exactly 100 words, fantacising on a dongle. The only condition was that it must not be rude. Over the succeeding few days I had five responses and, although I had not said that it was a competition (with, of course, the need for me to make a decision about the winner) an element of competitiveness entered into the blog comments. I now face the problem that I either ignore all the entries (potentially upsetting everyone who entered), select a winner and publish that entry (potentially upsetting all but one of the entrants) or publish everything (potentially upsetting all readers). I've chosen the last option on the grounds that it absolves me of all responsibility and you can turn the page if you don't want to know about dongles.

One person submitted two entries, the first of which was the *Dong with the Luminous Nose* by Edward Lear, but substituting 'dongle' for 'dong' (and thereby wrecking both rhyme and metre). I discount this on grounds of plagiarism, taste and length.

A submission from Christine. I hope that she doesn't mind me saying that it has a slight air of desperation about it

a dongle, a dongle, a dongle
I wish I had a dongle
actually I don't!
don't want a dongle
don't need a dongle
yet
I used to think the same about an eye pad
but now I have one of those
and have trouble wondering how I would
cope
without it
so,
dongle, dongle, dongle,
dongle, dongle, dongle
no
I can't seem to conjure up a fantasy about
a dongle
sorry
not only that, but I've only managed
seventy-eight words
well,
now of course that makes it ninety words
almost makes me wish I could think of
another ten!

For the avoidance of misunderstanding: this is my dongle

An entry from Jill Long. It scans and rhymes (more or less) and I see this as the most polished of the entries.

> John had a little Dongle
> He bought it for a song
> It's meant to re-connect him
> When WiFi has gone wrong
>
> When he stayed at Marsden
> He hoped that it would play
> Along with the brass band
> Practicing down the way
>
> Alas to say it failed him
> Despite all he had wished
> His blog remained in Marsden
> Twil go from Hebdon Bridge
>
> I've never met a dongle
> Though I've heard of them by name
> It paints a lovely picture
> But it's only in my brain!
>
> I think it has a smiley face
> And legs all long and thin
> But where do I connect it?
> Where does the thing plug in??

I have a little difficulty with the scanning of this offering from Deri Parsons but it is exactly 100 words and may be an attempt at free verse which was all the rage in the 1930s.

> I'm a little dongle,
> Short and stout,
> When John wants to chatter,
> He takes me out,
> As I get connected,
> Hear me shout,
> Fire me up and message out
>
> I'm a clever dongle,
> Yes, I know it's true,
> There really is no end
> To what I can do,
> I've got such a lot of digital clout
> When you fire me up and message out
>
> I'm a useful dongle,
> As John knows well
> I try to keep him on-line
> So his tale he can tell.
> But when there's a problem he starts to pout
> Fires me up but no message out!

John Moore went off on an entirely different tack, abandoning verse (which was not a requirement of the challenge) in favour of a word game. He said: "Been cogitating (in my armchair of course) over the dongle challenge. Here is my response. I tried to use every word derived from DONGLE once only in a story. Here goes (with certain liberties with grammar and pronunciation)":

> Lo, old Len Ogden on dole, one leg long-gone, don gel, go ogle lone golden doe. O! Den Noel done led olden Doge glen gold lode 'n no lego node, do log gen.

and then said "Cannot work in 'dong, dongle, god, lend, nod, and nog'. You've got plenty of time . . . .". This is so far out on the spectrum of conventional language use that I cannot decide whether it is genius or hallucination. Or it may be because of the gin alongside the armchair.

I leave readers to decide on their favourite. I'm saying nothing.

Ceramic panel inset on a waymarker post
showing Lady Anne being carried over
her Highway: see the page for day 43

Ilkley to Allendale Town

Date	Day	No	From	To	
10-June-2012	Sun	40	Ilkley	Pateley Bridge	GPX files for each day's walk can be downloaded from the internet and plotted using mapping software such as OS Getamap or Google maps. The download addresses are in the form http://www.wilmut.net/lejogbook/day40.gpx
11-June-2012	Mon	41	Pateley Bridge	Carlton	
12-June-2012	Tue	42	Carlton	Hawes	
13-June-2012	Wed	43	Hawes	Kirkby Stephen	
14-June-2012	Thu	44	Kirkby Stephen	Appleby	
15-June-2012	Fri	45	Appleby	Dufton	
16-June-2012	Sat	46	Dufton	Nenthead	
17-June-2012	Sun	47	Nenthead	Allendale Town	

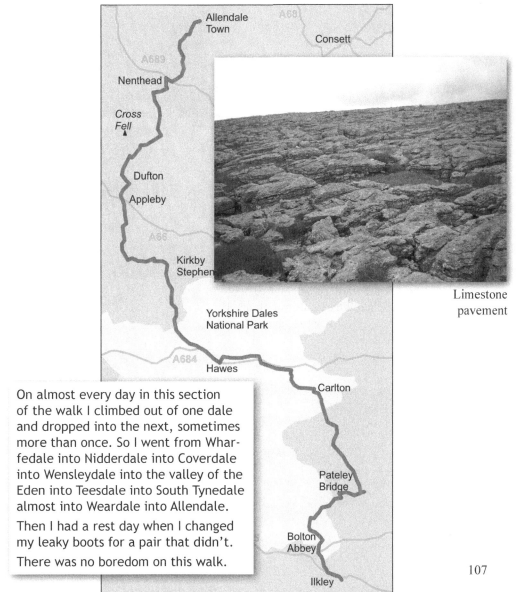

Limestone pavement

On almost every day in this section of the walk I climbed out of one dale and dropped into the next, sometimes more than once. So I went from Wharfedale into Nidderdale into Coverdale into Wensleydale into the valley of the Eden into Teesdale into South Tynedale almost into Weardale into Allendale.

Then I had a rest day when I changed my leaky boots for a pair that didn't.

There was no boredom on this walk.

DAY 40 **Ilkley to Pateley Bridge**

33 km (21 miles)
573 m of climb
51% completed

Left and Below: The Quaker
Meeting House at Farfield

Above: Bolton Abbey; Right: Crossing the Wharfe;
Below right: Coin Tree - for a discussion see
http://www.northernearth.co.uk/cointree.htm;
Below: Looking back into Wharfedale as I climbed
onto Craven Moor

FROM THE BLOG
A goodish half-way day

I've probably hinted before that today would be the halfway stage but, if I failed to mention it, it is. I'm not quite sure precisely when it occurs because I know that the route I've followed isn't exactly what I'd planned. And no doubt that will continue to be the case. But halfway has to be celebrated somewhere and Pateley Bridge is as good a place as any. So, as I type, I'm raising my glass of Black Sheep to the prospect of it all being downhill from now on.

I actually spent my rest day in Bradford which I'd never visited and which I enjoyed, though I didn't stray far from the city centre. There are some splendid buildings and the cathedral is well worth a visit. There was however, a sad lack of places where a hungry walker could eat in the evening and last night I ended up having a cold Morrison's quiche (perhaps that should be a Morrison's cold quiche) in the room of my hotel which was chosen for its cheapness and not for its elegance.

Unfortunately, when I took the decision to go to Bradford (mainly because I couldn't find a cheap B&B in Ilkley) I forgot that I would be trying to leave on a Sunday morning. It's hard to get out of Bradford on a Sunday! I had to leave the hotel very early, get a bus to Leeds and then another bus to Ilkley – the whole process took well over 2 hours. So a long day started rather late.

When I arrived, Ilkley looked elegant in passing sunshine and I set off up the Dales Way, following the River Wharfe. I can thoroughly recommend the walk – it's a beautiful valley and there's plenty to look at. I found a very small Quaker Meeting House at Farfield - built in 1689 and well-preserved, though no longer in use. Judging by the Visitors' Book it seems to attract a goodly number of people though not as many as Bolton Abbey, further upstream. The ruin is not as spectacular as other northern monasteries but the setting is very attractive and there are many opportunities for walks on the huge estate. There are also some stepping stones across the river that one small boy and his father were attempting as I passed - I think that they got across safely but with wet feet. One oddity was a felled tree; embedded in its bark were thousands of coins – all, as far as I could see were coppers and they looked as though they had been there for a long time. What was this about, I wonder?

Less good was the moorland crossing from Wharfedale to Nidderdale. The moors are very wet and bogs abound. Progress was slow and I got cross – then thoughts of the great mire into which the villain fell in The Hound of the Baskervilles came to mind and I got crosser. In the effort to avoid boots full of water I strayed off course and didn't end up very close to where I had intended – another navigational shortcoming! But the rain held off until 5 minutes before I got to the B&B.

I shall set off with renewed vigour tomorrow morning, knowing that the majority of the walk is behind me. In the meantime, bear with me if these posts sometimes appear in bits, with atrocious spelling/typing errors. Tonight's was being done in bits during a pub meal and while I was trying to hold a conversation. And I have to add the photos afterwards because I nearly always forget to download pictures from the camera before I start to write the blog. And you thought that I was efficient!!

DAY 41 · Pateley Bridge to Carlton

28 km (17 miles)
744 m of climb
53% completed

In my blog yesterday I forgot to mention the American lady who was staying at my Pateley Bridge B&B. I was projected into her company because she had been offered a lift to the pub and I was invited to ride in with her. I needed to write the blog so I took my netbook but I was looking forward to a pleasant bit of conversation; however, she brought a book with her which, for most of the time, she read!

I did discover that she was on her first visit to the UK and was spending time in Edinburgh, Stratford, Bath and London – I was never quite clear why she'd come to Pateley Bridge but perhaps she wanted to mix with some genuine northern agricultural folk. That may explain the book – I just didn't fit the bill. I think that she'd also done some walking that day and she seemed impressed with my efforts but am not sure that she knew where either Lands End or John O'Groats are. We left the pub just as the weekly bingo session started. You can't get more folksy than that.

A brace of mock castles. Left: Gouthwaite Reservoir dam near Pateley Bridge; Opposite: The shooting hut on Lofthouse Moor

FROM THE BLOG
Steelhouse Moor was my downfall

I have arrived in Carlton, have showered and sorted my gear and feel a good deal better than I did on Steelhouse Moor a few hours ago. But I need sustenance, so you'll have to wait for the story – possibly until tomorrow. But the walk continues!

I have now eaten, sorted out my gear and retired to my room in the excellent Foresters Arms at Carlton where I am the guest of Christian Aid supporter Jenny Walker. I'd like to be able to thank Jenny personally but it seems that she took a flight to Rome this morning so all I can do is to send her a note and to record my thanks in this blog.

I had a good start today from Pateley Bridge - walking up the Nidderdale Way which is not as smart as the Dales Way up Wharfedale but the valley is just as splendid. But I saw and spoke to nobody as I walked up the valley, noting the castellations on the Gouthwaite Reservoir dam. I turned off the path a mile or so north of Lofthouse and sweated up the steep side of the valley. There had been intermittent drizzle most of the way up so I had waterproofs on and got very hot underneath them.

At the top of the slope was a shooting hut which also had castellations on what may have been a chimney or an observation tower. The back part was unlocked so I went in, sat down and had my lunch before storming off across the moor on a well defined track. Apart from the drizzle, all was going well.

Now the authors of the Alternative Pennine Way, whose route I am following, were very clear about the next section across the moor: it was, they said 'rough going' with 'undefined' paths. You can say that again! First I had to locate a certain point on the path, then follow a compass bearing across a sea of grass and heather. It's a very tiring business with the constant extra hazard that a foot can easily go into a boggy patch and the boot fill with water – which mine soon did. It's also very featureless so maintaining a bearing is hard.

I was pleased when my first compass bearing got me to the right gate in the right fence – I was to go through this gate and then follow another bearing. I was just levering myself across a very boggy bit when my right calf muscle cramped violently and I was suddenly crippled. Legless on Steelhouse Moor comes to mind. It was, and still is, very painful and I hobbled for about 2 miles across the rest of the heather and grass using my sticks for balance and propulsion, and taking a very long time about it. I eventually reached the highest point of the crossing, located another stile and started the descent. Down proved easier than up and the muscle started to ease out a bit but I suffered again on the ascent into Carlton where I chose a bit of road rather than a convenient footpath.

I am going to hobble over to Hawes tomorrow (there's a nice title for the next post) – the hard bit is at the beginning, after which I can do a lot of road walking if I wish, giving the muscle a chance to ease out. I have come to the conclusion that my right leg is either accident prone or basically defective. I have been talking to it quite severely and am hoping that, once it gets over this current problem, it will behave.

Orange's waves don't reach Carlton so this blog, courtesy of BT Fon, is my only means of communication. Unfortunately, I failed to book some accommodation for the next 2 nights so will have to stop somewhere tomorrow where there's a signal and see what I can locate.

Roll on the next rest day, say I.

DAY 42   **Carlton to Hawes**

26 km (16 miles)
507 m of climb
54% completed

In a blog comment it was pointed out that there was a CCTV camera in Hawes connected to the internet and that I could walk up and down and be spotted, presumably to prove that I was really there. I didn't see this message before I

left Hawes but have to say that behaviour like that is why CCTV cameras are there and that I'm not risking arrest.

You'll see that I devoted quite a lot of the blog to stiles. Since writing it I've come across a splendid book by Michael Roberts, *Gates & Stiles*, which covers just about every variant you can think of and tells me that the gate in my photograph is called a lamb gate.

Left: On top of Carlton Moor;
Opposite Right: A classy footpath gate

FROM THE BLOG
Better leg; the Dutch and stile stories

I was not looking forward to this morning. First, I was leaving one of the most comfortable B&Bs that I'd stayed at and second, my leg as still very sore from the problems of yesterday. In the event, I've survived both and am now at Hawes.

The Foresters Arms at Carlton turned out to be a community-owned pub. The building had been a pub but it had gone up for sale some time ago and stopped functioning as a pub – a considerable loss in a remote dale where the nearest alternative was some 4 miles away. There had been an application to turn the building into cottages but this was turned down, at which point members of the community put up a scheme to set up a co-operative to buy the pub, refurbish it and re-open it.

On the evidence of my one evening there it seems a great success. The pub is well presented and seems well used. The food that I had was excellent and the room one of the best that I've had. I really was sorry to leave but I stumbled out of the door, turned left up the hill and hobbled to the top. I was not a good advertisement for long distance walking. But things improved; the first part of the walk was a fairly gentle climb up onto the moor followed a by a long descent into Wensleydale – a 4-mile workout that eased the damaged calf muscle which twinged less and less often and less and less painfully. Tomorrow will be another test but, once the stiffness has worn off, I think that all will be OK.

I did more road walking today than I'd intended – just to give the leg an easy time. For the most part I was using minor roads so wasn't traffic-dodging, but road walking is very boring and quite hard on the feet which suffer from the continual pounding on a hard surface. I stopped at a seat in West Burton, a small but perfectly formed village, to phone ahead for tonight's accommodation. Children from the primary school came out to play whist I was there – for a playground they used the sloping grassy area in front of the school that was also part of the village green. Despite the slope they seemed to manage a respectable game of football.

I feel a word or two about stiles coming on. I've crossed a lot in the last 5 weeks and they've varied hugely in quality, height, state of repair, ease of access and beauty.

A lot have been monuments to stonemasons of the past – dressed blocks of stone sticking out of a wall, to be climbed reverentially and with care. There are others that are little more than a gap in a wall with vertical slabs large enough for human legs to get through but too narrow for a sheep. Or one I encountered today that had a gate on it but where the mason had dressed the stones into curves lest the walker bruise his or her legs on rough stones.

Wooden stiles seldom show the same craftsmanship. On the moors it's common to find the two-ladder, up-and-over stile where you climb up one side, stand on a small platform and turn through 180 degrees and then climb down the other side. Not turning round commits you to climbing down with your back to the ladder – very hazardous! Other stiles are often no more than one or (preferably) two wooden platforms, arranged as a stair and sometimes either slippery or rocky or both. The best ones arrange the steps so that you can climb up, step over and climb down in a continuous movement with no feet shuffling.

All stiles suffer from the degraded approach – ground that has become worn away so that the step up or step down has become huge, or landing is into a sea of mud. There's not much pleasure in these. Staffordshire appears to have invested in the totally basic stile – just wooden bars like a gate that have to be climbed. Here the problem is balance – it's all too easy to fall off on one side or the other, especially when unbalanced by a rucksack. And while speaking of rucksacks, many kissing gates are not designed for someone with a large rucksack. There just isn't enough room to swing the gate over in front of one's belly. I could slim down, but that's not an immediate practical solution.

My room at Hawes looks down on the street from a great height. I witnessed the arrival of 3 vintage MGs with Dutch number plates and occupants wearing identical orange baseball caps. They decanted into the B&B with their luggage, leaving the cars somewhat strewn across the road. Eventually they moved these to a car park somewhere and I later saw them in the pub. Were these William's descendants planning a takeover? So soon after the Jubilee too!

Hawes to Kirkby Stephen

26 km (16 miles)
480 m of climb
55% completed

I saw more serious walkers in Hawes than anywhere else; tired and weary most of them and I think that most were on the Coast-to-Coast walk. This is a tough assignment, especially if you're walking from west to east and have just climbed into the Pennines having already crossed the mountains of the Lake District.

The mine/limekiln question remains unresolved but, thanks to Jan and Deri Parsons respectively, I have (on page 189) a lot more information about Lady Anne (whose Highway I used) and about the sculpture pictured opposite. This walk has been a magnificent education!

FROM THE BLOG

Lady Anne, railways, bluebells and muck

'Twas a good day today. The leg stiffness had eased further, the sun shone (now and again) and I took a route using Lady Anne's Highway.

Now I'm not sure who Lady Anne was and I've not been able to find out very much about her Highway. But, along the route there were a few small plaques fastened to posts showing a lady in a carriage being borne along. Tough on the horse since the Highway goes over the top of a fell that starts high above Mossdale at the Hawes end and ends, some 10 miles later, a few miles before Kirkby Stephen in the valley of the River Eden and, as it happens, in Cumbria, my nth county ($1 \leq n \leq 20$; I've lost count).

I liked what I saw of Hawes. It is surrounded by high fells and is clearly an important local centre high up in Wensleydale. A place to visit at more leisure, I think. But I headed up Mossdale, then climbed the steep slope up to Lady Anne's Highway. There was a splendid view down to the Settle and Carlisle Railway and the road over to Sedburgh and Kendal, with Whernside brooding in the distance. The last time I was in this area was in the 1970s on a visit to Whernside Manor which was then run as a national caving centre for scouts. This, of course, is Yorkshire limestone country with many of the UK's largest and deepest caves.

On the way up I came to a structure that I first thought was a mine entrance, then decided was a limekiln. But why here? Surely it would have been more economical to take the limestone down into the valley for burning using wood or, more probably, coal. Later I saw a similar structure and was fairly sure that it was a mine entrance – a matter for some more research I think.

Trains passed in the distance – goods trains working hard to climb from Kirkby Stephen. I've only travelled once on the Settle and Carlisle line, taking a train from near Penrith down to Skipton for the day. It's a line that

Above: The mine entrance that may be a limekiln

just escaped closure in the 1960s and is now something of a national treasure though it must have high maintenance costs. But it's encouraging to see it carrying so much traffic.

At the Kirkby Stephen end of the Highway is a sculpture that looks as though it has been there for some years, though there is no plate to identify the artist or the name of the work. It's very striking and I rather liked it, wondering whether it was making reference to Lady Anne or was a comment on the permeability of the limestone or perhaps just two people in conversation.

When doing O level Geography I heard of the Eden Valley and thought it very romantic. Up above Kirkby Stephen it is – a young river winding down a beautiful valley. Nearer Carlisle it looks pretty well like any other river. But up here bluebells were still in bloom – they have been since I left Lands End 6 weeks ago – and grass cutting and muck spreading are in progress. I had the pleasure of walking along a track into a farm behind a dripping muck spreader.

Not for the first time, the final stages of the day's walk did not do justice to the earlier part. I said before that I'm following the Alternative Pennine Way devised by Denis Brook and Phil Hinchliffe because I thought that it would give me a different view of the Pennines. And it has – Lady Anne's Highway is a good example. But it has also involved me in fiddling around with badly defined and roundabout footpaths that they seem to have chosen just to avoid road walking. Of course, I want to do as little road walking as possible but I also want to get to John O'Groats without walking any more miles than I have to and I don't want to waste time route-finding across farmland.

So I have been taking short cuts and will continue to do so.

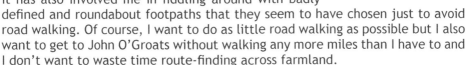

Top Left: Settle & Carlisle Railway train entering Moorcock Tunnel and Top Right: Dandrymire Viaduct; Middle: moorland sculpture; Bottom: Following the muck spreader

DAY 44   Kirkby Stephen to Appleby

25 km (15 miles)
465 m of climb
57% completed

I made a comment about the WI in this blog and was taken to task for criticising this venerable organisation. It wasn't meant as criticism but rather as an affectionate comment on the extraordinary range of activities that WI members are engaged in, though I should make clear that I base this view solely on my experience with the WI in our parish (where Viv is a committee member) and on the film *Calendar Girls*.

Having got that out of the way I can also point out that the best picture from this day appears over the page where I had a big space to fill and felt that a view of me clutching a Bounty Bar would give everyone a lot of pleasure. As I say in the blog, this picture was taken by the derelict farm where I was having sober thoughts about the fate of the family that had lived there. Hence my serious expression.

In the blog I mentioned Malham Cove and should have said that one of the most enjoyable experiences of my science teaching career was that for three years in the late 1960s a colleague and I conducted a maths and physics field course for sixth formers at Malham Tarn Field Studies Centre. We did interesting field experiments like towing boats across the Tarn and measuring the drag, measuring the variation of soil temperature with depth and over time and using resistivity measurements to detect underground cavities in the limestone. In all these cases we did some of the mathematics that goes with these problems and that students would not encounter in a normal A level course. We enjoyed our summer holiday weeks and it was a bit sad when we had to give them up as we moved on to other jobs.

Above: Regular goods trains carrying coal (apparently from Scotland) pounded up the hill through Crosby Garrett;
Right: Limestone pavement - a unique natural environment

Slowly cheering up

There are some days on this walk when I find it very hard to motivate myself. Could I just not stay here for another day? Do I have to get up now? Today was one of those days, and I didn't enjoy getting under way at all, choosing to stomp out of Kirkby Stephen along a minor road rather than taking to the fields as I should have done. But road walking is a debilitating business and I eventually gave up, crossed the Settle and Carlisle railway and started the field walking. I was cheered by the sight of a red squirrel in some woodland and by the grass underfoot – this is the dry strong grass of limestone country – none of your peaty, boggy stuff.

As I left the tarmac I encountered two ladies carrying a cage between them; one was also trying to control a wayward dog on a lead. I said 'Hello' as I passed and then looked in the cage where there was a teddy bear! Afterwards I realised that I should have asked whether it was fierce but I was so surprised that I missed my chance. I bet that it was a WI stunt – it's the sort of thing that WIs do.

The route took me down into a deep valley where there was a ruined farm amongst the trees, alongside a stream. A beautiful spot, very remote, and I sat on the footbridge eating a Bounty Bar and enjoying intermittent sunshine. The farm had clearly been abandoned for many years – the house was very derelict – and I wondered what had caused the family to leave. Had the economics of the farm not worked out? Had the family become disenchanted with farming or were none of the children willing to take on the farm? Had there been a falling out or had the isolation become too much of a burden? I am sceptical that places ever have an aura derived from past events but, having reflected on these questions, I began to see the place in a rather sad light, and was quite glad to leave.

A little later I was cheered by finding some limestone pavement to walk over. This is a surface feature of limestone (or karst) areas around the world – the best known in these islands is above Malham Cove in Yorkshire and on the Burren in Co. Clare in Ireland. The vertical cracks in the rock are opened up by the slow erosion from slightly acid rainwater, creating a pavement effect with deep cracks between the slabs of rock. The ecosystem of these cracks is special – the environment is very sheltered, the soils are alkaline and rarely dry out. The whole can be very mysterious and has a feeling of cragginess and remoteness.

I worked my way across to Great Asby – a pretty village where there was a bus shelter convenient for lunch. I never discovered whether there were any buses but the shelter was used as a distribution point for newspapers (villagers came to collect theirs from a bundle dropped off in the morning) and had a panel that described, in text and pictures, the inhabitants of the houses in the village in 1911. What a nice idea – you could step out of the shelter, look around, and identify who lived where, what they did for a living, what relations they had and so on. Good quality, unpretentious, living history.

Now I'm in Appelby, ready for a hard day tomorrow when I have to walk over the high fells, behind Cross Fell (the highest point in the Pennines) to Nenthead. I'm not looking forward to it – I need an early start and I'm hoping that I don't have to cope with bad weather.

From Day 44: You're never alone with a Bounty Bar

Beached in Appleby

I enjoyed the hospitality of Rev Roger Collinson in Appleby – he is an interesting person with whom I found I have a lot in common and I much enjoyed our after-dinner conversation about politics and education. An altogether refreshing experience, for which I'm very grateful.

I was on my way by 7am, walking to Dufton and expecting to cross the fells to Nenthead. But it was a wild morning with huge gusts of wind and by the time I reached Dufton I had decided that going onto Cross Fell (just about the windiest place on the Pennines) would be silly. So I abandoned the day, phoned my apologies to my intended hosts for that evening and got a bus back to Appleby.

These decisions can bite you in the bum. The wind dropped and the sun shone (just a little) in Appleby and I felt a bit of a wally. But the forecast is bad and I do tell myself that there's no point in taking unnecessary risks. So I will shortly spend the rest of the day sampling the delights of Appleby and will try Cross Fell again tomorrow.

I was interested to know that the brother of a friend of a friend was doing a long walk in the USA at the same time as I was striding across the UK. In a comment where he applauded my caution over Cross Fell, Deri Parsons said

"I think I've told you that I'm also following the blog of someone 'doing' the Appalachian Trail. Here's an extract from his posting of yesterday:

'Then it was on to The Climb of Death. I had an inkling things might be going south when we encountered a copperhead sunning himself on the trail. He wouldn't move out of the way even after we tossed sand and rocks his way. Eventually he slithered off the trail when I nudged him with a hiking pole. Not long after that we found ourselves climbing ever steeper rock formations. The only evidence there was a trail was the blazes. We negotiated six inch ledges using cracks in the wall for handholds. I was both afraid and angry that we had to make such an unsafe traverse'."

Cross Fell doesn't come into that sort of territory but, as the highest point in the Pennines and the highest point in England outside of the Lake District, it deserves respect. The summit, at 893 metres (2,930 ft), is part of a 12.5 km (7.8 mile) long ridge which also incorporates Little Dun Fell and Great Dun Fell. The three adjoining fells form an escarpment that rises steeply above the Eden Valley on its south western side and drops off more gently on its north eastern side towards the South Tyne and Tees Valleys.

The fell is prone to dense hill fog and fierce winds and can be an inhospitable place for much of the year. A shrieking noise induced by the Helm Wind is a characteristic of the locality which, in ancient times, was known as "Fiends Fell".

Not a great place to be in bad weather, I think.

DAY 46   **Dufton to Nenthead**

29 km (18 miles)
911 m of climb
59% completed

If you wanted an experience of the raw wildness of the north Pennines this would be a walk to choose, especially if it were a day following heavy rain, putting the streams and rivers into spate. It's demanding but not very risky walking but you would always be a long way from help if things went wrong. A tough place to live and work.

Left: Sculpture from 2002 by local artist Gilbert Ward identifying and celebrating the generally recognised start of the South Tyne River; Below: The trail down Trout Beck above where it joins the River Tees; the path can be seen to the left of the stream, though it has been eroded away in many places.

Damp but rewarding

Having aborted yesterday's attempt to climb out of the Eden Valley, I was determined that I'd not be thwarted a second time. A speedy breakfast and a prompt taxi allowed me to start walking at 7.45am from the bus shelter from which I'd slunk back to Appleby in the big Friday wind. I needed the full waterproofs today since it clearly wasn't going to be dry and, sure enough, the rain began within a few minutes and stayed with me for the next 9 hours.

Now you might assume that I was going to write a miserable piece, saying that this was a hard day, complaining at the rain and cursing the North Pennines for being so squelchy. Well, it was hard, though not as hard as I'd feared. And the rain was depressing – it's hard to be positive about rain unless you're viewing it from somewhere dry – but strangely friendly. And the squelchiness quickly resulted in a wet left foot and then a wet right foot as my boots once again failed to deliver the most basic of requirements – dry feet. But I did get more or less used to it.

So the whole day was curiously uplifting. I did the walk with absolutely no navigational errors. I kept walking continuously for the whole 18 miles, lying down only once when I slipped into a badly placed bog (that will give my daughter some pleasure – she only sank in up to her waist). And I climbed out of the Eden valley into the Tees valley, then over into the South Tyne valley and finally close to the head of the Wear valley. Well, all this water had to go somewhere and, in this small area, it would be possible to pee 4 times, feeding each of these 4 rivers once. Don't you find that an uplifting idea?

Of course I was tired at the end of it and my right leg is still rather sore. There was a lot of climbing – one lot on a cycle route in the company of a group of cyclists, mixed by ability and gender, who were slower than I was. And 18 miles of wet moorland was a bit depressing. But the experience reassured me that I wasn't yet past it – something that had begun to haunt me a little. I will stride into tomorrow with renewed confidence (which will probably be shattered by some horrid experience).

Highlights? The sight and noise of the Tees rushing down the fellside, already a mighty river of water, orange-brown from the peat with cream wavelets breaking over the rocks. Another moorland sculpture, this time celebrating the birth of the South Tyne River that flows to Hexham where it joins the North Tyne to become one of the great industrial waterways of Britain. Then, close to the end of the walk, getting caught up in huge hushes at a defunct Weardale lead mine and having to climb out to regain my path. No, I wasn't lost, just slightly diverted.

I was given a very warm welcome by Jo and Tony Pennell, their friends, dog and 4 cats at their farm near Nenthead. If you have an image of a Aga-heated farm kitchen where everything happens (a tractor dashboard was being rewired as dinner was being cooked as my wet clothes were being hung to dry as several conversations were being carried on at once) then you clearly know the Pennells.

And tomorrow is a short walk to Allendale Town and a rest day. Phew!!

Nenthead was, perhaps, the greyest place I visited. It is just on the western side of the summit which is at the head of Weardale and just over the summit is the Kilhope Mining Centre which I last visited a couple of years ago to discover that it is now a great deal more interesting than at my previous visit some 20 years earlier.

Lead mining was the major industry of this area and has left enormous scars on the landscape that include the hushes where artificial lakes were constructed and then the water released in a deluge that washed the surface soil away to reveal the lead deposits beneath. It was one such hush that I floundered through on my way into Nenthead the day before.

Go to Kilhope if you're ever close to Weardale; look at the bleak landscape and imagine the hard labour involved in extracting lead and the poverty of those who did the work.

Right: coming over the horizon with Robert Theobald
Above: Viv and I at Allendale Town.
Photographs by Lesley Theobald

It's sunnier in Allendale

It was a short day with a slow start. Breakfast at the Pennels was an opportunity for more conversation, cups of tea and coffee and the warmth of the kitchen Aga as the drizzle started outside. I was slow to get away and when I left it was in full waterproof regalia, expecting a repeat of the previous day. I walked into Nenthead and attempted to call ahead to say when I'd be arriving at Allendale but there was no signal. However, a BT phone box offered a traditional solution.

It said 'Coins' on the outside but the coin slot had been closed and there was a panel with extremely small print that said, in effect, that I was to swipe my credit card. But there was no credit card swipe slot so I read on. If there is no slot, it said, call this number. I did and was asked whether I wanted to make a national or international call. I then had to enter my credit card details and then the number I wanted to call. I was evidently too slow because a voice interrupted to tell me to wait for an operator. This was a man with a strong American accent – what had I got into? I was asked to repeat some of the credit card information and then give the number I wanted. It rang and I was connected. How this call was routed I have no idea; how much it will cost I will only find out much later. Not a good advert for BT – a pigeon would have been quicker had I had one handy.

I was careless in my estimate of how long it would take me to get to Allendale Town where I was to be met by Viv and friends. I suddenly realised that I had 10 miles to do in 3 hours – OK on flat streets with no rucksack but a tall order under these conditions. I belted along getting hot and wetter under my waterproofs than from outside. But gradually the day rewarded me – first with the end of the rain and then with tentative sun and then with sun that was so persistent that I could confidently remove the waterproofs and start to dry out.

Did I get to Allendale Town on time? To the minute, and the photograph to the left was taken one minute after my arrival in the rather pretty square. A triumph.

Oh, I forgot to say – shortly after leaving Nenthead I crossed into Northumberland. That means that I've connected the two most distant counties in England. Another triumph.

Suspension footbridge
across the River Allen

Allendale Town to Melrose

Date	Day	No	From	To	
19-June-2012	Tue	49	Allendale Town	Haltwhistle	GPX files for each day's walk can be downloaded from the internet and plotted using mapping software such as OS Getamap or Google maps. The download addresses are in the form http://www.wilmut.net/ lejogbook/day49.gpx
20-June-2012	Wed	50	Haltwhistle	The Eals	
21-June-2012	Thu	51	The Eals	Byrness	
22-June-2012	Fri	52	Byrness	Jedburgh	
23-June-2012	Sat	53	Jedburgh	Melrose	

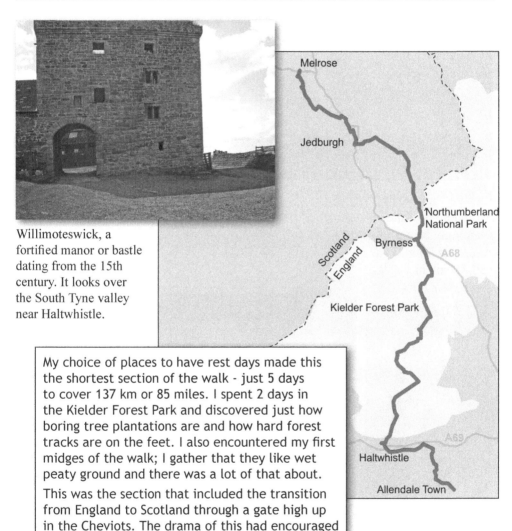

Willimoteswick, a fortified manor or bastle dating from the 15th century. It looks over the South Tyne valley near Haltwhistle.

My choice of places to have rest days made this the shortest section of the walk - just 5 days to cover 137 km or 85 miles. I spent 2 days in the Kielder Forest Park and discovered just how boring tree plantations are and how hard forest tracks are on the feet. I also encountered my first midges of the walk; I gather that they like wet peaty ground and there was a lot of that about.

This was the section that included the transition from England to Scotland through a gate high up in the Cheviots. The drama of this had encouraged me to think of Scotland as a foreign country and it took me some time to shake this off. I didn't feel quite the same about Devon but I had earlier seen Wales in the distance and it did look quite foreign. Could I be be a closet Cornish Nationalist?

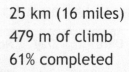
Allendale Town to Haltwhistle

25 km (16 miles)
479 m of climb
61% completed

Clockwise from top left: The South Tyne River near Beltingham; Ridley Hall (18th century house); The Allen River; Staward Peel (an early 14th century fortress built to guard England from the Scots but that later became a place of pilgrimage destroyed at the Dissolution).

The Staward Peel photograph © Copyright Peter McDermott and licensed for reuse under the Geograph Creative Commons Licence

I include here some photographs of the stunningly beautiful Allen and South Tyne valleys and my walk down them.

New boots, sun and water

First the boots. We did a visit to Cotswold Outdoor in Newcastle yesterday with a spectacularly successful outcome. They accepted that the old boots (sold to me at their Plymouth store) were defective, measured my feet very carefully and then offered me a selection of new possibilities. I eventually settled on a pair of Salomon boots – not a brand that I'd previously heard of - and they are great! Comfortable and, so far, absolutely waterproof. The assistants in Cotswold were very helpful indeed and the whole experience was much more positive than I'd expected. What a relief!

And in all other respects the rest day was a great success. It was very good to see Lesley and Robert Theobald and their new house (which they are building themselves). It's got to the point where it's looking very impressive – very suitable for camping out in for 2 nights. Viv had come up from Cornwall and we all went over to have lunch with the Theobald grandchildren – four girls who are a demanding delight. Altogether it was a great way to spend a rest day – no walking, just talk about walking, houses, other friends and plans for the future.

Back to reality this morning. There was fitful sunshine as I left Allendale Town but, apart from a few spots of rain, the day gradually improved and I am now bathed in full sunshine. My route was down the East Allen River which sparkled down through the deep wooded Staward Gorge, under a miniature suspension bridge, past the medieval fortification (against the Scots, of course) at Staward Peel to the more genteel landscape around Ridley Hall (an 18th century house that's now used as a school and conference centre). I then deserted the Alternative Pennine Way to do a walk up the South Tyne valley to Haltwhistle. This is gorgeous countryside and I'm looking forward to tomorrow's walk north into Kielder Forest.

I am delighted that the donations total has now topped £5000. We are trying to make sure that everyone is thanked for their support but, if we've missed you, do please accept our deep appreciation for your help. The ultimate target is £10,000. I am still optimistic that we can make this but I know that we need to continue to publicise the cause that I'm walking for. I'm already making plans for the follow-up to the walk but for now, if you know anyone who may be interested in the walk or in the cause for which I'm walking, please do let them know about the website and about this blog.

Above: Willimoteswick (a 15th century fortified manor or bastle) 127

DAY 50   **Haltwhistle to The Eals**

34 km (21 miles)
551 m of climb
63% completed

The Eals is midway between Bellingham and Kielder Lake.

Top Left: Whin Sill from the north; Opposite: Hadrian's Wall and Fort at Cawfield; Top Right: Alternative Pennine Way sign; Below Left: Wark Forest path and trees..trees..trees; Below Right: Fallen trees; Bottom: Anxious sheep (reminding me of Steve Bell's George Bush cartoon ears)

FROM THE BLOG
Kielder summer

The sun shone this morning and for much of the day as I climbed through the Wark Forest part of the Kielder Forest Park, as they call it. An awful lot of trees! I managed an early start and climbed first to Hadrian's Wall which sparkled today, waiting for its dose of sightseers. Its position atop the Whin Sill is spectacular when you walk through to the northern side and it's easier to appreciate the Ro-

man achievement in creating, maintaining and defending this barrier against the Scots. Northumberland weather must have been a sad experience for your average Roman soldier.

And so to the forest. I was following well-defined tracks along a route described in the Alternative Pennine Way and was very pleased to see a couple of route mark-

ers with an APW label. Fame for a now out-of-print book! I dutifully took to a bridle way shown as part of the route only to find it blocked by fallen trees. A notice, dated 2007, said that a temporary short by-pass route had been created to get round this problem. I eventually found it and it led off through the trees.

I don't know any walker who likes conifer forests. Stray from your track and you can be lost in no time, Every tree looks like every other tree and the gloom begins to conjure up the demons. The detour ended with no further route markers and a vast area of fallen trees. My only choice was to back-track and work out an alternative route. This cost me an additional 3 miles, a lost hour and some loss to my normal sunny nature.

So I arrived at my B&B later than on any other day of this walk so far. It didn't matter too much but I have a very elegant and comfortable room that I would have enjoyed just sitting in rather than immediately dashing out to the pub for a meal where I'm dashing off this post while I have WiFi, after which I'll dash back to the B&B and dash off to bed. Dashed nuisance, really.

Tomorrow is midsummer. I'm told that it will rain. Typical.

DAY 51 The Eals to Byrness

25 km (15 miles)
567 m of climb
65% completed

Above Left: Suspension footbridge
over the North Tyne River;
Above Right: Holiday teepee;
Right: Church near Greenhaigh;
Opposite: Limekilns at Belling
Rigg

FROM THE BLOG

Longest day; shortish walk; much rain

It bothers me that these posts are getting a bit pedestrian (pardon the pun). If I'm not careful every post is a short resumé of the walk (start, middle and end), a comment on the weather, a mention of some oddity (or oddities, if you're lucky) and a finish with an apt phrase or quip, perhaps linking to tomorrow's walk. Where's the originality, the zing that would make for a memorable blog?

Perhaps I should describe my day backwards.

I'm typing this sitting in what used to be the YHA hostel at Byrness. I'm in front of a wood fire that's lit in homage to the bleak midsummer downpour outside from which I'm a refugee. This place is now run as an independent hostel and B&B and very smart it is too; I've just spent an entertaining hour drinking tea in the company of some 7 or 8 gentlemen of various ages and many interests. Dinner has been ordered and will be ready in an hour or perhaps an hour and a half or perhaps ... Our hosts are, however, very helpful, so that I have an early breakfast booked, my waterproofs are drying and everyone is relaxing in comfort.

Byrness, you should know, is extremely small, sitting alongside the main road that crosses the border at Carter Bar. Scotland is only about 3 miles away and this has the feeling of a frontier place – a place of tension where people are in transit. Which is silly really – it's only Scotland over there, though perhaps centuries of conflict have left their mark on places like Byrness. A lot of rain may also have had some impact – it is a very clean place.

I wandered into Byrness along the Pennine Way which I'd chosen to follow today because last night's B&B was actually well to the east of Falstone, making my planned route quite inconvenient. I walked round the small group of houses and spotted two B&Bs, then realised I didn't know which one I'd booked. I was rescued by a Lech Walesa lookalike who said he thought that I was booked with him, checked and then gave me a royal welcome.

It was more forest today – another million trees passed but not saluted. Every one will eventually be turned into pulp, wood chips, pit props (if there are any pits left), kitchen worktops, newsprint or something else; in the meantime they grace the hillsides here in rather geometric sections of forest, separated by the graveyards of their predecessors. Kielder Forest is astonishingly big and walking through it is a sobering though rather tedious experience. Periodically Forestry Commission vehicles pass by checking, I assume, on some aspect of forest health and well-being.

And I passed a set of disused limekilns. I'm afraid that, despite the assertion of my esteemed friend John Moore, I am now convinced that the structures that I saw above Hawes were mine entrances and not limekilns, but I am perfectly sure that these structures were kilns, though why built here I have no idea.

This morning I was leaving what is the largest parish in England. (I did forget to say yesterday that Haltwhistle bills itself as the Centre of Britain – on what basis I'm not sure; I am honoured to have been in these two notable places). The Eals has a private suspension bridge across the North Tyne River which bounced quite violently as I crossed (and I remember the spectacular film of the Tahoma Narrows Bridge collapse that we always showed classes when doing waves in school physics – children were gobsmacked by such things in those days, perhaps no longer). The parish seems to have a lot of churches – including one close to my B&B and another, identical in design, passed as I climbed towards the forest this morning. For the Jubilee, the parish had produced a book, showing pictures of all the dwellings in the parish (much of which is covered in trees), accompanied in most cases by brief notes written by the current occupants. Copies had been distributed free to all households and the book is a high quality production of which people can be proud. What a nice idea.

Which brings me back to first thing this morning and my excellent and comfortable B&B near Falstone. I could easily have stayed for several days, enjoying Northumbrian hospitality. Is it any different from hospitality elsewhere? Probably not, though it is made more explicit and it is very easy to feel comfortable here though the accent sometimes defeats me.

That's England done, then. Just Scotland to go. And 4 weeks in which to do it. I'd better go to bed asap.

DAY 52   **Byrness to Jedburgh**

Scots Wae Hae (mentioned in the blog) is the party song of the SNP and is sung each year at the party conference. The lyrics were written by Robert Burns in 1793, in the form of a speech given by Robert the Bruce before the Battle of Bannockburn in 1314, where Scotland defeated the English army. I remember singing this at a concert a very long time ago; the lyrics are suitably bloodthirsty and the tune horrid.

Above: Catcleugh Reservoir seen from the hills above Byrness; Right: Approaching the gate into Scotland; Below: My first steps in Scotland - an occasion for celebration

Hallucinating in Scotland

Byrness at 6.30am is a doleful place. The occasional vehicle swishes through on the A69, heading either north or south as fast as it can. I stomped along the road looking for the Pennine Way; when I found the sign it pointed straight up the hillside through deep undergrowth on the edge of the forest. Clearly I would get very wet without waterproofs, so I stopped to put them on. Within 30 seconds the midges, all clearly refugees from over the border (they were singing *Scots Wae Hae*), homed in on me. This was not going to be an easy day.

Eventually I climbed out of the forest, wet, cross and midged, and set off across the Cheviots towards Scotland. On a sunny day this would be a lovely walk with 360 degree views of rolling hills and wooded valleys and an easy-to-follow route. The hills are criss-crossed with fences but I was aiming for that special fence that separates the Scots and the English. The crossing came at a smart new gate alongside an MoD sign that warned walkers to stick to the path or risk being killed by unexploded devices, with a graphic for those who needed to be shown what being blown up meant. I did make a sort of celebratory gesture as I stood by the gate, though this would have been more exciting if it hadn't been raining.

I had seen no-one on the way up to the border. I only saw a farmer on a quad bike as I descended into a long valley with hillsides that looked as though they were part of some model landscape. They owe their barren look to sheep, of course, and I have seen thousands and thousands of these as I've journeyed through the Pennines though I was told that shooting syndicates are buying up the land, removing the sheep and reserving the space for their own seasonal activities. I suppose that this will result in a return in some places to a more natural landscape with more trees (though fewer birds) and perhaps a bit more employment.

Then I joined Dere Street. Now this is a Roman road that connects various forts that the Roman army had in this area north of Hadrian's wall. I suppose that they pre-date the wall. Dere Street crosses the Cheviots and a good deal of it is walkable. At least in theory. A combination of damage by 4x4s and animals has made sections of it a mudbath. Perhaps it was a mudbath for the Romans as well, but I suspect that they at least paved their road with boulders so that their soldiers were not inelegantly dodging from tussock to tussock as I was.

Tracks like this do odd things to the imagination. I could have sworn that I heard a clanking of armour and a Latin oath; then I lost my footing and sprawled in the mud, fortunately still in my waterproofs. Quite thankfully, I left Dere Street a little later and walked into Jedburgh which is solidly Scots and sounds it. Odd that there seems to be little merging of Northumberland and Scots accents - the transition from one to the other is sudden. It's a good and comfortable B&B though and a rather nice small town, also lying on the A69.

Tomorrow to Melrose and a rest day.

Jedburgh to Melrose

23 km (14 miles)
502 m of climb
68% completed

FROM THE BLOG
Melrose mud and music

From one small border town to another – this was a day across a rolling and very breezy agricultural landscape. Good to look at and fairly easy walking. As I write it's early evening in Melrose where pipers have just started playing and a man in full highland dress has emerged from a house opposite, played a few notes in response to another piper in the distance and then disappeared again. Perhaps they are piping in Saturday evening or piping out the week. Or maybe it's a rehearsal for something else or a display for the tourists - *Scotland the Brave* is now being played. I did note that I wasn't piped across the border yesterday (a couple of sheep looked as though they might oblige, but ate wet grass instead) so perhaps this is just a delayed welcome. Bagpipes must get soggy in the rain.

In fact, I was sort of welcomed into Melrose. There was a race in progress when I got here and runners, whom I'd seen earlier on the Eildon Hills, were being applauded as they came back into the town. There was a small group in the Market Place serenading an appreciative audience that included me when I arrived. I like to think that they'd heard that I was coming but maybe they always do this sort of thing on a Saturday afternoon.

I left Jedburgh along minor roads that had plenty of interest including private pothole signs and a very elderly Citroën van of the sort that's not often seen in France now, let alone in the UK. This was my very last day with the Alternative Pennine Way which finished in Jedburgh but to which the authors added an addendum that

linked their route to the Southern Upland Way at Melrose. I didn't follow it faithfully today but did use the second part to get into Melrose. I appreciate that the book was published 15-20 years ago and that paths have changed. I also know that the representation on a map of a footpath in Scotland doesn't mean the same as in England, but my experience today was ridiculous.

The routes that I was using are shown on the OS map and were signposted. They evidently hadn't been used for ages (don't the Scots walk anywhere?) and were waist deep in grass, bracken, stinging nettles, brambles and the like. Walking through this, you can't see where you're putting your feet (which is a recipe for a twisted ankle) and it's very, very hard work. I probably had 2 miles of this and was very tired at the end.

OK, so these are little-used paths and I shouldn't be surprised. But what really got to me was that one path ended up on someone's back lawn. If I'd had the courage I'd have marched down the lawn and out of the front onto the road but they probably had bad tempers, a rottweiler, a claymore, or all three. So I sort of hopped over a fence into an adjoining field, in an attempt to sneak onto the road that way. Bad mistake. The field had a well-developed crop in it and the edges were head-high with wet grass. I headed to what I though was a gate but found that it was just a bit of fence. I straddled this and then had to climb down a bank onto a main road. I looked a mess when I stood on the road, knowing full well that I'd have the same problem later in the day with a path through a mile long strip of woodland. This was labelled Charlesfield Road!

After that things perked up a bit. I joined the St Cuthbert's Way which goes from Melrose to Lindisfarne in commemoration of St Cuthbert whose ministry began in Melrose in 650AD and ended at Holy Island. He had kindly arranged that the bit of his path that I was walking had been carefully signposted, with grass mowed to a bowling green finish and boardwalks over the messy bits. He hadn't quite managed to control the mud on the Eildon Hills which I crossed before descending to Melrose. There will come a time, I hope, when I don't arrive at a B&B with muddy boots.

The Eildon Hills are 3 peaks that dominate Melrose and the surrounding area. They are the remains of a complex volcanic system and are made of hard igneous rock that has weathered much less than the surrounding sandstones and greywackes. Most of the molten lava never reached the surface and cooled underground to form sills. Later eruptions threw ash and blocks of rock high into the air that can still be seen in layers on the hill sides.

Don't ever say that this blog is not an education in itself.

A rest day tomorrow so I'll not do a post unless something terribly exciting happens. Then I have 4 days walking across to the Forth Road Bridge west of Edinburgh followed by 2 days up to Perth. Then I really will be on the final stages!

Left: Melrose Abbey

Elegant and informative -
the ideal footpath signpost

Melrose to Perth

Date	Day	No	From	To	
25-June-2012	Mon	55	Melrose	Traquair	GPX files for each day's walk can be downloaded from the internet and plotted using mapping software such as OS Getamap or Google maps. The download addresses are in the form http://www.wilmut.net/lejogbook/day55.gpx
26-June-2012	Tue	56	Traquair	West Linton	
27-June-2012	Wed	57	West Linton	East Calder	
28-June-2012	Thu	58	East Calder	Dunfermline	
29-June-2012	Fri	59	Dunfermline	Kinross	
30-June-2012	Sat	60	Kinross	Perth	

Here was another part of Britain that I hardly knew at all. The Southern Uplands turned out to be hard going (as everyone said they would be) but extremely rewarding (except when I got lost). I avoided Edinburgh and the sad story of its chaotic tramway construction project (which was a very hot topic of conversation for many people that I met) and trundled through business parks and industrial estates, past the airport and onto the Forth road bridge in pouring rain. Then a quick climb up to Dunfermline and out into the country again; surely this was as painless a crossing of Scotland's central belt as could be managed.

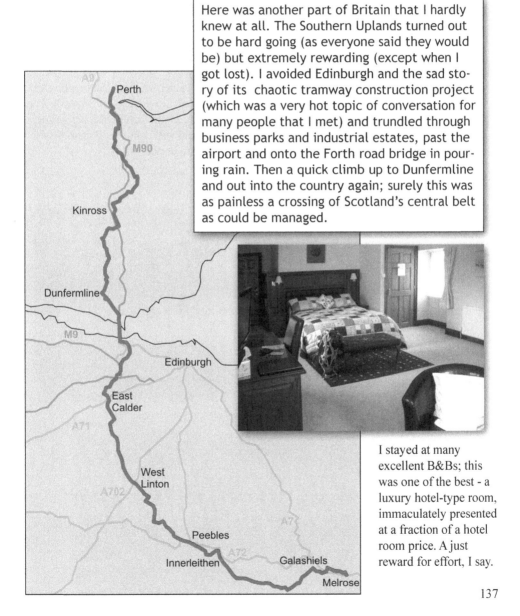

I stayed at many excellent B&Bs; this was one of the best - a luxury hotel-type room, immaculately presented at a fraction of a hotel room price. A just reward for effort, I say.

137

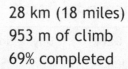

28 km (18 miles)
953 m of climb
69% completed

A fabulous day's walk along the Southern Upland Way

Opposite: The Eildon Hills with Melrose to the left; Left: The Three Brethren - a trio of massive cairns dating back to the 16th century; Below: River Tweed; Below Left: The Cheese Well, an ancient spring, now with an offering of coins; Bottom: *Point of Resolution* - a sculpture: the heather has been cut to stimulate new growth and as you walk from the Point the circles change shape and will continue to change with the seasons.

This was a splendid day

I don't know exactly what makes a good day's walk but today had all the ingredients. I got a reasonably early start; it was cool but quite sunny; I made no navigational errors; the views were splendid; I was alone on the hills; I arrived at my destination at the right time without hurrying ... and there are probably some other ingredients.

This was all on the back of a very relaxing rest day yesterday. Sunday is not good for a rest day if I want to shop but excellent if I just want to chill out and forget that I still have 300+ miles to do. I went to Melrose Abbey which stands at one end of St Cuthbert's Way which I mentioned yesterday. It's an interesting ruin to see though not the most exciting I've been to. But the setting, under the Eildon Hills and alongside the River Tweed, is splendid.

Which set me up well for today. Leaving Melrose I was walking up the Tweed valley – the river was rushing through, the result of heavy rainfall a couple of days ago. Then over Gala Hill and down to Yair Bridge. On the way down I encountered a flock of sheep being driven towards me by a farmer on a quad bike with the help of his dog – the only person I spoke to all morning. Across the Tweed at Yair loomed a hill covered with conifers and it was clear that I would have to climb through these. It was a steep 2 mile slog but the view from the top was stunning – a 360 degree panorama of hills stretching down into England and up towards the Scottish lowlands.

I was on the Southern Upland Way and it was easily the best-waymarked path of all those that I have so far used. I was helped by route descriptions taken from Robinson's book on the End-to-End walk which were precise and accurate and did not land me in bogs, long grass or nettles.

I met what I can only think was a class for schoolchildren on this high stretch of moorland – about 15 ten or eleven year olds with 3 adults - I assume teachers. They must have climbed the steep slopes to the ridge and I hope that they were enjoying the rewards of this high place as much as I was.

I discovered that this section of the Southern Upland Way is also known as the Minchmoor Road and is an ancient drove road that once provided the principal link across the Southern Uplands from west to east. Wallace and Edward II drove their armies across this path and Mary Queen of Scots travelled it. I came to a spring known as the Cheese Well which I suppose was there 800 years ago and where modern people had left coins on a slab of rock.

I'm now in Innerleithen enjoying the hospitality of Betty and Bob Scott, one more of the arrangements made by Christian Aid which have given me so much pleasure. Tomorrow I set off for West Linton and the last third of my walk.

Traquair to West Linton

34 km (21 miles)
820 m of climb
71% completed

It is a measure of the frustration with this day's walk that I took only one photograph and that was in the morning when I still felt moderately enthusiastic, walking up the Tweed valley from Traquair to Peebles. You can see that the sky

was blue and, though I was later than I should have been for a 21 mile day, things (like Peebles as viewed from the river) looked good.

The blog explains where it all went wrong and I don't think that it was anyone's fault. However, go wrong it did and I walked further than I intended and was later arriving in West Linton than I intended. It does illustrate the fickleness of this type of activity when, for no good reason, things don't go to plan. But I must put it in perspective: in the context of disasters that can befall people, this was very low down on the scale and it had no lasting impact. And the sunshine of Peebles and the kindness and generosity of people in West Linton more than offset the earlier problems. I can now look back on it and smile but I was gritting my teeth and worrying at the time!

To add to the blog: the West Linton area looked very damp and slightly knocked about. The road in had been hit by a big flood a few days before and great chunks of tarmac had been detached; the road sign simply said 'Road Closed' but cars were ignoring this since there was no sensible alternative route. As I walked in, a few people were trying to be jolly around a damp barbecue but I was surprised and pleased to find how well supplied with shops and services the (admittedly large) village was.

FROM THE BLOG

Poor day, long day, too late to blog

It started late, it was a long way, I made a mistake in my navigation, I arrived late, I am too tired to blog. Good night. Blog tomorrow.

Two for the price of one: Part 1 (written on Day 57)

I knew when I started this walk that there would be up days and down days and that the success of the walk would probably have more to do with what was happening in my head than what was happening in my feet (though, if my feet are reading this, don't take offence, lads – you still have to keep going across the rest of Scotland).

So I've already said that the Day 55 walk (Melrose to Traquair/Innerleithen) was a good day. You'll have gathered from my brief posting last night that yesterday (Day 56) was not a good day and I now have to report that today (Day 57) was excellent. In all cases it wasn't the state of the weather or the sate of my feet that made the day good or bad – it was my attitude.

This was conditioned, in part, by the news from home that our car was said to need a £1500 repair. I won't bore you with the details but Viv and I feel very strongly that we've been misled by the garage that we use; overnight I had been composing in my head very cutting and deeply effective letters that should be sent to this dealer, the manufacturer and anyone else who might listen. This doesn't put one in the frame of mind for walking.

Yesterday was always going to be a long day and I should have been more careful to get started early. It's not that early miles are better than late miles but that early miles *feel* better. Don't ask me why, though it probably has something to do with my lifelong obsession with not being late for things. So, though Bob Scott very kindly gave me a lift back to Traquair, the resulting 9 am start was, I think, my latest on this walk and it raised the anxiety level.

But all went well at the start; I did a road walk to Peebles to save time and then took to the footpaths, following Robinson's excellent directions. It fell apart when I encountered what was clearly a large new farm building that straddled the route that Robinson plotted some 5 or 6 years ago. Try as I could, I failed to work out the onward route which was through conifer forestry. After floundering through boggy long grass I eventually followed the edge of the forest onto open moor but was then much too far south. There followed a very trying and tiring trek over boggy heather and grass hillsides across two deep valleys before I regained the route.

Time had slipped away. It was clear that I would be a couple of hours late at my B&B. I was also due to make contact in West Linton with a friend of a friend of Viv's. When I eventually got off the moor and onto a road I sat in a bus shelter and tried to make some phone calls. I'm not very adept at using a mobile phone and I have a new one (a replacement bought in Newcastle) that I barely understand. I arrived in West Linton weary of foot and unhappy.

Then things turned round. I managed to make contact with the friend of a friend and he arranged for a friend of his to meet me at the pub where I was to have a meal. Wonderful! Then the lady who ran my B&B insisted on giving me a lift to the pub because it was pouring with rain. More wonderful! I had an enjoyable evening with the friend who, to my surprise, bought me dinner. Fantastic! I then slept very well.

West Linton to East Calder

21 km (13 miles)
329 m of climb
72% completed

I feel the need to convey what a wet day on the Scottish moors (or the Pennines or the Highlands) looks like. This is my best picture of a wet day and the only picture from Day 57 - the mist was down and the wet was up and the path, such as it was, looked like a small stream. This was the result of a season of substantial rain and is why I needed good boots!

In fact, as I say in the blog, this wasn't a bad day and I did enjoy myself. The drizzle was light and it was warm and I decided to abandon the waterproofs and put up with being damp. It is possible to get to the state where one isn't really getting any wetter from the rain than would happen under the waterproofs because of perspiration - it's just necessary to tolerate a bit of discomfort. It's surprisingly liberating though I did not go so far as to wear shorts. Attempts had been made to place wooden walkways across the worst of the bogs on this path so that it was possible to make reasonable progress, though intermittently. Because I'd coped well with the drizzle and with the navigation in the mist, I arrived at the end of the crossing of Caulderstane Slap feeling rather pleased with myself.

Two for the price of one: Part 2

Today was gloomy but I was cheerful as I left the good B&B, climbed out of West Linton (through an area that reminded me strongly of the Surrey commuter belt - same houses, same cars, a golf course - you get the idea). I crossed the Thieves Road over Caulderstane Slap leaving the Borders Region for Lanarkshire. It's an ancient drove road that is very sloshy underfoot but easy to follow - I made only a minor error that was easy to correct and I arrived in East Calder for a late lunch in a car park. I am about to meet another friend who has promised me a high class pub for my evening meal and I am typing this in another very comfortable and well-appointed B&B. It's drizzling outside but who cares? Euphoria rules.

Tomorrow is the crossing of the Forth into Fife. A big step since it puts me within 2 days of the gateway to the highlands at Perth. I am nervous of this last part of the walk for reasons that will probably become clear in later posts.

Good day, good end to the day

Just to add to my earlier post:

I had had a long-standing invitation to stay with Tony Baker in Edinburgh but for various reasons this didn't work out. However, this evening we met up for meal at a canal-side pub at Ratho and had a most enjoyable evening. Tony and I were engineering students in the early 1960s - he stayed in engineering for many years but then moved into education whereas I abandoned engineering immediately after graduating, in favour of teaching. It was great to catch up and turned a good day into a memorable one.

Another small milestone as a result of this walk!

Tony Baker is a very committed mountaineer which seems to be a principal reason for him to be living and working in Scotland. I discovered that he is now close to having climbed all the Munros in Scotland twice - I think that he said that he had five left to do and that he might manage those before the end of the year. Just in case you don't know, a Munro is any Scottish summit over 3000 feet in height and there are 283 of them though the list has required the Scottish Mountaineering Club to make some tricky decisions about what constitutes a summit. The original list was compiled by Sir Hugh Munro (1856-1919) who may have had nothing better to do with his time than to climb mountains. There are other lists: Corbetts are mountains between 2500 and 3000 feet and Grahams are those from 2000 - 2500 feet so you can have a merry time ticking all these off the lists. Most people have done no Munros; I think that I have done a dozen or so; Tony is one of very few people to have come close to the whole lot twice. I was very impressed.

The valley of the River Almond was spectacular, especially with the river in full spate. The photograph on the right shows it just above Lin's Mill aqueduct, completed with the rest of the Union Canal in 1822. This canal was built to link Edinburgh and Glasgow and the design of the aqueduct (by Hugh Baird) was strongly influenced by Thomas Telford's aqueduct at Chirk on the Llangollen Canal. It is a very massive and imposing structure.

The Falkirk Wheel (photograph opposite) was not part of the original canal but was built as a replacement for a flight of 11 locks that brought the Union Canal down to the level of the Forth and Clyde Canal which it joins just west of Falkirk. These locks were dismantled in the 1930s and it was not possible to reinstate them so the Falkirk Wheel was opened in 2002 to provide an alternative link. Boats are admitted to a channel that is closed off from the canal and then rotated in a huge wheel that brings the channel to the other level, either up or down. The wheel is nearly perfectly balanced so uses very little energy.

The photograph of the wheel was taken on another visit to Scotland a few years ago. The picture on the right was taken of the 19th century Forth railway bridge from the road bridge on this walk; it was raining from very low cloud.

A wet crossing into Fife

At the B&B I was very dolefully told that terrible weather was forecast for the Edinburgh area. In view of the gloom outside I put on the full protective clothing and set off through murk that came down almost to ground level. It certainly rained a bit but I get very hot under the waterproofs and I discarded the coat as soon as I could. I walked on a path above the River Almond that was roaring down its valley in full flood; my path ran alongside a feeder channel for the Union Canal that crossed the river at the impressive Lin's Mill Viaduct (this is the same

canal that we sat beside at dinner last night and that leads to the Falkirk Wheel – if you haven't seen the latter you've missed one of the most elegant pieces of modern engineering in Britain). So it was along the towpath towards the motorway junctions at the end of the Edinburgh airport runway. The murk was so low that planes were landing in the cloud – invisible until they touched down. Worrying for white knuckle flyers.

Then through Kirkliston and Queensferry on a cycleway that leads onto the Forth Road bridge. This is the one that was opened almost 50 years ago and where there have been concerns about rusting suspension cables. A second crossing is being built though is still in its early stages. The famous railway bridge was all but invisible in the cloud and the rain was lashing across as I walked over the bridge. This takes quite a long time to do and the bridge vibrates and bounces quite a lot. I could hear trains on the railway bridge but not see them but, almost as soon as I reached the north shore (and entered the Kingdom of Fife) the rain stopped and the cloud lifted enough to encourage me to discard the waterproofs again.

I walked up through Rosyth (which calls itself a garden city but which is best known for its naval dockyard) and into Dunfermline where I have a billet tonight. I have been here before but don't remember the town at all – the historic centre looks rather fine in a slightly dour way. But this was Scotland's capital for several centuries and would, I think, deserve a proper visit. I was surprised to see a church with a round tower, something I have only previously seen in Norfolk.

Rather a lot of road walking and noise today. I look forward to a quieter rain-free walk to Kinross tomorrow. We shall see.

PS Am adding the pictures after a rather good Italian meal with a walk into and back from the town in evening sunshine. Life is not all tired feet and rain.

DAY 59   Dunfermline to Kinross

23 km (14 miles)
366 m of climb
75% completed

Having consulted Wikipedia I can now repair the ignorance of my blog. Mary, Queen of Scots, was probably a victim of the complex and harsh politics of Scotland at a time when, as a Catholic, she occupied one side of a deep religious divide. She was less than a year old when she was crowned queen of Scotland in 1543, was married to the French king at the age of 15 but widowed 2 years later. Her second marriage to Henry Stuart, Lord Darnley gave her a son who became James VI of Scotland and later James I of England. After 2 years of marriage Darnley was murdered and Mary quickly married for a third time but faced increasingly strident opposition from both Catholics and Protestants. As a result, for about 10 months in 1567-8 she was imprisoned in the island castle on Loch Leven near Kinross, during which period she was forced to abdicate the Scottish throne. She fled to England but was imprisoned there by Elizabeth I and later executed.

You can visit Loch Leven Castle which is a picturesque ruin accessed by boat from Kinross.

Left: Loch Leven seen from Bishop Hill. The castle island is visible just above the trees. Photograph © Copyright Alfred Fyfe and licensed for reuse under the Geograph Creative Commons Licence

Opposite: Loch Leven Castle (photograph taken in 2007).

FROM THE BLOG

Lakeside dreams

The heavy rainfall is following me up the country. I have escaped before the downpours in the south west, Hebden Bridge, The Tyne Valley and the Southern Uplands and I've been dodging heavy showers today, peering over my shoulder to see what might be catching up with me. You'll gather that it's been a wet day, but where's the news in that? If I'd known what sort of June this would be I'd have left my sun hat at home.

My B&B last night was exceedingly smart – quite the classiest I've been in (and most of those I've used have been excellent, so the standard is high). In the evening I trekked into Dunfermline to an Italian restaurant that was good, though the prices were a bit high and the service a bit slow. But I'm not being profligate on this walk so an occasional good meal is, I think, well justified. Then today has been largely a road walk, much of it through forestry on the higher ground north of Dunfermline. I left Fife (called a Kingdom but I think that was long ago) and came into Perth & Kinross.

I came back to motorways yesterday for the first time since walking underneath the M62 in Yorkshire just over 3 weeks ago (it seems longer!). The noise was something that I have been glad to have missed and I have already said how noisy the Forth Bridge was. Well, I'm still dodging motorways – Dunfermline, Kinross and Perth are all fed by the M90, speeding traffic from the Forth Bridge up to the A9 and the Highlands. Kinross sits among the Lomond Hills and alongside Loch Leven where, a few years ago, Viv and I took the boat trip out to the island upon which Lochleven Castle sits. I've forgotten the details of the story but Mary Queen of Scots was incarcerated here for some time. What would Scottish history do without Mary? Anyway, the lake is very attractive, though wet. I

spent 2 hours, a baked potato and 2 coffees in the café there this afternoon while I typed this post; it started raining again when I was ready to leave.

My waterproofs are very effective at keeping the rain out. I would enjoy wearing them if they didn't also trap the wet in – I sweat rather a lot when walking and the absorbent material in the waterproofs can't cope so it all gets very clammy. You probably won't want to know this, but the problem is a consequence of my concern about weight – the best quality waterproofs have multiple fabric layers and so are relatively heavy. But they do keep you dry. Mercifully, my new boots continue to keep all the wet out.

Because I'm running a day late I will be arriving in Perth on Saturday afternoon and leaving on Monday morning. This has scuppered my plan to collect the tent, sleeping bag, cooking gear and other items that Viv was due to mail to the Perth post office. We've now switched this collection to Pitlochry so that I'll still have the camping gear available for my Cairngorm crossing two days later. I shall be walking up Glen Tilt from Blair Athol, over the saddle and down to the Linn of Dee where there is a bridge across the River Dee; this is where I plan to camp. Then, next day, it's up over an ancient drove road through Lairig Ghru that is a high pass between Cairngorm peaks, leading down to Aviemore. I've not done this route before but I've spoken to several people who have and, provided that the weather is not awful, I'm reasonably confident that I can get through to the northern highlands this way. It's an exciting but slightly daunting prospect with no blog to say how I've got on until I've arrived in Aviemore.

But tomorrow it's more pedestrian plodding to Perth.

Old, but not, I think, very old tractors in a rally with their old but not very old drivers; all very cheerful.

Below: Looking down over the Tay estuary. Right on the horizon is the Tay railway bridge built to replace the original that collapsed in a major storm in 1879 when a train was crossing. William McGonegall's poem recorded the event; one verse reads:

*So the train mov'd slowly along the Bridge
    of Tay,
Until it was about midway,
Then the central girders with a crash gave way,
And down went the train and passengers into the Tay!
The Storm Fiend did loudly bray,
Because ninety lives had been taken away,
On the last Sabbath day of 1879,
Which will be remember'd for a very long time.*

McGonegall, often described as the world's worst poet, got the death toll wrong - it is now reckoned to have been 75 people.

Trousers on, trousers off, trousers on, trousers off …

Don't get all excited – there were no funny goings-on in Perth & Kinross. Read on to find out the truth about the trousers.

My B&B in Kinross was poor; in comparison with the splendid one in Dunfermline, which cost the same, this was a paltry effort at hospitality. The room smelled as though the windows had never been opened and was poorly equipped. It was actually a room with a double and two single beds; how 4 people would have coped in that space beats me. I was offered, and foolishly accepted, an £8 in-house dinner. It was raining outside and this would save me a wet trek to the pub. Well, there wasn't much of it (the dinner, I mean) and what was offered wasn't very attractive. I was then quite offended at a blatant attempt to charge me more because I had had a pudding! Selecting a B&B from a list is a lottery and I got it wrong in Kinross.

But the sun shone this morning – rather fitfully, but the clouds were high and only showers forecast. At the last moment I revised my route to Perth, feeling that what I'd previously planned was unnecessarily roundabout. This turned out to be a good choice for the most part, introducing me to the very best of direction posts for footpaths and a rally of old tractors and older drivers. But it also led to the trousers game.

The waterproof trousers went on first because what appeared on the map to be a track turned out to be a very overgrown path with grass very wet from the previous day's rain. Trousers on for about half a mile then off when I reached a bit of road. I then lost the track across a hillside where a wind farm had been sited and new fencing put in but quickly corrected that mistake and arrived at a well-sited felled tree overlooking a very small lake. A good spot for lunch which, on this walk, is generally a very quick affair conducted without tableware, napkins or cutlery.

A heavy shower steamed over the horizon – having not even got the lunchbox out I quickly closed up the rucksack and sprinted (well, hurried) for some tree cover. That was the wrong decision – I got quite wet whilst 'sprinting' and made a mistake crossing a stream so that both boots went into the water over their tops. No boot, however waterproof, can cope with that so I once again had two quite wet feet. Shortly after I was forced to shelter under a rather scanty tree and put on full waterproofs (including the trousers). I squelched on and was glad to have the trousers on as there was another heavily overgrown footpath to contend with. Lunch was eaten on the trot – two pieces of shortbread provided by an earlier B&B and an apple but I did get a splendid view of the Tay estuary with the railway bridge in the far distance.

Then the sun came out and the storm clouds went off to annoy someone else. I sat on a seat in Bridge of Earn and took off my waterproofs and walked into Perth in quite reasonable sunshine and in time to do some essential shopping. Tonight's B&B is much more homely which is as well as I'm here for 2 nights.

Three little PSs

A comment heard from a resident of Innerleithen and omitted from my blog for that day: "A day spent out of Innerleithen is a day wasted". Isn't that nice!

The dongle is working! When all else fails you can, after all, depend on a dongle. It is winking at me as I type.

Tomorrow is July. Traditionally a wet month.

The sculpture to the left suggested to me that the man at the front was pushing forward and the one at the back was making progress impossible. But it is apparently called 'Pensive Man'. Sitting on a seat (above) is a bronze 'Fair Lady'. And I was pleased to see Smeaton's name on the bridge over the Tay. It was he, of course, who built the Eddystone Lighthouse that now adorns Plymouth Hoe.

Rest day pics

I haven't previously written a rest day post and I'm not really going to do one now. But I had a good few hours mooching around Perth which was pretty dead when I arrived there this morning but which gradually filled up with people as shops and cafés opened. So here are a few pictures with captions, just to fill a space.

I had a gentle Sunday in Perth, drinking coffee, reading the paper and taking a few photographs. I heard a pipe band in the town playing 'Men of Harlech' which was a bit surreal for Scotland and then later saw a performance outside the concert hall (left) by the Perth and District Pipe Band which included a sturdy lad who had some difficulty in supporting his very large drum – he had to lean back some way in order to balance and, after taking a rest between items, needed some help in getting the drum aloft. A real Health and Safety issue, I'd say.

Clockwise from the top left below are the City Hall, St John's Kirk (which disappointingly closed its doors to visitors after the end of morning service) and museum and art gallery (which opened too late for me that day); all are impressive buildings in a largely pedestrianised town centre whose shops slowly came to life as the day wore on.

The old bridge at
Carr Bridge

Perth to Inverness

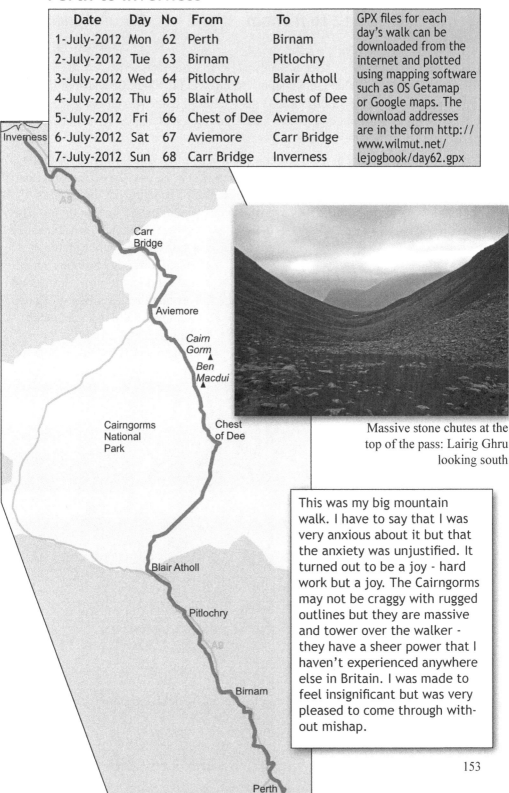

Date	Day	No	From	To
1-July-2012	Mon	62	Perth	Birnam
2-July-2012	Tue	63	Birnam	Pitlochry
3-July-2012	Wed	64	Pitlochry	Blair Atholl
4-July-2012	Thu	65	Blair Atholl	Chest of Dee
5-July-2012	Fri	66	Chest of Dee	Aviemore
6-July-2012	Sat	67	Aviemore	Carr Bridge
7-July-2012	Sun	68	Carr Bridge	Inverness

GPX files for each day's walk can be downloaded from the internet and plotted using mapping software such as OS Getamap or Google maps. The download addresses are in the form http://www.wilmut.net/lejogbook/day62.gpx

Massive stone chutes at the top of the pass: Lairig Ghru looking south

This was my big mountain walk. I have to say that I was very anxious about it but that the anxiety was unjustified. It turned out to be a joy - hard work but a joy. The Cairngorms may not be craggy with rugged outlines but they are massive and tower over the walker - they have a sheer power that I haven't experienced anywhere else in Britain. I was made to feel insignificant but was very pleased to come through without mishap.

153

DAY 62   Perth to Birnam

28 km (17 miles)
264 m of climb
79% completed

The (rather obscure) reference to happy birthday in the blog title was that it was 2 months since I had left Lands End. I also believed that I was entering the last quarter of the walk though, as I now know having re-calculated the distances, I had passed that point before arriving in Perth.

When I arrived in Birnam it was obvious that it and Dunkeld (which were really just settlements on opposite sides of the River Tay) must once have been dominated by the traffic on the A9 and were now at least able to benefit from the by-pass, though the noise from traffic was ever-present. I was surprised by two things. The first was that the Post Office, a café and the police station shared a wooden building - a real economy of use. The second was that there is a Beatrix Potter Memorial Garden since, when she was a child, Beatrix came to Birnam and Dunkeld on holiday.

I did not see any rabbits.

Photographs taken on a sunnier day than mine: Above: The entrance to the Beatrix Potter Memorial Garden; Right: Bronze Peter Rabbit in the Garden.

Photographs © Copyright Eugene Birchall (above) and © Copyright Snaik (right) and licensed for reuse under the Geograph Creative Commons Licence

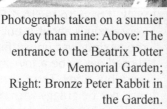

Happy birthday; into the last quarter

Best wishes for the successful end to the walk were extended as I left my B&B in Perth this morning – nice and early this time – only a spot after 7.30. It was a very comfortable and welcoming place, reasonably priced and well-placed, though they had suffered over the weekend through the Scottish Game Fair being abandoned because the ground was waterlogged. This Fair (which has, I'm afraid, more to do with dead meat than with Nintendo) is said to attract 30,000 visitors to Perth and is held by the River Tay in the grounds of Scone Palace (where Viv and I camped a few years ago on the way back from Orkney). Today the whole area looked sorry and sodden in the drizzle as I walked past on the other side of the River.

[Incidentally, I have been thinking about how I will write up this walk when it is finished. I think that it will be in the form of an e-book, available to download, and I will include a list of the B&Bs where I've stayed. You will have to look at my comments in the blog to decide whether I enjoyed my stay at each one.]

So you'll gather that today was drizzly. Everything dripped as I walked out of Perth along the river bank on a path through a parkland area called North Inch (there is a corresponding riverside area that I walked through on Saturday called South Inch and, taken together, these are valuable green spaces close to the city centre). Perth has an attractive city centre but rather ordinary suburbs though the occasional striking building sneaks up on you as you walk around.

It also has raised flood walls and flood gates, suggesting that the Tay sometimes bursts its banks and threatens the city. Indeed, some parts of the golf course on North Inch looked as though they were below today's river level; that conjures up all sorts of comic images of a golfer standing knee-deep in water with club raised. Such a silly game.

The A9 is beginning to dominate the walk. The motorway around Perth feeds into the A9 which then powers its way northwards towards Dunkeld (where I am tonight) before following the Tay up the valley to Pitlochry and Blair Atholl (my next two stops). I then leave the A9 to go through the Cairngorms but join it again at Aviemore and then follow it down to Inverness and beyond. It's about as unpleasant as any fast road and walkers and cyclists are very vulnerable. Today I managed to keep off it for all but about half a mile but that was quite enough. There is a narrow strip of tarmac bounded by a solid white line and I think that I'm meant to stay on that. Well, it's often overgrown by the verge or has debris in it or is so narrow that it's impossible to walk on it. Vehicles swerve around me – nothing ever slows down – leaving gaps that are sometimes frighteningly small and sometimes ludicrously great. When the road is wet there's a shower from every lorry. I don't like walking on main roads.

Fortunately, I managed a reasonable spread of footpaths today though tomorrow may be harder. I will be embarking on the last quarter of the walk and the end feels eerily close though I know that I still have 3 weeks to go. But today is 2 months since I left for what has been a strangely isolated existence – I have been in a bubble that seems entirely separated from my normal life.

Really quite cathartic.

Apologies for the lack of personal photos. It was all misty.

DAY 63 Birnam to Pitlochry

24 km (15 miles)
473 m of climb
80% completed

Pictures of signs are the poor man's way of filling a page. The difficulty is that what looks funny, interesting or relevant at the time looks dull and uninteresting later on and to everyone else. But I'm going to put the pictures of signs here anyway since I have few other pictures for today's walk which was only fairly interesting otherwise. Before I do, a word about Dunkeld which is a small and attractive town whose cathedral (now partly ruined) was one of the principal ecclesiastical sites of Scotland, dating back to the 9th century. Following the building of Telford's stone bridge across the Tay, new roads were constructed with Regency buildings in clear contrast to the earlier traditional architecture close to the cathedral, bishop's palace and other sites. I took a wrong turning in the town and so saw more of this than I intended - no bad thing at all.

Right: A disused railway bridge over the River Tay at Logierait, now being used as a roadway

The tale of the parcel, the convenience and the slug

I needed to get to Pitlochry in good time today because Viv had sent a parcel that was due to be waiting for me to collect from the Post Office. It was; had it not been, some radical changes to the arrangements would have been needed as it contained the last set of maps and my tent and other camping gear. I can now go into the Cairngorms on Thursday, completely equipped (I think).

Pitlochry is full of tourists - coach loads being dropped off and wandering up and down its main street eating ice creams and browsing gift shop windows. I've not seen tourists like this for the last 2 months and they are part of an alien world. Jill Long has commented that Pitlochry has stunning public conveniences; that may be true but, when I needed them, they were nowhere to be seen. Perhaps hiding public conveniences is a way of keeping them stunning.

The walk from Birnam through Dunkeld started under dark grey skies that became steadily brighter as the cloud base lifted to reveal the surrounding hills. I walked out of Dunkeld past the medieval cathedral which is a partial ruin. The path then followed the Tay (past a very upmarket Hilton Hotel) until I crossed on the A9 bridge to join a couple of minor roads that went all the way to Pitlochry. Not ideal, but these two roads were very free of traffic and I enjoyed the walk. The views over the valley (first of the Tay and then of the Tummel) were splendid and the weather slowly improved. A highlight was the old railway bridge that is now used for light traffic, walkers and cyclists.

This was, in fact, a cycleway which was very clearly signposted. This is generally the case - I wish that footpaths were as well marked. Cycleways don't make ideal walking since they are generally hard surfaced - either tarmac roads or gravel tracks. But, from a walker's point of view, if I want to get somewhere quickly and don't mind some road walking, they're good value.

I did come across three signs that I thought worth showing though I saw no salmon, hedgehogs or red squirrels today. It did occur to me that the salmon might, given the choice, prefer the odd stone to the hooks of fishermen. But what I have seen on many days of this walk are huge numbers of slugs and snails setting off across wet roads, I suppose in pursuit of glory or better food on the other side.

They don't seem to notice that they are passing the flattened remains of their friends who attempted similar crossings on previous days.

The most ambitious slug that I passed (a few days ago) was marching purposefully across the Forth Road Bridge in the pouring rain, heading for Fife. It had only just started when I saw it and, assuming that it avoids boots and tyres and finds enough to eat along the way, it should reach the other side late in 2014.

That's courage for you.

Blair Atholl is a small place in the Cairngorms National Park; its chief attraction is Blair Castle, said to be one of Scotland's premier stately homes. I didn't see this castle but I have discovered that the Duke of Atholl, owner of the castle, is the only British citizen allowed to raise a private army. Had I known that at the time I would have very carefully studied all the people I met.

In fact, now I come to think of it, that may explain the curious incident in the tea room. You can see a photograph below of a small event being run for Riding for the Disabled; this event was attended by a man in a kilt and plaid and wearing a long and ostentatious sword. Just of the right of the picture there is a tea room and I went in there to drink a cup of coffee and read the newspaper (since it was far too early to go to my B&B). This kilted man came in and went to the counter; standing beside him in the queue was a woman. They got into a conversation that was of the 'chatting up' type rather than the 'polite chat' type; suddenly the man drew a very large and lethal-looking knife from the folds of his plaid, brandished it in front of the woman and put it away again. He also fingered his sword. This was all done with much laughter and joking and, I think, some innuendos. Perhaps he was a Duke of Atholl's soldier; if he had brandished those weapons (or even carried them) in a city street the police would have been there in a trice with an armed response team. In Blair Atholl it probably passed as normal behaviour and the man's presence at the Riding for the Disabled event probably increased the interest and, perhaps, the profits.

Next day I would walk out of Blair Atholl through the Atholl estate which seemed to go on for miles. That's what comes of owning a castle and being able to raise an army. We do live in a curious sort of society.

Wettish, drying later

This is, I think, my shortest planned day and I find it hard to say much about it, other than it was raining when I started and not raining when I finished. Such is the advantage of going north. I went into a hardware shop before I left and commented that it was a miserable morning and the lady said "at least it's what was forecast" as if that would make me feel better about it.

I will fill a little space with a comment on my rucksack which has got heavier with the addition of the tent and other camping gear, offset to some extent by the package of stuff that I mailed home from the Pitlochry Post Office this morning. I took a big risk and included my sun hat in this package, a spare T-shirt and a redundant pair of socks. My B&B (another excellent choice – in the middle of Pitlochry and most convenient) provided a set of bathroom scales and I checked the new weight which was 13 kg – heavy but not as heavy as I'd feared. I'll see how it feels in a couple of days – if I'm suffering under this load I may have to thin stuff out even more. The big weight saving would be to dump the netbook, camera and associated charging equipment but that would mean the end of the blog as we've come to love it and I'm very reluctant to do that.

I gather that there's an article about the walk in *Christian Aid News* but, sadly, probably only included in the edition which goes to the SW England region. I'd be glad to know if that's right – if it is I may try to get a scan added to my website so that the misguided people who don't live in SW England can read it. If you know anybody who may be interested please forward a copy to them.

I arrived in Blair Atholl ridiculously early but tolerably dry. It took me all of 5 minutes to see the sights, buy a newspaper and locate a place where I could drink coffee. On the field outside the coffee shop the local Riding for the Disabled Association was holding a fund-raising event so I took a picture (the only one today) that will please Jill Long (I hope).

And that's all the news for today. Tomorrow the Cairngorms with a post highly unlikely.

Glen Tilt, featured on the next page, was a lovely place; I guess that most of the land was part of the vast Atholl estate. This is a picture taken early on Day 65, put here to fill a space and to whet your appetites.

159

DAY 65 | **Blair Atholl to Chest of Dee**

33 km (20 miles)
666 m of climb
83% completed

This was more like your popular perception of an end-to-end walk - a remote valley with a path winding up between mountain peaks, the sun shining, sheep baaing and water rushing down the river. Fording the said river and camping would be wholly consistent with this perception, ignoring the fact that most of Britain just doesn't fit that rugged sort of image.

In hindsight this was probably the most memorable part of the walk and I'm very glad that I chose this route. It was not the biggest climb of my walk but almost the whole day was a gradual ascent amongst splendid scenery in good weather.

Pictures taken in Glen Tilt:
Top Left: River Tilt; Top Right:
A sheep on a beat; Above: Forest
Lodge; Middle Right: Gaw's
Bridge; Right: Waterfall above
Bedford Bridge

Splendid Cairngorms, part 1

What a splendid day! I got away early, the weather was good and the scenery, oh! the scenery was magnificent. A day to relish and remember. I'm lying in my very small tent typing this – there's not enough height to sit up so I'm lying on my sleeping bag, typing with one finger and watching out for midges (none seen yet). But I do have frogs hopping about – it's a tad boggy and I guess that I've invaded their home. Of course, this post won't get added to the blog until tomorrow evening at the soonest by which time I should be over Lairig Ghru and enjoying the fleshpots of Aviemore.

But what about today? After a short road walk out of Blair Atholl I joined a track that serves two lodges on the Atholl estate, high up in Glen Tilt. This is a long glen that runs for about 15 miles northeast from Blair Atholl and which turned out to have a magnificent tree-lined gorge through which a fairly hefty river flows over rapids and waterfalls, always noisily. Some parts of the lower glen were almost Alpine with broad flower meadows alongside the river but, higher up, the valley became much narrower with very steep sides.

People were on holiday in both lodges, though it was 8 miles down a gravel track to Blair Atholl from the larger one. I met only one other walker and a couple of mountain bikers (who later gave up the track when it became too rough and returned to Blair Atholl) and a small group of young people of varied cheerfulness carrying large rucksacks. Later on, as I walked into the valley of the River Dee there were a few other walkers, probably making their way back to cars parked at the end of the road up from Braemar.

The route included crossing the Bedford Bridge – it is a 19th century suspension bridge erected in memory of Francis John Bedford, an 18 year old who was drowned on this spot in 1879. Behind the bridge is a very splendid waterfall and I guess that many walkers stop here to read the plaque, admire the scenery and perhaps rest on the grass below the bridge. A lovely spot.

The Cairngorms are not so obviously rugged as the Western Highlands but they are large and imposing mountains that have to be taken very seriously, particularly when the weather is bad. This approach to Lairig Ghru from Glen Tilt shows a very forbidding view of the Cairngorms and I think that tomorrow will be a testing day – I hope that the weather doesn't add to the difficulties.

Thank you for all the comments on this blog and I'm glad that my travels evoke others' memories. I try to respond where appropriate but I rarely have enough time in the evenings to keep properly up to date. I should also say that I've taken far more photographs than I've included in the blog and aim to make most of these available in a higher resolution once the walk is over.

Chest of Dee to Aviemore

28 km (18 miles)
477 m of climb
84% completed

This was a vast empty space. The photographs show the ascent to Lairig Ghru past Carrour Bothy (left); two views of the top of the pass (middle) and (bottom) my tent and looking back up the pass from the descent towards Aviemore.

Splendid Cairngorms, part 2

This was a hard day – but no less splendid for that. It exposed the deterioration in my capacity for mountain walking (I am not as flexible and supple as I once was), the fact that I was carrying a heavy pack and the demanding nature of the walk. The weather was kind again, so that wasn't a factor, but I felt very tired by the end of today's walk and could easily have dived into bed and stayed there until morning.

I should point out that this was the highest point that this end-to-end walk will achieve. Lairig Ghru is a pass at 835 m or 2733 ft with some of the highest Scottish peaks (including Ben Macdui and Brae Riach) on either side. It it an ancient routeway connecting Aviemore in the north to the valley of the Dee and Braemar in the south and in the 18th and 19th centuries was used as a drove road. It is now only a walking route. There is no habitation in the pass or on its approaches or in the valleys that link into it except for the Carrour bothy and it is as remote an area as one is likely to find on the British mainland.

I didn't sleep very well in my tent so it was no hardship to get up at 5am and start walking by 6. From where I was camped I had first to walk up into the pass for some 5 miles, climbing all the way and passing the bothy which is normally busy though not apparently this morning. This approach to the pass is on a grand scale – towering mountains that loom over the valleys and topped this morning by cloud. It was over 4 hours to the top of the pass which is a chaos of boulders at the foot of rock slides from both sides. There was no-one else in the pass until I met, at the summit, a man who had climbed from the north side to do a bird count in one of the high corries.

It was the boulders on the scree slopes that exposed my lack of agility. The pack spoiled my balance and I was far more cautious (and therefore far slower) in crossing them that I would once have been. In one sense that was prudent – it's all too easy to make a mistake and break an ankle or leg - but it is also very wearing to take so long over a mile or so of boulder slopes.

It was huge sense of achievement, however, and I've no regrets about choosing this route which will stick in my memory for a very long time. And some of the excitement was to discover that the northern approach was very different from the southern. The mountains did not overwhelm the valley in the same way and one could look down and see Aviemore in the far distance. The descent was rough and slow but, on the lower slopes, there was far less sloshing through peat bogs and the end of the pass fanned out into several onward routes. I met more walkers here and the last 5 miles into Aviemore was along quite heavily used paths.

I was able to sit in the sun and drink a pot of tea (a cup at a time) before walking into the village to find my B&B at about 4pm. I then started booking accommodation for the next 3 nights and found that Inverness is hosting a golf tournament, with all the B&Bs already fully booked. It was only with the help of a lady called Pearl that I eventually found a bed for Sunday and Monday nights; I will be having a rest day in Inverness.

Speaking of rest ...

DAY 67 **Aviemore to Carr Bridge**

17 km (10 miles)
208 m of climb
85% completed

I do apologise for the rant about Windows 7 (and all the other rants in this blog). Re-reading the posts I see myself as a very intolerant person. But if you can't have a rant in a blog, written in a B&B or a pub at the end of a long day's walk, where can you? Some of the problems have stemmed from poor WiFi connections that have failed me just when I was loading a picture or had just edited but not saved some changes to the text. Everyone who uses a computer will know the feeling!

A short day like this, particularly in the rain, generates few photographs so I am reduced to showing a slug, an ants nest (with my map case to show its size) and a picture of Carr Bridge taken the next day, after heavy overnight rain. With water pouring through like this, the bridge looks extraordinarily frail but a plaque on an observation platform did say that stabilisation work had been done fairly recently. As for the slug, it is probably still walking north as I write, 3 months after leaving Scotland. Good luck to it, I say. I wish that I'd given it a name. Robert Burns would probably have written an ode to it.

Above: Carr Bridge after heavy rain;
Top right: The slug, manfully (or womanfully) marching northwards;
Right: A large ants' nest in a wood near Carr Bridge - the white blob is my map case

164

Steam, the slug and a bridge

This should not have been 10 miles – more like 15. I made a daft mistake when I booked my B&B in Carr Bridge, thinking that I was making today and tomorrow more equal in length. In fact, I'm now committed to another 20-miler tomorrow to get me to Inverness. However, unlike the long walks over Lairig Ghru, I don't face any significant gradients so it will just be a matter of grinding it out along the flattest and shortest tracks and roads that I can find including, I hope, some bits of one of General Wade's Military Roads that were built in the wake of the 1745 rebellion.

I've had a wet walk from Aviemore, the first part alongide the Speyside Railway where steam and diesel trains whistle and hoot as they ply the Spey valley. I did try to get a photograph but was too slow in getting the camera out from under my waterproofs but I can vouch for the prettiness of the trains which do not, however, recreate the glory days of early 20th century Scottish railways. But who cares – a steam train is a steam train, whatever the type and colour. I diverted to Boat of Garten in order to make the walk more interesting but there was not a lot to see though the village did remind me of settlements in British Columbia – newer timber frame houses tucked amongst the conifers with a sprinkling of older stone buildings. The drizzle was similar as well.

Carr Bridge (which the OS map has as Carrbridge) is a pleasant village which has a spectacular old bridge that was originally built in 1717 but then seriously damaged in a major flood in 1829. It's now a thin skeleton stone arch that is strangely reminiscent (though on a smaller scale) of the bridge at Mostar in Bosnia. Possibly the young men of Carr Bridge are tempted to show their prowess (and physique) by diving off their bridge occasionally (but possibly not).

I met the Forth Bridge slug again! I swear it's the same animal – it was still sliding along a wet road, heading north, just as before. It must have come up by train – it could not have made it to the northern part of the Cairngorms National Park without mechanical assistance. Perhaps it is bound for Inverness or maybe, just maybe, it is actually doing the end-to-end walk for charity. Someone should tell it that using the train is cheating.

Some of the impact of this (and the previous) post is lost because I have a (temporary, I hope) problem with the photo editor that I'm using for the pictures. I should have loaded a copy of some dependable friend such as Photoshop but I found on the netbook this product that came with Windows 7 and I've been using it, though with several hair-tearing glitches over the past 10 weeks. I will labour at this problem and solve it in the next day or so; in the meantime you have my honeyed words but not, I'm afraid, my epic pictures. I am, incidentally, increasingly irritated by Windows 7's tendency to organise everything for me and to dress up simple tasks as if they were the best thing since Bill Gates' hairdo. I want to do things for myself!!!!

DAY 68   Carr Bridge to Inverness

39 km (24 miles)
452 m of climb
87% completed

I said in the blog that I was not sure that General Wade actually supervised the construction of the roads that bear his name. That was, indeed, the case; most of the network was created by Major William Caulfield whilst Wade went on to higher things, including being MP for Bath for 25 years and becoming a field marshal.

Left: The Moy Viaduct;
Below: Vanity - self portrait taken in a traffic mirror

FROM THE BLOG

Oh my feet are sore!

I said that I'd made a mistake in booking the B&B at Carr Bridge didn't I? No problem with the B&B itself - it was one of the very good ones that I've stayed at and it had a pub a couple of doors away where the food was good and the atmosphere very pleasant. The problem lay in the fact that it left me with a long distance to do today and I just had to switch onto automatic and walk. I had only three very short breaks, it took 9 hours and, I'm afraid, included rather more road walking than I'd wanted. It was also beset by drizzle, varying from intense to very little so the waterproofs got another outing.

At least, unlike the Lairig Ghru crossing, there was limited up and down and the going underfoot was easier. But 3 of the last 4 days have topped 20 miles and that's bad planning - I'm glad it's over and I don't want to do another few days like these. Consequently, I'm close to making some decisions about changing the final stages of the walk. There are several factors.

My planned route to John O'Groats involved several days camping. The tent that I collected in Pitlochry is one that I've had for some years and not used very much and now turns out to have a leaky groundsheet; that's something that wasn't apparent when we put it up on the lawn at home on a hot sunny day but which became obvious when I camped on wet peaty grass three nights ago. Bad news – everything gets wet! It's also a very small tent that I can't sit up in. Fine in good weather but a real drag if it's raining – imagine cooking and eating everything lying down. Or typing this blog in a horizontal position. So I've somewhat gone off the camping bit which also involves extra weight in my rucksack. That's OK if the camping is going well but it's hard to justify otherwise.

I've looked at the weather forecasts for the next few days and they don't make good reading. If I have to walk in the rain it's nice to feel that I can have a shower, a good meal and a comfortable bed at the end of it. I may have become a wimp but ending a wet day in a wet tent, preparing for another wet day has become rather unattractive.

Finally, and most importantly, I have reached the stage of this walk where I just want it to end. Not prematurely – I still want to get to John O'Groats and have the satisfaction of having done the whole thing – but I want that as quickly as possible now. Any route which gets me there sooner is better than one that takes more time. Sadly, though, the quickest route is up the coast which means road-walking the A9 for the best part of 2 days. Everyone agrees that it's a miserable business, which is why I originally chose an inland route across the Caithness Flow Country; this is the route shown on my website but it requires at least 3 nights camping – there's no accommodation available because almost no-one lives there.

I will make the final decision tomorrow – I need to work out the changed route and sort out accommodation. I also need to either park the camping gear somewhere in Inverness, to be collected on my way home or post it back to Cornwall. I'll let you know how it pans out.

Just a final word about today's walk. The road walking was following a cycle route for some of the way – this used minor roads and paths including one bit close to but not on the A9 over Slocht Summit at 405 m (1328 ft) – a dismal place with none of the grandeur of Lairig Ghru and only half the height. But it did have some nice foxgloves. Also on the way was the Moy Viaduct, the last remaining timber viaduct on any mainline Scottish railway. It was built in 1887 and, in 2003, was repaired with the addition of some new timbers and the treatment of the old ones to prevent further decay. It is not a pretty structure but it is interesting.

I also trod part of one of General Wade's military roads built after the Jacobite rebellion of 1715. I seem to remember that Wade, though credited with this network of roads built to enable the army to get about the Highlands, was neither the architect nor the overseer of most of the work but there are many places where it is still possible to walk the routes and see the bridges that Wade initiated.

A day off tomorrow – the next post will be from somewhere beyond Inverness, but I'm not sure where.

The stacks at Duncansby

Inverness to John O'Groats

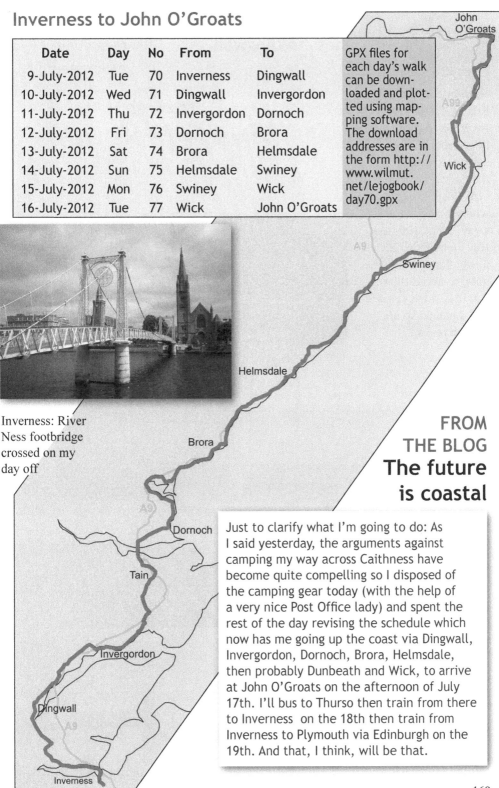

Date	Day	No	From	To
9-July-2012	Tue	70	Inverness	Dingwall
10-July-2012	Wed	71	Dingwall	Invergordon
11-July-2012	Thu	72	Invergordon	Dornoch
12-July-2012	Fri	73	Dornoch	Brora
13-July-2012	Sat	74	Brora	Helmsdale
14-July-2012	Sun	75	Helmsdale	Swiney
15-July-2012	Mon	76	Swiney	Wick
16-July-2012	Tue	77	Wick	John O'Groats

GPX files for each day's walk can be downloaded and plotted using mapping software. The download addresses are in the form http://www.wilmut.net/lejogbook/day70.gpx

Inverness: River Ness footbridge crossed on my day off

FROM THE BLOG
The future is coastal

Just to clarify what I'm going to do: As I said yesterday, the arguments against camping my way across Caithness have become quite compelling so I disposed of the camping gear today (with the help of a very nice Post Office lady) and spent the rest of the day revising the schedule which now has me going up the coast via Dingwall, Invergordon, Dornoch, Brora, Helmsdale, then probably Dunbeath and Wick, to arrive at John O'Groats on the afternoon of July 17th. I'll bus to Thurso then train from there to Inverness on the 18th then train from Inverness to Plymouth via Edinburgh on the 19th. And that, I think, will be that.

Inverness to Dingwall

27 km (17 miles)
304 m of climb
89% completed

High bridges like the Kessock Bridge at Inverness, with traffic relentlessly thundering over, are hard on the pedestrian's sensibilities, especially when they bounce or sway. Some walkers fear them and I have to say that it would be good to avoid them. But they do save time and distance so are hard to resist.

Top: Inverness City Hall;
Above: Kessock Bridge that carries the A9 over the Beauly Firth;
Right: On the Black Isle footpath signposts are metric!

From Testaccio to Kessock with a little poo

Excitement, excitement. I'm in a B&B right alongside a railway level crossing and from the window in my room I can watch the trains go by! The downside is that it's the line from Dingwall to Kyle of Lochalsh and there are only 4 trains each way each weekday. Miss one and there's 3 hours to wait for the next. There are no gates so I assume that the citizens of Dingwall can be trusted to stop when the red lights flash.

An interesting walk today. It started in Inverness city centre just as shops were opening and continued out through the dockside area to the Kessock Bridge over the Beauly Firth. I enjoyed Inverness city centre yesterday – it was a bustling place, fully justifying its claim to be a regional capital. A good mix of local and national shops and the streets were still quite lively in the evening.

I went to an Italian restaurant which was packed to the doors and with people queuing to get tables – remarkable for a Monday evening. It was warm, very noisy and busy – absolutely reminiscent of one that Viv and I went to in Testaccio in Rome some time ago. The food was a bit disappointing however – for me it lacked the flavour and interest that the menu prices led me to expect and the service was rather slow. I have found that the cost of eating out in the evenings has risen quite sharply as I've come up through Scotland. The cheap and good quality pub food that's widely available in England is harder to find here.

The Kessock Bridge is my third estuary crossing and was as noisy as the other two and almost as wet as the walk over the Forth Bridge (but I didn't see the slug who, perhaps, took the inland route). Nor is the bridge as high or as exposed as the Forth Bridge but it does represent an important link, taking me into the northern highlands and onto the last leg of the walk (in a manner of speaking).

I dropped down from the bridge to walk a very quiet minor road along the north bank of the Beauly Firth. It was very secluded – the tide was out and the mud flats alive with birds. In front of me the highlands were cloaked in low cloud and the rain was fairly incessant, though not too heavy. Then up footpaths (waymarked in km!) across the middle of the Black Isle and down on a cycleway to Conon Bridge and Dingwall at the head of the Cromarty Firth. I associate the Black Isle with the late George Black (chief geologist to the Nature Conservancy Council for many years) who did his PhD there. I learned more of the practical realities of the conservation of the natural environment from George than from anyone else and I wrote about this in the *Old School News* some time ago.

I'm sorry to say (and this will be the last time that I mention it) that the problem of dog poo is worse in Scotland than in England. I don't think that it's that there are more dogs – in fact, I think that there may be fewer per head of the human population. It's possible that they poo more but more likely that there is not as strong a pick-up culture and, I think, fewer disposal bins. The mind wanders as I walk and I did speculate on the possibility of marketing an automatic poo collection and disposal device but the details became rather sordid.

A train went through as I was typing this. Rather tame – the lights flashed and klaxon sounded and, almost immediately the 2-coach train trundled through at a very sedate pace. Nearly a non-event.

Above: A spare oil rig waiting for
something to happen;
Below: An oil rig in the Invergordon
dry dock being refurbished.

As on so many days, I arrived in Invergordon quite early and needed to kill some time before going to my B&B. Sometimes this was easy, sometimes not. The ideal would be that I walked into a town and immediately came across a coffee shop which had free WiFi where I could sit in peace and quiet for a couple of hours to write my blog before sauntering off to the B&B. It was rarely as simple as this, usually because there was either no coffee shop or (as in Invergordon) no WiFi.

172

I learn about oil rigs

I won't moan on about the weather again – after all, there was a short burst of watery sunshine today which is more than some places have had. They tell me that through to the weekend will be better – I hope that they're right.

Here I am in Invergordon which turns out to be the place where they refurbish oil rigs. There are 4 or 5 here at the moment plus a few bits of rigs that seem to have been left here and forgotten. Close to, an oil rig is an impressive structure and there is one in dry dock being given a facelift. I have just been talking to a fellow B&B inmate who is working on this rig which is, apparently, a 1980s model that is now quite slummy but that has a good deal of life in it yet. He is working on the installation of ROVs (don't you envy my command of technical jargon? – Remotely Operated Vehicles) which are sent down to do inspections and tasks on the sea bed. They install things like blow-out preventors (the thing that failed in the Gulf of Mexico oil spill) and other pieces of gear that I barely understand and so can't bore you with. He's made his career on rigs, working in India, off the coast of Africa, in the Gulf and in the North Sea so he was an interesting person to talk to as I prepared and ate my dinner.

Invergordon is not much of a place though no doubt somebody loves it. The opportunities for eating out are very limited indeed so I went to the Co-op and bought a ready meal and some accessories, walked them back to the B&B (about a mile away) and used the kitchen there to make myself a meal that would have gladdened their hearts on Master Chef. That's when I learned about the rigs, only tearing myself away so that I could write this blog for your pleasure and education. However, Invergordon is on the Cromarty Firth which is a delightful spot where it's possible to see whales and dolphins if you're in the right place at the right time. For me, one of these conditions was wrong but I will let you know if I see a dark shadow in the water though I will tomorrow be leaving this firth for the Dornoch Firth where, for all I know, there may be neither whales nor dolphins.

I thought Dingwall a very pleasant small town and Alness, which I walked through today, is also rather nice. Both have a good spread of shops, some national names and some clearly local. Both places put my local town to shame though I did not see anywhere to compare with Trewarthas (which, if you've not heard of it, is an incredible hardware emporium in Callington). "My, you've got some stuff in here" was the reaction of one customer entering Trewarthas for the first time. He was right.

Truth to tell, this was a rather downbeat day when I worried about the worthwhileness of this walk. It may have been because of the rain or because I was road-walking again or because my right foot still produces a niggling pain after all these weeks. I think that this is probably just because it's all coming to an end and places like Invergordon do not lift the spirits. But then my spirits were lifted by the news that some Christian Aid supporters will meet me when I arrive at John O'Groats next week and will put me up for the night and get me to my train at Thurso the morning after. That's really great – it would have been a lonely celebration otherwise (I had thought that, to cheer myself up, I would get one of those miniature bottles of malt whisky and down the contents as I stood under the signpost, but now I don't need to bother.)

I see that the rain has stopped....

DAY 72   **Invergordon to Dornoch**   30 km (19 miles)
261 m of climb
92% completed

This (edited from Wikipedia) makes me glad I didn't visit Dornoch Cathedral:

'Dornoch Cathedral was built in the 13th century as the cathedral church of the diocese of Caithness. In 1570 it was burnt down during local feuding. Full 'repairs' (amounting to one of the most drastic over-restorations on any important Scottish medieval building) were not carried out until the early 19th century by the Countess of Sutherland. Among the 'improvements' carried out, the ruined but still largely intact aisled medieval nave was demolished and a new narrow nave without pillars built on its site. The interior was reordered in the 1920s with the removal of Victorian plasterwork (but note that the medieval church would have been plastered throughout). The site of the medieval high altar was raised and converted into a burial area for the Sutherland family, who introduced large marble memorials alien to the original appearance of the building.'

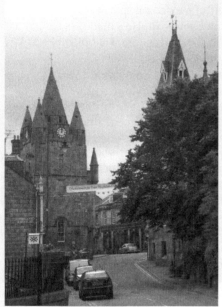

Top: Six legs sit in the Cromarty Firth;
Above: Tain has interesting buildings;
Bottom: Causeway and bridge take the A9 across the Dornoch Firth

The outlook improves

All sorts of things looked more positive today. First, the weather looked better – not a tropical blue sky but a light grey one with the occasional blue streak, the temperature may have reached 15, there was a reasonable breeze and NO RAIN appeared. Bliss.

Then I had a good early start and a steady walk – too much road, but that's going to be the story of the last few miles of this marathon (there's only about 80 miles left to do!!!). It was an interesting walk that took in Tain, a bridge and Dornoch and plenty of interesting bits in between. And I began to see some advantages in this coastal route. I certainly won't get bored and, although I have to put up with the A9 and its traffic, it isn't as busy as I had expected and there's plenty to see. I do hanker after the inland cross-country route but there would be long sections of that without much variety – just mountains, lochs, streams, mountains, lochs, streams and so on. Anyway, that's what I'm telling myself.

So, to the details. The first part of the walk was along the northern shore of the Cromarty Firth. I left the oil rigs behind but got a better view of the 6 huge oil rig legs that stand in the water on the southern shore waiting, I gather, for the resolution of a financial dispute that's been going on for years. They look like the fat lady's legs on a 1950s Blackpool postcard but I guess that they may rust where they stand. Then inland, up through forestry on minor roads until I was walking down a lane into Tain which sits close to the south shore of the Dornoch Firth. As I approached I was accosted by an aggressive lamb that strutted along its side of the fence as I walked along mine. Most lambs beat a retreat when they see me but this one was bleating loudly; was it warning me off, wanting favours or just bored? I walked on into Tain, a little unnerved. As I came into the town I passed the old poor house, now converted to residences but still clearly betraying its origins. There is a wonderfully informative website about workhouses by Peter Higinbotham (Google 'workhouses' to get to it); it includes a full description of the Tain Poor House which was one of three in Ross & Cromarty.

Tain is a very attractive small town, no doubt sustained by the nearby Glenmorangie Distillery. It retains some grand buildings and many smaller traditional houses and shops. With the A9 now diverted around the town it is a pleasure to walk through and I had enough time to enjoy a large cappuccino and to catch up with the newspaper. Then on to the bridge that crosses the Dornoch Firth. This was my fourth and last estuary crossing which (a notice told me) was opened in 1991 by the Queen Mother. The bridge has approach causeways on either side and then an 890 m bridge that is apparently the longest in Europe built by the cast-push method. If I understand this correctly it is a process where a completed section of a bridge (such as a single span) is launched outwards on special supports mounted on a previously completed span, then joined to the previously completed sections. This then forms the basis for the launch of the next section.

There's a sandy beach on the north shore and I had my first beach lunch of the walk, though the tide was out so that paddling was not an option. But here is another compensation of this coastal route and it set me up for a stroll into Dornoch, smaller than Tain but with many more tourists and my very comfortable B&B for the night. It is called Amalfi but the sun doesn't shine like it should.

DAY 73   **Dornoch to Brora**   31 km (19 miles)
244 m of climb
94% completed

Above: The iron age Carn Liath Broch
Above right: Golfers, but aren't the
grass contours nice? Right: this is an
oddly funny sign; Opposite Top: The
ruin of Skelbo Castle; Opposite Below:
Dunrobin Castle near Golspie;

FROM THE BLOG
A two castle day

It was hard to leave the B&B in Dornoch;
apart from the comforts of the place I had interesting conversations about Kansas and the Battle of Embo at breakfast, together with a check on the best onward route for me to take. It seems such a shame to leave B&Bs like this after just one night – I feel that I don't do them justice.

But I strode out on dry roads under a grey sky out of Dornoch to which, again, I haven't given enough attention. My route took me past the local golf course, backed by a suitably impressive hotel. Not many people playing – it reminded me of a comment by my host in Innerleithen earlier in the walk who said that local gold courses were struggling to get members. There may have been few players but there was an impressive number of machines being used to mow the greens. The North Sea didn't exactly sparkle but it made a good backdrop.

The route was along a disused railway track that went through Embo and then joined a minor road that ran along the southern edge of Loch Fleet - a small tidal loch at the heart of a National Nature Reserve. Along the way I passed the ruins of Skelbo Castle, which brings me to the Battle of Embo which probably took place in about 1260. A party of Danes landed at the mouth of Loch Fleet and camped near Embo. Richard de Moravia of Skelbo Castle engaged the Danes and held them in check until the Earl of Sutherland could get there with a stronger force; however, in the course of the battle Richard was killed. The Earl apparently then slew the Danish leader with the leg of a horse (detached from its body and picked up off the battlefield). Richard is buried on Dornoch Cathedral and there's now a horseshoe on Dornoch's coat of arms. I can vouch for the horse story as I saw this morning a drawing of the incident done on the bat-

tlefield by the well-known medieval artist Macasso.

I then had a dose of the A9 for a couple of miles before escaping down a track through some woodland, then past another golf course (where I think no-one was playing) into Golspie which was, I thought, a bit nondescript. But it did give me access to the dunes and a seat overlooking the beach where I could have a late lunch. Lest you think that I indulge in an orgy at lunchtime let me say that, throughout this walk, I've dined on a mixture of nuts (peanuts or cashews) and sultanas, followed by a choccy bar (usually a Bounty but I have been seduced by the occasional Snickers) and an apple, all washed down with water. Anyway,

it was good to sit and look at the sea and then walk on across the front of Dunrobin Castle, the seat of the Earls and Dukes of Sutherland.

The Castle as it is today is a 19th century building in a baronial style and it certainly cuts an impressive picture. However, I'm not particularly well-disposed to Earls, Dukes, Countesses and the like and particularly not to the Sutherlands who, in the late 18th and through the 19th centuries played a major part in the highland clearances that were the brutal removal of people from

the land in order to 'improve' agricultural production, especially by the keeping of sheep. The suffering was immense with the destruction of communities and culture and a major loss of the Gaelic language that is said to now be more widely spoken in parts of Canada than it is in Scotland. So I hurried past Dunrobin despite entreaties from the Countess to join her for afternoon tea.

And so, with another small dose of the A9, I arrived in Brora where I am in another elegant B&B where I have received a splendid welcome. Tomorrow I have an easy day that will take me to Helmsdale which will be the launch pad for the final 3-day push to JOG. I can't wait.

FROM THE BLOG

Another golf course and more A9

This wasn't the most demanding day of the walk; it was pleasant enough but did use the A9 quite a lot. It started alongside another golf course built on the dunes north of Brora where I had a very comfortable stay and one of the best night's sleep of this whole adventure.

Before I started the walk I went to the optician to get some new contact lenses. I've worn contacts since the mid 1980s, though rather less since I retired, and they're much better than glasses when it's raining or when I get very hot and glasses begin to slide down my face. I have worn the lenses every day of the walk but, shortly after I got into Scotland, I began to get trouble with my eyes feeling as though they had grit in them. The problem has come and gone but yesterday was a bad day; one eye was very sore and I was crying as I walked along. I took the lenses out but, by yesterday evening, the eye was very uncomfortable. The good night's sleep has more or less cured the problem but I'm wearing glasses today as a precaution.

I should say that I'm writing this in a cafe in Helmsdale and there's a large family sitting opposite with a small child called Archie who is extremely noisy and who looks like a small Alex Salmond. He's clearly stressed out by this family (especially when goaded by his older sister) and probably hungry so I can only hope that the arrival of food will silence him.

The golf course walk out of Brora was followed by a long stint on the A9 made easier because it's Saturday with few lorries on the road. It is boring and sometimes worrying since many drivers prefer to swerve round me rather than slow down. I have another long dose of this tomorrow and then I think that things will improve.

It's clear that I have moved from being an object of curiosity to being commonplace. Until Inverness most people I spoke to had never previously met an end-to-end walker. Now, I'm taken for granted - just one of the eccentric minority that chooses to walk rather than ride. I think that people are still approving though I have had a small number of annoyed horn blasts as drivers have swerved past me on the A9. Some cyclists have also passed me, bikes laden with luggage and only a few hours away from

Above: I see no reason why sheep should not take an intelligent interest in golf; Opposite Top: The Last Wolf in Scotland; Opposite Bottom: Helmsdale Harbour

the finish. I respect cyclists for their general fitness and girth of thigh but I can't help feeling that the use of a mechanical aid is something of a cheat.

I passed the plaque which records the killing, in the 18th century, of the last wolf in Sutherland. The plaque was put up in the 1920s when someone presumably thought that this was an event well worth recording, though whether it signalled approval or sadness I can't be sure. Wolves, could they see the plaque, would no doubt have a view on this.

TO MARK THE PLACE NEAR WHICH
(ACCORDING TO SCROPE'S "ART OF DEERSTALKING")
THE LAST WOLF IN SUTHERLAND
WAS KILLED
BY THE HUNTER POLSON,
IN OR ABOUT THE YEAR 1700,
THIS STONE WAS ERECTED BY
HIS GRACE THE DUKE OF PORTLAND, K.C.,
A.D. 1924.

And so to Helmsdale which is small, with a harbour with some inshore fishing boats in it and a pleasant demeanour; this is where I ate a late lunch. Like most of the places I've been through recently it has a railway station on the line that winds around NE Scotland connecting Thurso and Wick with Inverness and which I will travel back down next Wednesday. It has, I think, 4 trains a day in each direction but none on Sundays and it's strangely reassuring that a line as eccentric as this should have survived the cuts and rationalisations that beset the railways in the 20th century.

And speaking of travelling back, I'm not sure that I've been explicit about the last days of this walk. So, tomorrow is a 20+ mile haul to a B&B near Lybster, all on the A9. Then, on Monday, I have a shortish walk to Wick (I had considered going to Watten but almost certainly will not). All being well, Tuesday is then the final day when I'll walk from Wick via Keiss to Duncansby Head and then to John O'Groats.

And that will, at last, be that. And I have to report that the noisy family is leaving and I can enjoy my second cappuccino in peace. As people have stood up I see that Archie will shortly have a younger sibling; whether this will send him over the top or silence him forever I shall never know.

PS (later in the evening) I've just returned from the local chippy. This is no ordinary chippy - it is a restaurant called *La Mirage* and has been rated by Clarissa Dickson-Wright as one of the 6 best chippies in Britain. If she sampled all the chippies in the country before coming to this conclusion we have an explanation for her imposing appearance. It's not something you'd expect to find in a small place like Helmsdale but it had a very varied menu, expert, efficient and cheerful service and a wine list. The fish and chips were excellent and the place was packed, with tables reserved in advance; I was lucky to get in. It was my first and almost certainly my only fish and chip dinner of the walk and I will cherish the experience.

Swiney is a very small settlement 1km west of Lybster.

Top: The narrow white line - a monotonous view of the A9;
Middle: I was welcomed;
Bottom: Soft Bed sign

FROM THE BLOG
I march into Caithness

Yes, this is my last county; beyond this I have to swim. It chucked it down soon after I left my B&B in Helmsdale and I had to go for the full wet gear. It's a three-mile uphill haul out of the village and the rain had stopped by the time I reached the top; the sun came out and the North Sea appeared bluish in patches. So off with the gear and a nice day for a walk – even along the A9. In fact, there was little traffic during the morning. The lorries and white vans were all still in their beds and only a few cars disturbed my peace. It's a splendid coast with tiny harbours at Berridale, Dunbeath and Latheronwheel and a roller-coaster of a road connecting them. Being road walking, it was possible to make quick progress and I knocked off the miles in 8 hours that included a lunch stop and a couple of other short breaks.

This is wild country. The road, with nowhere else to go, hugs the mountainsides above the sea, slowly giving way to farmland as I walked north. It's a very open landscape and, for much of the way, I could see the road snaking away into the far distance. There are snow gates on each section of road and, once shut, these would completely isolate the small communities. There is a steep drop and several hairpin bends at Berridale which is a very lush valley enclosed between the bleaker hills. There were, of course, escape lanes on the hills - I had never before seen them referred to as 'soft escape beds' which conjured up quite the wrong sort of image. Then, as I neared my B&B, farmers were cutting, turning and bailing grass - taking advantage of the relatively settled weather, which I hope will persist for two more days. After that, I don't care!

I passed the track down to Badbea which was one of the settlements established by the displaced victims of the highland clearances. Here they attempted to scratch a living on the very marginal land at the tops of the cliffs and it was said that parents used to tie down their children and animals to prevent them being blown off the cliffs into the sea. The settlements were doomed from the start

– there was no possibility that the villagers could scratch a living from that land and people gradually left, mostly as emigrants to North America or Australia. I haven't seen Badbea (something else to come to on a more leisured visit) but I understand that it's a sad and ruined place – a monument to the grossest inhumanity.

I was not the only traveller to John O'Groats. I passed a group of cyclists getting ready to depart from Helmsdale and they later passed me as we all ground up the long hill. They were expecting to make JOG today but I was secretly pleased to see that their baggage was being carried in a support vehicle – it makes me proud to be a walker!

The A9 doesn't boast much in the way of cycle lanes – only the newest parts of the road have a lane marked off with a solid white line where cyclists and walkers can travel in reasonable safety. There are pavements in the few villages but everywhere else one treads the white line at the edge of the road, trying not to stumble off the tarmac onto the verge or over the line into the road. I prefer to walk on the left of the road, only crossing to the right when I risk being out of sight on a left hand bend. That way, I can legitimately plod on, leaving the drivers to either swerve round (which most do without slowing) or to slow behind me until it's safe to pass. Facing the traffic, I feel obliged to step onto the verge when there's oncoming traffic but motorists simply take advantage of this and zoom past as quickly and as closely as possible. Perhaps the day will come when every larger road has wide pedestrian and cycle lanes along its entire length, acknowledging the entitlement of pedestrians and cyclists to safe passage.

Finally, I have reflections on banana skins and widgets. Banana skins first: have you realised that we are in the midst of an in-car banana consumption craze? And that, once finished with, the banana skins are thrown out of the cars (and lorries and vans for all I know)? I have seen dozens of banana skins in the gutters and on the verges and I have a confession to make. As a 14-year old I went to Bordeaux as part of the Bristol-Bordeaux exchange. I was taken out by my host family in their Citroën (one of those sleek 1950s ones that looked like a sucked lozenge). I was in the back seat alongside Olivier, my exchange partner and we were given bananas to eat. At Olivier's urging I wound the window down and threw the banana skin out only to be told (by a gleeful Olivier) that this had wrapped itself round the face of a cyclist whom we were passing at speed. I have never before confessed to this misdemeanour and I trust that no elderly French cyclists are reading this blog.

Mixed with the banana skins by the sides of the road are widgets. A widget is any small artefact that makes things work – it could be a bolt, a nut or a washer or a small plate, lever or pulley. There's a huge number of these objects on our roads all, I suppose, having fallen off vehicles. How many break-downs or, worse still, crashes have occurred because a vital widget has been lost? Think what a haul of scrap metal there would be if all the country's lost widgets were collected together. Special vehicles with powerful magnets could patrol our roads collecting the haul which could be melted down and sold to pay off the deficit. Think Osborne, the widget wonder.

And I have to say that it doesn't stop with widgets. There is an unaccountable number of discarded rubber gloves on our verges. But never in pairs.

DAY 76 Swiney to Wick

24 km (15 miles)
143 m of climb
98% completed

The top photograph shows the view over Pulteney Harbour in Wick from my B&B. The lower picture is of the harbour in the 1860s at the height of the herring trade when over 1000 boats operated out of Wick in the summer season and ten thousand migrant workers from the Highlands and elsewhere joined the locals to fish for and process the herrings, mainly by salting for the Baltic trade. Overfishing and revolutions in key markets greatly diminished the industry at the end of the nineteenth century although it limped along into the 1950s.

FROM THE BLOG
Upbeat and informative. That's me.

I have been encouraged to be more positive in these posts and instructed to include conversations with locals. Though this is the penultimate post of the walk (though not, I expect, the last word) I will try to comply. However, I would say that it was not the purpose of this walk to try to hold conversations with people in bars or cafés, I have not been in many bars or cafés except in pursuit of essential sustenance, many of the people I've met have not been local or have not had much of interest to say (apart from complaining about the weather) and I hope that I've made it clear that this walk has had its share of ups as well as downs.

I am, at the moment, in a B&B overlooking part of Wick harbour and out to the North Sea. The sun is shining, the sea is blue and all the locals that I can see are smiling. As a last B&B of the walk this is precisely what I could have hoped for, particularly since the walk this morning was in unrelieved gloom and rain. Neither the gloom nor the rain nor the sunshine was forecast - I was led to expect light cloud and dryness. I am now in an optimistic mood because the weather has improved and the outlook from my window is good, because I have located somewhere to have a meal this evening, because I've managed to get some clothes washed that will dry quite quickly, because this B&B has WiFi (so that I will easily complete this post to the blog) and, especially, because I have less than 20 miles to go tomorrow before I celebrate at JOG. I couldn't be more upbeat.

There is little enough to say about this morning's walk. I did it along the road because I was so brassed off with the weather that I wanted it to finish as soon as possible. I tramped into Wick in the pouring rain and made for the station where I stripped off the waterproofs and ate my lunch. That alone was sufficient to encourage the sun to come out so I walked around Wick, found a café and a cappuccino and read the newspaper. I have not been to Wick before and may not come here again; in the sunshine it looks reasonable enough but in the rain it would not be my holiday resort of choice. But Wickers or Wickmen or Wicks (or whatever they call themselves) look pleasant enough and I see in the guide to Caithness that Wick in the 19th century was Europe's largest herring port with 1000 boats working out of the harbour. Indeed, such was its importance that Thomas Telford, no less, redesigned the harbour which I'm looking over now.

One local accosted me as I was heading for the B&B. He was of my age I think and had probably been having a pleasant time at a bar somewhere during the morning. He had a nondescript dog with him. "Are you on a walking holiday then?" "Yes, sort of." "Are you having a look round Wick?" "Yes, I've not been here before so I thought that I'd take a walk around." "Did you know that Wick has the shortest street in the country, possibly in the world?" "Yes, I had heard that." "If you go along there you'll see Mackay's Hotel - it's where two roads meet at an apex and that's Ebenezer Street that's just 6'9" long. The Hotel is no 1 Ebenezer Place - there's a 1 on the doorway" (I am paraphrasing here - the description was a little less succinct and I think he said 9'6"). "Yes, I saw Mackay's Hotel earlier - I'll go and have another look." He was, I think, about to show me the way.

Mercifully, at that moment, a car pulled up and someone hailed my local gent - he was distracted long enough for me to make my escape. Consequently, we didn't get onto the topic of Scottish independence or the status of women in the kirk but I'm sure that he had information and views on both matters. I didn't speak to the dog.

So tomorrow is it - the last day of this walk and I do hope that the sunshine stays with me all day - it would make the whole experience that bit more memorable. If I forget to say it tomorrow, thanks for reading this and many many thanks for the comments and encouragement. The walk wouldn't have happened without all the support of all kinds and I'll always be grateful for that.

TTFN (younger readers will need to Google that).

DAY 77 **Wick to John O'Groats**

33 km (21 miles)
417 m of climb
100% completed

Right: Oil pipeline assembly tracks;
Left: Keiss Castle (built about 1595);
Below: On the approach to Duncansby
Head

FROM THE BLOG
Well, that's that then

I am pleased .. very pleased ... relieved ... very relieved ... to say that I'm here – at sunny John O'Groats which looks remarkably like Lands End. I walked, partly on the road but largely on a cliff path above a blue and glistening North Sea, to Duncansby Head (which is as far from Land End as you can get) and then on to John O'Groats where I was met by a very friendly group of Christian Aid supporters who took my photograph, bought me coffee and said some very complimentary things. I am overwhelmed by all this and the enormity of finishing the walk has yet to sink in.

I will try to write a more comprehensive post tomorrow; in the meantime I will go to bed to sleep off the physical and emotional stresses of the day

It was buttercups all the way

I don't think that this whole thing will come into focus for some time. I am neither elated nor depressed at the moment – just wanting to get home and to stop living out of a rucksack, planning routes and organising B&Bs and being a slave to the nightly blog posting. This post is just a reflection on yesterday, to bring the report of the walk to a proper conclusion. I would have written it last night but was so tired that only a very short post was feasible.

As days have gone, yesterday was one of the best – not just because I got to the end but because of my route, what I saw, the weather and how it all went. In the end it was 21 miles and, the night before, I had called the lady organising the welcome to say that I'd get to John O'Groats by 4 o'clock. Well, that turned out to be optimistic. I left Wick good and early along the A99 past Tescos and the airport and stomped up to the point where the road crossed the pipeline railway. This was a railway track built to assemble and then move long sections of oil pipeline down to the shore to be laid on the seabed connecting the rigs to land. It's derelict now but there is still a cluster of buildings at the site, presumably servicing existing pipeline installations. The access road also leads to Sinclair Bay which has a beach to dream of. It's a couple of miles of wholly unspoiled, unoccupied sand; some sun and a palm tree and you'd have a tropical paradise. Instead it's the North Sea which, yesterday, was gentle and blue.

I went from the bay through the village of Keiss and things then got more difficult. The cliff path started well enough but got less and less clearly defined and my progress became slower and slower. Parts of the path had collapsed so I had to take to the fields, climbing fences and wading through long grass though the buttercups glowed cheerfully as they had in Cornwall over two months earlier. The chances of arriving at JOG at 4pm looked increasingly remote so I gave up on the clifftop and went back to the A99 and marched northward as quickly as I could, eventually phoning to change the arrival time to 5pm. That enabled me to walk through Stirza and out onto another clifftop path that was considerably better and much more interesting.

There are geos along this coast – inlets in the cliffs, some of which go back 200 or 300 metres and are home to many nesting sea birds. They are spectacular with the clearly bedded sandstone creating shelves and stacks that make the whole very impressive. I could see the lighthouse on Duncansby Head in the distance and was able to stride across the heather and grass towards it – a very satisfying way to read a goal such as this.

There were quite a lot to people at Duncansby (there's a road out to it from JOG); they were walking the cliffs looking at nesting gannets and seals basking on rocks, walking dogs or just looking at the lighthouse. I took some photographs of myself draped over the trig point. Then it was a mile or so west along the cliff, looking across the Pentland Firth to the Orkneys, to the muddle and mess that is John O'Groats. The famous hotel is being revamped and, with its towers surrounded with scaffolding, it could be a perfect Hitchcock gothic horror film set. But my welcoming party marched over and it was wonderful to be greeted, photographed, given coffee and have the walk enthused over. I wouldn't have missed it for worlds.

I stayed the night with Christian Aid friends at Dunnet but wasn't the best of guests – I think that I was just too tired to be properly sociable. Then Jane kindly took me to Thurso this morning to get the train down to Inverness – and I was on my way home.

Arrival photographs are on the next page

DAY 77   Arrival!

Right: At the trig point at Duncansby Head, the furthest point from Lands End and with the Pentland Firth and Orkney in the background; Below: I celebrate at John O'Groats

Below: Welcomed by Christian Aid supporters at John O'Groats

These photographs by Owen Pugh

BLOG COMMENTS

My blog was started when I was doing my training walks early in 2012. From the start the posts attracted comments and I report the extent of these in Chapter 5. In this Chapter, I have incorporated some of the points made into the additional notes that I have written for some of the days of the walk. However, there are some comments that are either too large to fit in the space I have available for each day or that are not really specific to a particular day. I am putting a few of these in this footnote to Chapter 3 but I don't think that I should attempt to reproduce the great majority of the comments which were appropriate and very welcome at the time but probably don't add a great deal to this narrative of the walk.

Day 1: Encounter. A comment from Ralph and my response

Ralph: Hi. I'm the man with the Canadian or American accent. Actually it's Scottish but I have lived many years in Norway. Just on holiday in Cornwall and thought it was a pleasure to meet you. Good luck with the walk and when I get back home, there might be a small donation for your cause.

Me: Thank you for the comment and I'm sorry that my guess about your nationality was so wide of the mark. There's a lesson there somewhere. I hope that I didn't totally misrepresent our conversation and I'm grateful for your interest and even more grateful for your offer of a donation. Best wishes.

Day 26: Farewell Severn. A comment from Deri Parsons

Sorry to see you leave the Severn valley as you were walking in the footsteps of my forebears. My earliest link to the area is Henry Kirkham who died in Pattingham in 1595 - he was my 10th great grandfather. Distant cousins still live in the area and they occasionally send me old photographs of family members they unearth. The latest was one of a 3rd great grandfather on his barge taking stone from his quarry down river.

Day 28: Walsall and the 60s. Comments from Andy Marsh and me

Andy: I don't think Kate approves of all this talk of ladies and their 'attributes'... not sure if she's more put out by learning such things about her dad, or that her husband is reading it as he settles down to sleep!!

Me: The 60s as I remember them weren't all they're now cracked up to be. Either we were too old or too young or in the wrong place but our preoccupations were much the same as students everywhere - surviving the course as well as possible, having some enjoyment and getting a job at the end of it. People may have been doing unmentionable things in Hyde Park but that was another world. Men still wore flat hats.

Day 32: Greetings. A comment from John Moore

You could be more adventurous with your greetings. Regard it as a challenge to evoke a spark of life in those you meet! What Ho! How ya doin' (Mate?)! May the Blessings of the Day surround you! Trouble is, we don't need to greet each other these days. We all have what we need, we all have maps and know the way (well, apart from those who seem to get lost rather frequently by their accounts), we drive round in cars insulated from the world at large, run indoors and shut the door lest anyone asks us for a favour. We should communicate more and the more articulate and outgoing should stimulate dialogue in others. Or what's the point?

Day 36: The M62 farm. Comments from Deri Parsons and me

Deri Parsons: I know a little about this [farm in the middle of the M62] as a friend lives close by and we've visited him a few times. The commonly held myth about its odd location is that the farm was/is owned by a bloody-minded farmer who refused to sell the required land for the construction. The more prosaic truth is that the geology of the area meant that it was far cheaper to split the motorway rather than have the carriageways side-by-side. The farmer was happy to remain living in his old home.

Me: It still beggars belief that a family is willing to spend their lives in such an atrocious noise. It must go on 24 hours a day, every day and no amount of insulation could prevent some noise getting into the house. And the residents would never have the pleasure of sitting in the garden on a nice day

Deri Parsons: You'd be surprised at how regular exposure can get you habituated to noise. I was brought up in the lee of a pit and coke works and that was a real noisy environment. But it didn't intrude into life at all.

Day 40: Coins in trees. A comment from Laurie Hayward and two responses from me

Laurie Hayward: Near the NT car park, at the bottom of Aira Force, Ullswater in the Lakes is another fallen tree in which there are hundreds of coins embedded – copper and silver. I haven't been able to determine the significance or instigators.

Me: I think that http://www.northernearth.co.uk/cointree.htm gives a lot more information. Me (not added to the blog): On a very recent walk through Dovedale I saw several examples of logs with coins in them. Perhaps forestry workers are on to a good thing.

Day 42: Stiles. A comment from Dave Wood

You may have noticed whilst passing through the Peak District, that many stiles are being replaced by gates. Having installed a few I can advise that whilst they are said to increase the access for all, the main reason is that the rangers are getting older.

Day 43: Lady Anne's Highway. A comment from Jan Parsons

She was Lady Anne Clifford who was born in 1593 at Skipton Castle. She was a wee bit upset when her father didn't leave his estate to her but to her brother. Her first husband did not support her claim but her second husband did. He was the Earl of Pembroke and many buildings bear her initials AP. In 1643 she finally came into her inheritance and embarked on a massive programme of building and renovation. She rebuilt Skipton, Pendragon, Appleby, Brough and Brougham Castles and many almshouses and churches to boot. There is a 100 mile walk through places associated with our Lady Anne and that I presume is her highway. It runs through Skipton to Wharfedale and Wensleydale and finishes at Brougham Castle near Penrith where she died in 1676. She was supposed to have been a formidable lady with a real appetite for building as described. You may see her initials somewhere along your route. Ponder no more!

Deri and I first came across this lady when we first stayed near Penrith. There was a memorial to a last meeting between Lady Anne Clifford and her mother on a lonely stretch of road. It said little more than that and I was intrigued. Many years later we visited Skipton Castle and there we came across our Lady Anne again and her story was revealed. I like this lady. She wouldn't let the injustice of her times deny her her birthright – as she saw it. She fought and fought until she won.

Day 43: Sculpture. Deri Parsons' comment and a note from me

Deri Parsons: The sculpture is, I believe, called the Water Cut and was erected to commemorate the Millenium. Can't recall the artist but I'm sure Google would reveal.

Me: Google did reveal: This is one of 10 sculptures by different artists placed along the valley of the River Eden. It is by Mary Bourne, carved from Cumbrian Salterwath limestone. Initially the two halves looked different as one had been exposed to weather for longer prior to carving. Now they have weathered down to match each other. It is shaped rather like a tombstone riven from top to bottom by a serpentine space representing the river.

Day 49: Salomon boots. A comment from Emilie Sigel in the USA

My brother hiking on the Appalachian Trail (eastern USA) is wearing Salomons. After 1200 miles he literally wore them out, and a new pair was shipped gratis to him on the trail. The company apparently stands behind their product even unto the extreme.

Day 66: Cairngorms. A comment from John Roynon

For me your description of your route through the Cairngorms Mountains from Blair Atholl to Aviemore revives some happy memories from my youthful pedalling days when one summer I cycled around Scotland starting in Glasgow looping up to Inverness and back via Aviemore and the not so busy A9 (no fancy bike trails in those days), but with a respite at the YHA hostel by Loch Morlich. This provided me with the opportunity to hike (in fine weather) to summits of Cairn Gorm and Ben Macdui which served as ample compensation for poor weather that had preventing me from being able to "summit" Ben Nevis the previous week.

Your route through these mountains sounds wonderful - I just hope for your sake you have fine weather - it's a sweltering 35°C and dry here in Toronto - too bad we cannot do a transfer - a bit of your precipitation in exchange for a few degrees Celsius. Be sure to take a picture of the waterfall at Linn of Dee.

Happy camping!

Day 73: Golf. A comment from Cris Rainbow and my response

Cris Rainbow: Rob is getting a bit concerned about a certain lack of respect for the noble game reflected in your blog!

Me: I acknowledge my lack of enthusiasm for golf which seems to use up a lot of space with little to show for it. I think that I know that Cris's husband understands this.

Chapter 4

It's not finished yet

The last blog posting

Shortly after returning form the walk I started work on this book whilst trying to pick up the threads of my normal life. Within the first week I posted my last blog entry; here are some extracts from it.

FROM THE BLOG
Aftermath

I've been home for a week and the walk seems like another world as I adjust to the more everyday issues that have piled up whilst I was away. It is ironic that, as soon as I got back, the weather improved across most of Britain, to the point where I now feel the need to re-acclimatise.

I more or less closed this blog a week ago, not intending to write any more. But things have moved on a bit and I thought that I needed to share some of the developments of the past week. I won't keep doing this – without the collection of new experiences to write about every day it's not easy to compile new posts and I will probably become quite boring if I try.

...

To my surprise a welcome back party had been organised for me at our community centre which is a superannuated Victorian school. I wasn't supposed to know about it and was to be enticed there on some pretext, to be confronted by masses of local supporters. Inevitably, I did hear about it but was still overwhelmed by the number of people who came and the degree of enthusiasm that they showed. It was a rather wonderful evening which added (through new donations and the proceeds of a raffle) more than £500 to the sponsorship and boosted my ego (and my level of embarrassment) very considerably. It's made me look at the walk in a new light – seeing all the people who have donated, given encouragement, offered supporting prayers, stood in for me whilst I was away, given me accommodation, read and contributed to the blog and in many other ways, as collaborators in a jointly owned project. I may have been doing the walking but I no longer think that I own the walk. It's a good feeling.

...

And finally ... someone has said that they'd like a picture of the feet that walked more than 1750 km. I'm not about to indulge this sort of fetish – here is a picture of the left foot which performed well; the picture of the right foot has been withheld as a punishment and to protect the innocent.

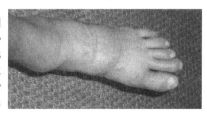

The money raised

By the end of 2012 the sum raised from donations (including Gift Aid) was well past the £10,000 target. However, the owners of the Just Giving website will take a small sum to cover expenses (the basis of this is explained on the site). I list the donors in Chapter 5 where there is also other information about the costs of the walk.

The panel opposite has been provided by Christian Aid. It was never the intention to itemise the spending of the money raised from the walk and, whilst the work in Sierra Leone was used to highlight the need for support for education in developing countries, it was always possible that some of the money raised would be used on other similar education projects elsewhere. What the panel does provide is an idea of the types of expenditure involved in supporting education so giving us a fairly precise picture of how the walk money will eventually be spent. What is clear is that, although the details of educational need vary somewhat from country to country, the broad areas where monetary support is needed are very similar and all stem from the effects of poverty that afflicts individuals, communities and governments.

My hope is that donations from those who enjoy this book will push the total well beyond the £10,000 target so that we can further enhance the impact that this walk has had.

What have we learned?

There is a very short list of messages that I would like to take from this experience and offer to anyone contemplating something similar.

- If you are fund-raising, establish a close contact with your charity as early as possible. Set a target that you believe you can achieve, though not too low as it may become a ceiling that you cannot easily break through.

- Do not under-estimate the amount of advance work you will need to do in order to set up an efficient way of managing and maximising donations.

- Be honest about what the activity will cost you personally; can you afford to do it?

- The success of the activity will depend as much (or perhaps a lot more) on your mental attitude as on your fitness.

- Isolating yourself from normal day-to-day concerns and concentrating on the activity may be the only way of managing the pressures that it will bring.

- That isolation will probably demand a considerable amount of support from someone else who will need to be as committed as you are.

- Develop plans for the activity only to the point where you are confident that you have covered all the angles. Over-planning may be as damaging as under-planning.

- Be prepared to answer the same basic questions (such as "How are your feet?") over and over again!

Where the money will go

It's too early to be able to update the news about the support that Christian Aid is giving to education in Sierra Leone. However, we can use another example from Africa that shows the way in which money is being spent to improve educational opportunities; this is from **Sudan** and illustrates the way in which money raised in the UK and elsewhere is translated into local action by a local partner.

Mundri Relief and Development Association (MDRA) was set up in 1991, seven years after Sudan's second civil war began, to provide relief for people affected by the conflict and to support education and agriculture in Mundri county, Western Equatoria. Christian Aid began supporting MRDA four years later and continues to have a strong partnership with them – even inspiring their own fundraising week which has raised money to pay for a community library and a clinic for young children. The focus of Christian Aid's support is on supporting teacher training and improving school infrastructure.

Here are some examples of how money is being spent (showing cost per item, not total spent).

- A six month teacher training course to improve teaching quality for one teacher - £596
- Classroom construction in a school in southern Sudan - £4820
- Desks for 50 children - £1500
- A three month English course for one teacher returning from Arabic-speaking north Sudan to improve their confidence teaching in English, the medium of all schools in southern Sudan - £320
- Training a school's Parent Teacher Association so that they can take responsibility for looking after the school and fundraising - £400
- A session with a Parents Teacher Association to raise awareness of the importance of educating girls - £51
- Rehabilitating a school kitchen to ensure a school has a good standard kitchen allowing them to secure World Food Programme support for school feeding - £1,067
- Rehabilitating a school latrine to maintain pupils' health and encourage older girls to stay in school - £800

Another example ... education politics in the Caribbean

Christian Aid is also continuing to invest in the *4% for education* campaign in the Dominican Republic. Just 2.3% of its GDP is spent on education, compared to 12% in the UK and 6% in other Latin American countries. In 2010 Christian Aid spent £10,000 on helping partner organisation Centro Montalvo build the 4% campaign. By May 2012 all presidential candidates had signed the pledge to fulfil the mandate of 4% if successful in the election. Continued investment is needed to follow up on those pledges and ensure that the Dominican Republic gets the investment in education it so clearly needs.

Was it all worthwhile?

I have no doubts that the answer is 'yes' on all counts. At a personal level and despite the weather and my various ailments I know that I gained more from the experience than the effort that I put into it. It enabled me to re-connect with a lot of people whom I'd lost touch with, to connect with friends and family in a new way and to meet a whole new set of people. Doubts about whether I could manage it dissipated quite early on in the walk and I gained levels of confidence that I haven't felt for some years. The walk enabled me to have a private personal space that I could probably not have achieved in any other way and it has given me an experience that is absolutely unique and absolutely personal. I am still reflecting on the impact that the time by myself has had on my beliefs and will need some time to come to terms with this.

I am relieved that we have now exceeded the monetary target that I set (see page 192). I know that I would have been secretly disappointed and that my self-esteem would have taken a knock if I'd fallen far short of that and I'm confident that the money raised will be used in a constructive way. In the context of the need it is a drop in the ocean but I believe that it's the best that I can do for the time being. Whether I'll make this kind of effort again I don't know though I'm fairly certain that another end-to-end walk would not have the same feeling of personal discovery and adventure about it.

At several points in this book I have claimed that this was not just my walk, attracting a lot of support, but a joint enterprise amongst a community of people. I don't think that I came to this perception until after the walk had finished and I realised how much interest, support and effort it had engendered. Of course, this wasn't a community effort in the sense that people living in one area might club together to support a common cause. Here we have people who don't know one another who have been willing to be involved in one way or another because they felt that this walk was worth doing and worth supporting. I certainly don't know all the members of this community and I know that several of those who have donated or otherwise supported this walk don't know me personally.

I have to say that I find this a very enjoyable and refreshing idea. I'm sure that it's not the first time that it has happened and I'm sure that it will happen again since, as a species, we have learned that co-operation and collaboration are more rewarding than competition. So, whilst children in Sierra Leone (or somewhere else with similar needs) are the most obvious beneficiaries, members of our temporary and disparate community can, I hope, celebrate the success and personal rewards of our joint efforts.

One of the purposes of this book was to make a record of the walk that would both identify the achievement and provide a source of information that could be of use to others who were contemplating something similar. To everyone in that position I can say: don't hesitate, you should go for it, enjoy yourself and we all wish you the best of luck.

Chapter 5

Thanks, facts and statistics

This is the chapter with all the small details that, taken together, form the backbone of the walk. It's also the chapter where I finally say 'thank you' to those people who became involved in this walk and whom I've mentioned in the text of the earlier chapters. I hope that I don't leave anyone out and I hope that I have already given personal thanks to everyone listed here. If not, please accept my apologies and please let me know.

Thanks for the help

Before I started the walk I put these two acknowledgements on my website.

I was thinking about doing this walk for some years before I made the commitment to do it, late last year. It started out as a walk to fulfil my own ambitions and then became a walk to support the education of children in the developing world. But it might never have happened had I not been inspired by the end-to-end walk of Nancy and John Eckersley in 2011, also for Christian Aid's work in Sierra Leone. I've never met them, but it seemed an example worth following! I was also shamed into the effort by the example of a long-standing friend and colleague, Bob Rainbow, who accompanied his son and a friend on a LEJOG cycle ride last year. If he could do it, so could I! And finally, I do the walk remembering one of the world's good guys and a good friend; the late Dave Lukes did the cycle ride for charity a few years ago and stayed with Viv and I on the first leg through Cornwall.

There are many people that I want to thank for their help with this walk. I'm writing this a few weeks before I start and I will be adding my appreciation for the help of others as I near departure date.

My commitment to this walk probably surprised my family, but they've accepted it without question or reservation and I'm very grateful for this. Viv will be providing backup from home and Ian, Kate, Ruth and Andy have given help in many ways as I've been preparing for the walk. At Stoke Climsland, Deri Parsons and Peter Hammond have very kindly taken on extra work to cover for my absence and many others have offered good wishes and support. Kathryn Carnegie at Stoke Climsland Parish Church has enthusiastically committed to publicising the walk as part of the church's work for Christian Aid week and this has been an enormous encouragement for which I'm very grateful.

Helen Burgess and Martin John Nicholls in the Exmouth office of Christian Aid were enthusiastic right from the start and have provided all the information I needed to support my fund raising and have made a host of arrangements to link my efforts into those of other people. This introduced a whole new dimension and has added immense value to the idea of the walk.

With the kind help of their Community Champion Alan Woollcombe, Tesco in Callington, Cornwall has generously paid for some of the consumables for my walk (such as clothing, first aid supplies, batteries and food items). I also am very appreciative of the help that Alan has given with publicity for my walk.

Now the walk is finished I can complete this vote of thanks.

More than anyone else, my wife Viv provided support and help in the planning of the walk, in managing our home, the cash and the communications while I was away and in bringing the walk to the attention of a lot of people that I barely know but whose support has been enormously welcome. The walk would never have happened without Viv's support. And that goes for our children Ian and Kate and their partners Ruth and Andy who gave moral and specific support from afar; in particular, I am very grateful for Andy's help with checking and proofreading.

And, while on the subject of proofreading, I am very grateful for the help and support that Helen Burgess of Christian Aid gave during my walk, for her help with additional material for this book and her comments and ideas as the book took shape.

In Stoke Climsland, Derrick Parsons and Peter Hammond took over my role in producing *The Old School News* and the Trustees of The Old School and members of the Parish Council covered for my absence. I have particular gratitude for the way in which the Trustees and Edah Joll and their co-conspirators organised the welcome home party at The Old School which was an evening of real joy.

Also at home in Stoke Climsland, Kathryn Carnegie and others at the parish church continued to publicise the walk and organise the collection of donations to the cause. Staff at the Exmouth office of Christian Aid continued their support which included organising my send-off at Lands End and my welcomes at both John O'Groats and Plymouth as well as circulating information to local papers, in Christian Aid News and on the Christian Aid website.

I was very pleased to have the help given by John Moore and other fellow-students from the 1960s who circulated information amongst those who were at college with us and who have followed the walk and commented on the blog.

And that goes for everyone who contributed to the blog - your support was very welcome, very interesting and good fun.

John Moore also put me in touch with Richard Franklin of Arima Publishing who patiently dealt with all my enquiries and has given me help and encouragement in preparing this book; for this I am most grateful.

To everybody, many thanks and I do hope that you all feel that it was well worth while.

Help with accommodation

I am very grateful to the following Christian Aid supporters and personal friends who gave me overnight accommodation for 1 or 2 nights during the walk.

Doreen & Tony White, Fraddon, Cornwall

Dee Edwards and Dave Williams, Luxulyan, Cornwall

Jenny & Neon Reynolds, Bridestowe, Devon

Richard Law, Tedburn St Mary, Devon

Judy & Keith Norwood, Nailsea, Somerset

Jane & Laurie Hayward, Filton, Bristol

Shirley & Matt Welsh, Cam, Gloucestershire

Rosemary & Mike Ellis, Gloucester

Sue & Kevin Cowen, Kidderminster, Worcestershire

Ruth & Andrew Stilton, Blakeshall, Worcestershire

Anne & David Jones, Wolverhampton

Chris & Robert Ray, Abbots Bromley, Staffordshire

Marie & Julian Raffay, Churchtown, Sheffield

Jenny Walker, Carlton, North Yorkshire (at the Foresters Arms)

Rev Roger Collinson, Appleby, Cumbria

Jo & Tony Pennell, Nenthead, Cumbria

Lesley & Robert Theobald, Stocksfield, Northumberland

Betty & Bob Scott, Innerleithen, Borders

Jane & James Coll, Dunnet, Caithness

In the blog and elsewhere in this book I have said how much I appreciated my send off at Land End, my reception on arriving at John O'Groats and my welcome at Plymouth Station, all from Christian Aid supporters. Their willingness to turn out to meet a perfect stranger and the pleasure that they showed in being involved in the walk was very rewarding and I will always remember this with pleasure and deep appreciation.

Donors

The list that follows is of the donors whose names we know and who have donated either on the website or directly to us, as at January 2013. Donors who made more than one donation are included once only in this list. The Anonymous donations include individual donors and the collection during the pre-walk session at Tesco, Callington.

Val Adamson
Pauline Ager
Boz, Mark and Charlie Allen
Bob Anderson
David Andrew
Peter Andrews
John and Sim Bailey
Hugh Baker
Ann Baldwin
Ann and Ray Barnes
Anna Barnett
Susan Bell
Gordon Berrie
Dan and Denise Birkett
Patrick Boylan
Roger Boysen
Patricia Broadfoot
John and Joan Brown
Jane Browne-Clayton
Mrs Bruce
Nancy Bruna
M G Bullen
Diana and Luc Bujold
David and Chrys Bundy
Neil Burden
Peter and Lois Burke
Bryan and Sandra Bushell
Helen Cadiot
Ruth Cadiot
Adrian Carey
Alastair Carnegie
Lisa and Robert Chaffer
Brian and Pauline Champness
Michael Clements
Roger A Collinson
Barbara Cooper
Jane Coumbe
Kevin Cowen
Tim Court
Michael and Brigitte Cox
Ann Craig

David Crawley
John Curtis-Rouse
Diana and Vernon Daniel
Emma Davies
Fred G Davies
Robert Davies
Jo Deeley
Lloyd and Anne Down
Mrs Downer
Kay Dunleavy
Helen and Graham Dunster
Rosemary and Michael Ellis
Marilyn Elliott
Per Evans
Christine Ford
Andrew Fromant
Gordon Gerrie
Sarah Gregson
June Grindley
Alistair Guy
Margaret Harris
Laurie and Jane Hayward
Christine Haywood
Reg and Sylvia Hamley
Wynne Harlen
Pamela Hasell
Margaret and John Herod
Rob and Helen Hopkins
Hilary Howarth
Russ Humphrey
Indian Queens Methodist Church
Barrie James
Angela Jenkins
Kam Johal
Edah Joll
Mary Jones
Mary Joshi
Josie Kells
Phillipa Kells
Clive Kidman
Naomi King

Tim Kingston
Lanlivery Parish
Richard Law
S Leonard-Williams
Steve Lewis
Alan and Helen Lewis
Diana Lewis
Dennis Long
Jill Long
Eileen Lukes
Nicola Lukes
Sheila Macintosh
Jane and David Maher
Sarah Mansbridge
Andy Marsh
Ann Matthews
Pauline McKenzie
Claire and Bob McWilliam
Noel Mitchell
John Moore
Roger Murphy
Leora Murray
Grace Myerscough-Tournoff
Dominic Nelson
Ruth Nevill
Judy and Keith Norwood
Ruth Oaks
Old Fairfieldians Society
Old School raffle proceeds
Ann Paddon
Nicholas John Dennis Parkin
Jan and Deri Parsons
Bernice Pegler
Allen and Judith Pengelly
The Printing Press
Dea Price
Owen Pugh
Rosy and John Plumb
Cristina and Robert Rainbow
Jane Rawson
Mr A Ramage
Richard's Ramblers
Val and Roger Robertson
June Rogers
David Royle
John and Jean Roynon
Arminell Rule
David Rycroft

Robert Scott
Tom Scott
Margaret and David Seward
John and Chris Shepherd
David Short
Maureen Sibbons
M Sierre
Tracy Sisson
Colin Smith
Iain Smith
Mrs H Smith
Margaret and Geoff Smith
Megan Smith
Sallie Smith
Hugh South
Alan and Val Spargo
Caroline Starkey
David StPierre
Sheila Stipling
Robert and Lesley Theobald
Harry Tolley
Lesley Tranter
Sue Tudor
Graham and Jenny Turner
Jennifer Tuson
Hilary Twist
Rita Vickers
David Vowles
Jenny Walker
Paul Warmington
Amanda Weld-Blundell
Sandra West
William Pengelly Cave Studies Trust
Dave Williams
John and Annette Willis
Bob Willmott
Kate Wilmut
Mabel Wilmut
Avril and Michael Wilmut
Vicki and Richard Wilmut
Ann Wilson
Betty Wilton
John Winkley
David Wood
Don and Miriam Wright
Sarah Wright
Anonymous (8 donations)

Statistics of the route

Date	Day	Day No	From	To	Distance km	miles
2 May 2012	Wed	1	Lands End	Penzance	17.32	10.76
3 May 2012	Thu	2	Penzance	Four Lanes	30.65	19.04
4 May 2012	Fri	3	Four Lanes	Truro	20.23	12.57
5 May 2012	Sat	4	Truro	Fraddon	21.70	13.48
6 May 2012	Sun	5	Fraddon	Nanstallon	19.43	12.07
7 May 2012	Mon	6	Nanstallon	Camelford	25.17	15.64
8 May 2012	Tue	7	Camelford	Launceston	27.86	17.31
9 May 2012	Wed	8	rest day	at home		
10 May 2012	Thu	9	Launceston	Bridestowe	22.56	14.02
11 May 2012	Fri	10	Bridestowe	West Gooseford	25.88	16.08
12 May 2012	Sat	11	West Gooseford	Crediton	23.74	14.75
13 May 2012	Sun	12	Crediton	Tiverton	25.47	15.83
14 May 2012	Mon	13	Tiverton	Thorne St Margaret	24.08	14.96
15 May 2012	Tue	14	Thorne St Margaret	Taunton	17.33	10.77
16 May 2012	Wed	15	rest day	Taunton		
17 May 2012	Thu	16	Taunton	Cossington	33.41	20.76
18 May 2012	Fri	17	Cossington	Axbridge	21.81	13.55
19 May 2012	Sat	18	Axbridge	Nailsea	21.16	13.15
20 May 2012	Sun	19	Nailsea	Almondsbury	30.44	18.91
21 May 2012	Mon	20	Almondsbury	Berkeley Road	30.47	18.93
22 May 2012	Tue	21	Berkeley Road	Gloucester	30.11	18.71
23 May 2012	Wed	22	rest day	Gloucester		
24 May 2012	Thu	23	Gloucester	Tewkesbury	15.71	9.76
25 May 2012	Fri	24	Tewkesbury	Worcester	30.46	18.93
26 May 2012	Sat	25	Worcester	Blackstone	30.38	18.88
27 May 2012	Sun	26	Blackstone	Blakeshall	17.06	10.60
28 May 2012	Mon	27	Blakeshall	Nurton	25.79	16.03
29 May 2012	Tue	28	Nurton	Penkridge	25.86	16.07
30 May 2012	Wed	29	Penkridge	Abbots Bromley	31.26	19.42
31 May 2012	Thu	30	Abbots Bromley	Ashbourne	33.09	20.56
1 Jun 2012	Fri	31	rest day	Ashbourne		
2 Jun 2012	Sat	32	Ashbourne	Youlgreave	33.61	20.89
3 Jun 2012	Sun	33	Youlgreave	Hathersage	25.99	16.15
4 Jun 2012	Mon	34	Hathersage	Flouch Inn	31.34	19.47

Cumulative Distance		% done	Height gain[1]	Height loss[1]	Terrain /km[2]			Times /hh:mm[3]		
km	miles		m	m	tracks	minor roads	A/B roads	Start	Finish	Walk
17.32	10.76	1	332	367	10.9	4.3	2.1	11:28	16:00	04:32
47.78	29.68	3	481	283	13.1	15.1	2.5	07:41	15:39	07:58
68.01	42.25	4	285	478	10.6	8.8	0.8	08:24	14:20	05:56
89.71	55.73	5	416	312	3.9	17.3	0.5	07:43	13:59	06:16
109.14	67.80	6	316	403	9.6	9.1	0.7	07:45	13:52	06:07
134.31	83.44	8	504	321	19.5	4.9	0.8	08:00	15:22	07:22
162.17	100.75	9	417	466	7.4	19.5	1.0	07:39	15:21	07:42
184.73	114.77	11	422	392	5.9	15.4	1.3	07:53	13:54	06:01
210.61	130.85	12	535	482	14.8	10.9	0.2	08:34	16:39	08:05
234.35	145.60	13	343	534	6.4	15.4	1.9	08:18	14:46	06:28
259.82	161.43	15	539	513	10.1	13.7	1.7	08:21	16:12	07:51
283.90	176.39	16	231	188	21.5	2.6	0.0	08:05	15:13	07:08
301.23	187.16	17	98	180	12.2	4.3	0.8	08:19	12:45	04:26
334.64	207.92	19	147	138	21.8	10.8	0.8	08:04	16:16	08:12
356.45	221.47	20	138	162	13.4	7.7	0.7	08:01	13:25	05:24
377.61	234.62	22	235	222	17.8	2.0	1.4	08:24	15:21	06:57
408.05	253.53	23	526	471	22.6	5.0	2.8	08:08	16:21	08:13
438.52	272.46	25	177	229	14.7	11.5	4.3	08:15	17:00	08:45
468.63	291.17	27	108	129	22.5	6.5	1.1	08:05	17:34	09:29[4]
484.34	300.93	28	83	82	14.3	1.4	0.0	08:49	13:50	05:01
514.80	319.86	29	156	144	25.2	3.3	2.0	07:36	16:43	09:07
545.18	338.74	31	216	213	29.1	0.2	1.1	06:15	14:36	08:21
562.24	349.34	32	339	260	13.9	3.2	0.0	09:15	15:06	05:51
588.03	365.37	34	379	353	20.3	4.9	0.6	07:06	14:18	07:12
613.89	381.44	35	196	244	21.1	4.3	0.5	08:05	14:46	06:41
645.15	400.86	37	210	176	28.0	2.6	0.7	07:30	16:10	08:40
678.24	421.42	39	362	353	22.6	8.0	2.5	07:47	17:11	09:24
711.85	442.31	41	691	643	25.6	7.1	0.9	07:44	16:09	8:25
737.84	458.46	42	586	603	21.3	3.8	0.9	07:44	15:15	07:31
769.18	477.93	44	954	824	28.6	1.3	1.4	06:40	16:30	09:50

Date	Day	Day No	From	To	Distance km	miles
5 Jun 2012	Tue	35	Flouch Inn	Marsden	27.04	16.80
6 Jun 2012	Wed	36	Marsden	Hebden Bridge	27.09	16.83
7 Jun 2012	Thu	37	Hebden Bridge	Haworth	13.49	8.39
8 Jun 2012	Fri	38	Haworth	Ilkley	20.34	12.64
9 Jun 2012	Sat	39	rest day	Bradford		
10 Jun 2012	Sun	40	Ilkley	Pateley Bridge	33.83	21.02
11 Jun 2012	Mon	41	Pateley Bridge	Carlton	27.73	17.23
12 Jun 2012	Tue	42	Carlton	Hawes	25.68	15.95
13 Jun 2012	Wed	43	Hawes	Kirkby Stephen	26.11	16.23
14 Jun 2012	Thu	44	Kirkby Stephen	Appleby	24.68	15.34
15 Jun 2012	Fri	45	Appleby	Dufton	6.65	4.13
16 Jun 2012	Sat	46	Dufton	Nenthead	29.08	18.07
17 Jun 2012	Sun	47	Nenthead	Allendale Town	18.33	11.39
18 Jun 2012	Mon	48	rest day			
19 Jun 2012	Tue	49	Allendale Town	Haltwhistle	25.33	15.74
20 Jun 2012	Wed	50	Haltwhistle	The Eals	34.10	21.19
21 Jun 2012	Thu	51	The Eals	Byrness	24.51	15.23
22 Jun 2012	Fri	52	Byrness	Jedburgh	29.63	18.41
23 Jun 2012	Sat	53	Jedburgh	Melrose	23.16	14.39
24 Jun 2012	Sun	54	rest day	Melrose		
25 Jun 2012	Mon	55	Melrose	Traquair	28.29	17.58
26 Jun 2012	Tue	56	Traquair	West Linton	33.51	20.82
27 Jun 2012	Wed	57	West Linton	East Calder	20.54	12.76
28 Jun 2012	Thu	58	East Calder	Dunfermline	25.51	15.85
29 Jun 2012	Fri	59	Dunfermline	Kinross	22.84	14.19
30 Jun 2012	Sat	60	Kinross	Perth	31.94	19.85
1 Jul 2012	Sun	61	rest day	Perth		
2 Jul 2012	Mon	62	Perth	Birnam	27.50	17.09
3 Jul 2012	Tue	63	Birnam	Pitlochry	23.64	14.69
4 Jul 2012	Wed	64	Pitlochry	Blair Athol	10.93	6.79
5 Jul 2012	Thu	65	Blair Athol	Chest of Dee	32.95	20.47
6 Jul 2012	Fri	66	Chest of Dee	Aviemore	28.40	17.65
7 Jul 2012	Sat	67	Aviemore	Carr Bridge	16.79	10.43
8 Jul 2012	Sun	68	Carr Bridge	Inverness	39.42	24.49
9 Jul 2012	Mon	69	rest day	Inverness		

Cumulative Distance		% done	Height gain[1]	Height loss[1]	Terrain /km²			Times /hh:mm[3]		
km	miles		m	m	tracks	minor roads	A/B roads	Start	Finish	Walk
796.22	494.73	46	559	653	23.1	2.2	1.7	08:09	16:30	08:21
823.31	511.56	47	903	920	19.9	5.9	1.3	07:58	17:40	09:42
836.80	519.95	48	414	403	6.9	5.2	1.4	08:55	12:53	03:58
857.14	532.59	49	536	619	14.2	3.9	2.2	08:56	15:52	06:56
890.97	553.61	51	573	550	23.7	7.2	2.9	08:25	17:58	09:33
918.70	570.84	53	744	604	21.7	5.7	0.3	08:44	17:51	09:07
944.38	586.79	54	507	531	5.9	17.5	2.3	08:07	15:47	07:40
970.49	603.02	55	480	543	21.9	1.6	2.6	08:38	16:33	07:55
995.17	618.36	57	465	495	10.0	14.7	0.0	07:45	16:05	08:20
1001.82	622.49	57	131	91	0.0	6.7	0.0	07:07	08:35	01:28
1030.90	640.56	59	911	689	20.4	8.7	0.0	07:47	16:36	08:49
1049.23	651.95	60	377	543	1.3	15.5	1.5	08:45	13:03	04:18
1074.56	667.69	61	479	526	12.9	11.3	1.1	08:34	17:12	08:38
1108.66	688.88	63	551	611	24.3	9.3	0.5	07:38	18:05	10:27
1133.17	704.11	65	567	484	19.1	5.4	0.0	09:11	15:57	06:46
1162.80	722.52	66	682	811	17.6	11.6	0.4	06:47	16:21	09:34
1185.96	736.91	68	502	504	9.7	10.0	3.5	08:28	16:01	07:33
1214.25	754.49	69	953	884	26.8	1.4	0.1	08:00	16:00	08:00
1247.76	775.31	71	820	744	18.3	0.0	15.2	08:59	18:39	09:40
1268.30	788.07	72	329	451	10.3	7.2	3.0	08:10	13:25	05:15
1293.81	803.92	74	267	325	17.5	2.1	5.9	08:30	14:48	06:18
1316.65	818.11	75	366	309	1.9	16.6	4.3	08:15	13:46	05:31
1348.59	837.96	77	414	500	14.9	8.0	9.0	08:11	16:21	08:10
1376.09	855.05	79	264	232	14.9	6.0	6.6	07:41	14:00	06:19
1399.73	869.74	80	473	435	4.9	7.8	10.9	08:20	14:16	05:56
1410.66	876.53	81	168	131	0.7	0.0	10.2	09:17	11:49	02:32
1443.61	897.00	83	666	364	31.7	1.1	0.2	07:49	17:11	09:22
1472.01	914.65	84	477	705	25.6	0.7	2.1	06:00	15:51	09:51
1488.80	925.08	85	208	161	10.0	5.2	1.6	08:21	13:31	05:10
1528.22	949.57	87	452	678	10.9	14.2	14.3	08:24	17:27	09:03

Date	Day	Day No	From	To	Distance km	miles
10 Jul 2012	Tue	70	Inverness	Dingwall	26.93	16.72
11 Jul 2012	Wed	71	Dingwall	Invergordon	24.01	14.92
12 Jul 2012	Thu	72	Invergordon	Dornoch	30.32	18.83
13 Jul 2012	Fri	73	Dornoch	Brora	30.83	19.16
14 Jul 2012	Sat	74	Brora	Helmsdale	18.68	11.61
15 Jul 2012	Sun	75	Helmsdale	Swiney	33.64	20.90
16 Jul 2012	Mon	76	Swiney	Wick	23.78	14.78
17 Jul 2012	Tue	77	Wick	John O'Groats	33.33	20.71

total distance	1749.93	1087.32

Christian Aid Week

Bank Holidays

total days	77	
walking days	68	
rest days	9	
average distance/day	25.73	15.99
longest daily distance	39.42	24.49
shortest daily distance	6.65	4.13

1 The height gains and losses are computed by adding together the gains or losses in altitude between successive waypoints. The results are approximate since the figure does depend on the intervals between the waypoints; two waypoints a long distance apart may show, for example, zero height gain but conceal a hump between them. Most of my waypoints were taken at 2 minute intervals so the errors should be small.

2 It is difficult to get clear distinctions between tracks, minor roads and major roads. I have taken minor roads to be those shown in yellow on OS maps and tracks to be paths shown as such or roads shown in white, a few of which may have been laid with tarmac. A few minor roads were gravel roads but most had tarmac surfaces. Some B roads had very little

Cumulative Distance		% done	Height gain[1]	Height loss[1]	Terrain /km²			Times /hh:mm[3]		
km	miles		m	m	tracks	minor roads	A/B roads	Start	Finish	Walk
1555.15	966.29	89	304	334	6.0	18.9	2.0	08:53	15:25	06:32
1579.16	981.21	90	233	232	0.0	11.9	12.1	07:53	14:44	06:51
1609.48	1000.04	92	261	263	1.5	19.2	9.6	07:42	15:16	07:34
1640.31	1019.20	94	244	235	14.6	8.3	7.9	08:23	16:12	07:49
1658.99	1030.81	95	245	245	3.5	2.2	13.0	08:46	12:55	04:09
1692.63	1051.71	97	637	580	0.0	0.0	33.6	08:18	16:33	08:15
1716.41	1066.49	98	143	207	0.0	0.0	23.8	08:47	13:28	04:41
1749.74	1087.20	100	417	417	16.2	5.3	11.8	08:11	16:40	08:29
1749.93	1087.32	100		sum	991.6	503.4	254.9	total time	493:27	
				%	56.7	28.8	14.6			
	total climb		28144	28174						

traffic, most of the A/B road walking shown was in Scotland and some was on pavements or in cycle lanes. It would be reasonable to say that approximately 85% of the walk was on paths and virtually traffic-free minor roads and 15% was road walking.

3   Some of these times are approximate. The total time walking (including short stops) was 493 hours spread over 68 days; this is an average of 7¼ hours per day. The average speed over the whole walk was 3.6 kph or 2.2 mph. This average speed generally increased over the period of the walk by about 0.4 kph or 0.25 mph, probably largely due to the higher incidence of road walking in the later stages.

4   Day 21 included a break of 1½ - 2 hours at Frampton on Severn

The full spreadsheet upon which this table is based can be downloaded from http://www.wilmut.net/lejogbook/walkendfile.xls/

Equipment list

	item	weight (g)	notes
basics	Osprey Talon 44 rucksack	1110	
	liner	80	strong plastic sack
	rucksack cover	150	lightweight nylon
	Silva compass + whistle	120	
	Blizzard emergency bag	370	
	500ml water bottle + water	610	
	spare bootlaces	20	
accessories	sewing kit/safety pins/strong plastic bags	80	
	pens/paper/elastic bands/chequebook/cards	250	
	OS maps (cut down)	580	average weight
	Meridian map case	100	
	printed direction sheets	50	average weight
clothing	North Face waterproof jacket	510	
	Mountain Equipment waterproof trousers	660	
	Grasmere ankle gaiters	110	
	sweater	420	
	bush hat	70	
	spare outer socks	80	Tesco
	Coolmax liner inner socks	50	
	spare T shirt	40	
	indoor light trousers	330	Tesco
	underpants + handkerchief	40	
	trainers	580	Tesco
	washing liquid	150	for hand-washing clothes
medical/ toiletries	towel	120	Trektowel
	basic toiletries + bag	380	
	ibuprofen/paracetamol; Compeed blister pack; plasters; micropore tape; Rennies; antiseptic cream; bite cream; stretch bandage (2); small bandages (2); support bandages; water tablets; ear plugs; midge repellant	520	total weight with First Aid bag
	contact lens fluid/lenses case and glasses case	240	

electrical	head torch	230	including batteries
	Pentax Option L40 camera + charger	370	including battery, sd card
	small gorillapod	50	
	mobile phone + charger[1]	140	
	T-Mobile 3G dongle	40	
	Sony audio recorder	85	including batteries
	Samsung N145 netbook + sleeve & charger	1460	
	Garmon etrex10 GPS	160	including batteries
	Kindle (basic type) + case	220	
	spare batteries	170	
	memory stick	30	
	various cables	150	
food	emergency food bars + lunch	500	variable weight
TOTAL		11425	
wearing/ carrying in pockets	Mountainlife walking trousers	640	could be used as shorts
	boots[2]	1460	Salomon Mens Quest 4D GTX
	walking poles	500	
	T shirt, underpants, socks	210	
	small knife/scissors	40	small Leatherman
	watch, money, wallet with credit & debit cards/YHA card/NT + EH cards/railcard	300	
TOTAL		3150	
camping	North Face Mountain Marathon tent	1690	
	Berghaus Flare 850 sleeping bag	920	lightweight 1-2 season bag
	silk sleeping bag liner	120	
	Thermarest sleeping mat	740	
	Outlander stove	160	
	Coleman 250 gas cylinder	360	
	pots + cup	180	
	cutlery	20	
	gas lighter	100	
TOTAL		3990	

1 This phone was a replacement bought in Newcastle; it replaced a failing phone that weighed 320 g
2 These were the replacement boots; the first (Berghaus Explorer Trek GTX) pair weighed 1260 g

List of B&Bs

This list does not provide full details of each B&B but, probably without exception, these can be found on the internet, usually by Googling the place name + 'guesthouses' or 'accommodation'.

Day	B&B
1	Keigwin House, Penzance TR18 4LZ
2	Loscombe House, Four Lanes TR16 6LP
3	Truro Lodge, Truro TR1 1QE
5	Countryman Hotel, Camelford PL32 9XA
10	Gooseford Farm, Whiddon Down EX20 2QQ
12	Bridge Guest House, Tiverton EX16 6PE
13	Thorne Manor, Thorne St Margaret TA21 0EQ
14/15	Salisbury House Hotel, Taunton TA1 3NN
16	Brookhayes Farm, Cossington TA7 8LR
17	The Old Manor House, Axbridge BS26 2ED
23	Lower Lode Inn, Tewkesbury GL19 4RE
24	Wyatt Guest House, Worcester WR1 1HU
28	The Bridge House Hotel, Penkridge ST19 5AS
30/31	Compton House, Ashbourne DE6 1BX
32	Bankside Cottage, Youlgreave DE45 1WD
33	Hartley Hotel, Glossop Road, Sheffield S10 2HW
35	New Inn, Marsden HD7 6EZ
36	Birchcliffe B&B, Hebden Bridge HX7 8JA
37	Rosebud Cottage Guest House, Haworth BD22 8QQ
38/39	Westleigh Hotel, Easby Road, Bradford BD 7 1QX
40	Bewerley Hall Farm, Pateley Bridge HG3 5JA
42	Herriot's in Hawes, Hawes DL8 3QW
43	Black Bull Hotel, Kirkby Stephen CA17 4QW
45	Bongate House, Appleby in Westmoreland CA16 6UE
49	The Mount Guest House, Haltwhistle NE49 9NS
50	Eels Lodge Bed & Breakfast, Tarset NE48 1LF
51	Forest View Inn, Byrness NE19 1TS
52	Kenmore Bank Hotel, Jedburgh TD8 6JJ
53	Briadwood, Melrose TD6 9LD
56	West Lynn Grove Bed & Breakfast, West Linton EH46 7HK
57	Glenalmond B&B, East Calder EH53 0ET
58	Grange Farmhouse, Dunfermline KY11 3DG
59	Roxburghe Guest House, Kinross KY13 8DA
60/61	Dunallan Guest House, Perth PH2 7HT
62	Byways, Birnam, Dunkeld PH8 0DH
63	Atholl Villa, Pitlochry PH16 5BX
64	The Firs, Blair Atholl PH18 5TA
66	Ardlogie Guesthouse. Aviemore PH22 1PU
67	Craigellachie House, Carrs Bridge PH23 3AS

Day	B&B
68/69	6 Broadstone Park, Inverness IV2 3LA
70	Moydene, Dingwall IV15 9LE
71	Craigaron Guesthouse, Saltburn, Invergordon IV18 0JX
72	Amalfi, Dornoch IV25 3LY
73	Bay View House, Brora KW9 6QS
74	Kindale House, Helmsdale KW8 6JF
75	The Croft House, Swiney, Lybster KW3 6BT
76	Harbour House, Wick KW1 5HB

Cost of the walk

It is almost impossible to provide an estimate of the equipment costs since either I was using gear that I already possessed or I was buying equipment that I will use again and which I can't realistically 'charge' to the walk. Anyone doing a walk like this will almost certainly be the same position and will wrestle with the same problem - how to carry the smallest weight whilst spending the smallest amount of money. Apart from food, travel and accommodation I brought back everything I took (I actually lost nothing during the walk!) and can reuse it (I will even reunite the fragments of maps).

This leaves the costs of the consumables, principally accommodation, travel and food. I do not have a complete record of what I spent on each (for example, I do not have a record of my spending on lunches) but I have sufficient information to make pretty reliable estimates of cost. It is important to remember, particularly in relation to accommodation, that I was walking a particular route between May and July 2012 and that costs on other routes at other seasons and in later years may be different.

I stayed at B&Bs, guesthouses, hotels, pubs and hostels for 54 nights. There is no clear distinction between these types of accommodation so I lump them together; the only conditions that I applied in choosing them were that each was in the right place, likely to give me access to a place to eat in the evening and would cost £45 or less. I was generally quite successful in meeting these conditions; I have mentioned in the blog some occasions when I failed.

From the 54 nights I have records for 48 costs. The highest cost was £50 and the lowest £25 with an average of £39.80. From this figure I estimate that I spent £2159 on accommodation. Without help from Christian Aid supporters and personal friends that figure would have been about £1000 higher.

I ate evening meals in pubs, restaurants, fish and chip shops, at the B&B using food bought elsewhere and at the B&B when a meal was supplied as an extra (not included in the accommodation cost). I estimate that I spent around £3 per day on lunches and £13 per day on dinners, giving a likely total of £933 for food. My clear impression was that I was spending perhaps 20% more on meals in Scotland than in England and that it was harder to find pubs doing food, particularly later in the evening.

Car travel from home to Lands End and from Plymouth to home can be estimated as £65 (at 25p per mile) and the rail fare from John O'Groats to Plymouth was £70. So my best estimate of the total cost to me is about £3230. Had I paid for everything it would have been about £4440.

The blog

I started the blog on March 7th 2012, feeling that I needed to make sure that people who were hearing about the walk and donating would have some feedback about the preparation process. Then, from the start of the walk, I managed to maintain a daily blog though some postings were not made until the following day. On several days I did not have time to put the photographs in; these were often added a day or two later than the text. I felt that it was imperative that I maintained the postings to the blog on as regular a basis as possible.

I made 89 posts in all, most of which are included in whole or in part in Chapters 3 and 4. The blog attracted 366 comments (of which about 70 were my replies to comments or questions posted by others) and I have drawn on these in compiling Chapter 3 and in the blog footnotes on pages 187 - 190.

At the time of writing (January 2013) the blog has been viewed about 9600 times with 220 on the day that I finished the walk. Of these viewings, 266 were in the run-up period whilst I was reporting my training and other preparations. Viewings were still running at about 100 a week 3 months after the walk finished but are now tailing off. 80% of viewings are from the UK but there have been regular contacts from Australia, New Zealand, Canada and the United States and elsewhere.

Time spent reading

I suppose that a walk is an opportunity to read. *War and Peace* is a traditional choice for a prolonged exile like this, but I tried that once before (20+ years ago on a winter 6-day train ride from Beijing to Moscow) and got only about a third of the way through it.

I took a Kindle, bought specially for the walk because it was light, could hold a huge number of books and was more likely to survive the rigours of a rucksack than would most paperbacks. In the first instance I had no clear idea about what I wanted to read so I loaded *The Girl with The Dragon Tattoo* by Stieg Larsson (likely to be an easy read) and *Thinking the Twentieth Century* by Timothy Snyder and Tony Judt (which I knew to be a demanding read). Tired at the end of my first day, I opted for the easy read; later I needed to find out what happened so I downloaded the other two books in the Larsson trilogy, *The Girl Who Played with Fire* and *The Girl Who Kicked the Hornets' Nest*, and read those. Once used to the slightly intense style, I enjoyed these books which took me as far as the Pennines.

Still avoiding Snyder and Judt, I went for *Bring Up the Bodies* by Hilary Mantel (the recently published successor to her book *Wolf Hall*) and enjoyed it hugely. In

Scotland, and needing some easy reading, I then downloaded two recent Ian Rankin novels and was very disappointed; though not Inspector Rebus books they were still about police, still set in Edinburgh and Fife and still in the same style. Slightly ashamed at having spent time on these I downloaded *Absence of Mind: The Dispelling of Inwardness from the Modern Myth of the Self* by Marilynne Robinson. I have greatly admired her exquisitely written novels (*Home*, *Gilead* and *Housekeeping*) about small town America; this book is a series of lectures that she gave about supposed tensions between science and religion. I found the book disappointing: the style felt ponderous and the points over-written and sometimes clumsily made. I read two chapters, skim-read two more and then abandoned the book. But, if she writes more novels, I will certainly read them.

I am amazed at the amount of reading that I did. That's what being on your own in strange places does for you but you may begin to doubt that I did any walking at all.

I finally tackled Snyder and Judt when I got home. I find it a great book - a worthy successor to Judt's history of Europe since 1945, *Postwar* and is the result of conversations between the two men in the last few months of Judt's life. It's very demanding but is a thought-provoking read about major issues in recent history such as the Holocaust and Marxism and about the nature of historical enquiry. Having read it I put the Kindle away and went back to real books.

It was only very recently that I read Robert Macfarlane's *The Old Ways*, kindly presented to me by Bob Rainbow my return from the walk. I do wish that I'd read it before I left on the walk; it is a wonderful book that gave me a whole new perspective on the nature of walking and of journeys and of the relationship between people and landscapes. Armed with these insights I might have written a much better blog and compiled a much better book. Oh dear!

References to sources mentioned in the text

Denis Brook & Phil Hinchliffe (1992) *The Alternative Pennine Way*. Cicerone Press

John Butler (2011) http://www.jbutler.org.uk/e2e/

John Hillaby (1970) *Journey Through Britain*. Paladin

Robert Macfarlane (2012) *The Old Ways*. Hamish Hamilton

Andrew McCloy (1994) *Lands End to John O'Groats*. Hodder & Stoughton

Andrew McCloy (2002) *The Lands End to John O'Groats Walk*. Cordee

Mark Moxon (1995-2012) http://www.landsendjohnogroats.info/

Michael Roberts (2001) *Gates & Stiles*. Gold Cockerell Books

Andy Robinson (2007) *The End to End Trail*. Cicerone Press

Ordnance Survey Getamap service http://www.getamap.ordnancesurveyleisure.co.uk/

Jenny Uglow (2002) *The Lunar Men*: *The Friends who made the Future 1730-1810.* Faber and Faber

CPSIA information can be obtained at www.ICGtesting.com
Printed in the USA
LVOW010916280213

3403LVUK00001B/3/P

9 781845 495688